THE HOMEOWNER IDEOLOGY

AFRICAN PERSPECTIVES
Kelly Askew, Laura Fair, and Pamila Gupta
Series Editors

The Homeowner Ideology: Economic (F)Utility of Real Property Rights in Four African Cities
Singumbe Muyeba

Typologies of Humor in African Literatures
Adwoa A. Opoku-Agyemang

Between HIV Prevention and LGBTI Rights: The Political Economy of Queer Activism in Ghana
Ellie Gore

Protest Arts, Gender, and Social Change: Fiction, Popular Songs, and the Media in Hausa Society across Borders
Ousseina D. Alidou

The Imaginative Vision of Abdilatif Abdalla's Voice of Agony
Abdilatif Abdalla, edited by Annmarie Drury

Congo Style: From Belgian Art Nouveau to African Independence
Ruth Sacks

Lagos Never Spoils: Nollywood and Nigerian City Life
Connor Ryan

Continuous Pasts: Frictions of Memory in Postcolonial Africa
Sakiru Adebayo

Writing on the Soil: Land and Landscape in Literature from Eastern and Southern Africa
Ng'ang'a Wahu-Mũchiri

In Search of Tunga*: Prosperity, Almighty God, and Lives in Motion in a Malian Provincial Town*
André Chappatte

A complete list of titles in the series can be found at www.press.umich.edu

The Homeowner Ideology

Economic (F)Utility of Real Property Rights in Four African Cities

Singumbe Muyeba

University of Michigan Press
Ann Arbor

Published in the United States of America by the
University of Michigan Press
First published March 2025

A CIP catalog record for this book is available from the British Library.

Library of Congress Cataloging-in-Publication data has been applied for.

ISBN 978-0-472-07732-8 (hardcover : alk. paper)
ISBN 978-0-472-05732-0 (paper : alk. paper)
ISBN 978-0-472-90493-8 (open access ebook)

DOI: https://doi.org/10.3998/mpub.14418455

Publication of this volume has been partially funded by the African Studies Center, University of Michigan.

The University of Michigan Press's open access publishing program is made possible thanks to additional funding from the University of Michigan Office of the Provost and the generous support of contributing libraries.

Cover image: Kibera neighborhood in Nairobi, Kenya (2019).
Photograph by Singumbe Muyeba.

For the Late Professor Ambassador Mwelwa C. Musambachime,
beloved uncle and mentor

CONTENTS

Digital materials related to this title can be found on
the Fulcrum platform via the following citable URL:
https://doi.org/10.3998/mpub.14418455

FIGURES

TABLES

PREFACE

During a July 2009 walkthrough of some of Cape Town's new racially mixed housing projects, I was astonished by the poverty. At the time, I had just completed my MPhil in development studies with a thesis on the effects of foreign aid on poverty reduction in Zambia. As a newly minted graduate still figuring out what was next, I joined the Center for Social Science Research at the University of Cape Town as a research associate. My first assignment was a study commissioned by the provincial government of the Western Cape Province led by Professor Jeremy Seekings. The research was concerned with the critical national question of whether the new housing projects had achieved racial desegregation among these new homeowners. Poverty would emerge as a widespread issue among our research participants. At the time, I had peripheral awareness of the conventional thinking that homeownership reduced income poverty. So, there was something strange in the familiar—our participants were homeowners, but they were poor. They had a place to lay their heads at night, but little food in their stomachs. I wondered how it was that these homeowners remained poor to the extent that a token shopping voucher would represent their only meal that day. My experience in Cape Town became an obsession, a quest, and ultimately the present book.

My wonderings and wanderings brought me into my PhD program and postdoctoral research. It drew me to summer schools at Brown University, where I sought to understand development and inequality, and the University of Amsterdam, where I was taught about urban sociology. It took me to Yale University as a Fox International Fellow, where I sought to understand urban poverty, policy, and social problems; economic thought and analysis; and statistical methods. I sought knowledge at Harvard's Joint Center for Housing Studies, which produced seminars and papers on homeownership theory. I even took a job as a research specialist at a Boston nonprofit on homelessness shortly after earning my PhD. Finally, as a professor at the University of Denver in the United States, my quest took me on research trips back to Zambia—the land of my birth—and to Kenya and Angola. I continue to obsess and to ask questions born from my early obsession with poverty.

In these pages, the reader will find what I learned on my quest as I examined the economic, social, and ideological significance of real property rights for poverty in four African cities. The story that unfolds explains why decades of development studies on the subject are inconsistent with the realities of the urban poor in African cities, and why the use of homeownership as an intervention persists despite evidence that it is ineffective. The conventional view advanced by market fundamentalist neoclassical economists is that real property rights, where the poor have ownership rights to land and housing, improve the economic chances of the urban poor and can eradicate poverty in cities of developing countries. While homeownership has clear benefits among the poor—including important measures of human welfare—the book shows that the utility of real property rights as an economic resource is severely limited. Yet the idea persists because of the social production and reproduction of a preference for homeownership tenure driven by the homeowner ideology, family intergenerational production, transmission of homeownership culture, and the state's support for homeownership tenure.

A major contribution of the book is that it interrogates long-held, ideologically based assumptions about real property rights using causal analysis methods not previously utilized in studying property rights among the urban poor in the African context. Drawing on 11 years of study, fieldwork involving four large-scale housing surveys, and in-depth semistructured interviews in Cape Town, Lusaka, Nairobi, and Luanda, *The Homeowner Ideology* fills an important gap by illustrating the significance of real property rights among the poor in sub-Saharan Africa. These cities used different means to deliver property rights to the poor, thereby providing an opportunity to comprehensively examine the effects of homeownership.

The book thus expands knowledge in the field by showing that causal analysis in combination with qualitative research reveals a richer story of how taken-for-granted claims about homeownership work differently in the African context.

ACKNOWLEDGMENTS

I am so grateful to have received generous support throughout my quest and in writing this book. First, I thank Almighty God, from whom I draw inspiration, faith, intelligence, knowledge, and direction. I am especially grateful to my doctoral supervisor, Professor Jeremy Seekings, for unwavering guidance, and financial and other continuous support throughout my career. I extend my gratitude to colleagues at the Centre for Social Science Research who engaged with various parts of my work on the cases of Cape Town and Lusaka.

I am thankful to colleagues and mentors at the University of Denver and the Josef Korbel School of International Studies, in particular, who provided generous feedback, especially in the initial stages of the book's development. Ilene Grabel heard my ideas from very early on and provided much-needed guidance and feedback. Till the day I signed my contract, she was someone I could turn to for immense wisdom and light. Aaron Schneider read the very first version of the book proposal. My mentor and associate dean for research, Rachel Epstein, who has kept me honest and accountable in my career progression, in December 2019 organized a book workshop where I could present my work and receive feedback. At that workshop, I subjected my colleagues, Dean and Professor Frederick "Fritz" Mayer, Marie Berry, Jack Donelly, Rachel Epstein, Rebecca Galemba, Ilene Grabel, Micheline Ishay, Sandy Johnson, Aaron Schneider, and Frank Laird to raw book ideas. The feedback I received went on to define the development of the book. I am forever grateful for the grace and patience shown to me by senior colleagues. I am also grateful for the support of Alan Gilbert, Oliver Kaplan, and all colleagues at the Korbel School.

Gratitude goes to the University of Denver for the Professional Research Opportunities for Faculty (PROF) grant (84379-207421). The grant funded my fieldwork in Nairobi and Luanda and supported a research assistant. I am also grateful for professional development funds that made travel and accommodation possible.

I also received funding for a book manuscript workshop at the recommendation of Dean Fritz Mayer and Rachel Epstein. I received invaluable feedback from Anne Pitcher and Caroline Wanjiku Kihato, to whom I am forever grateful. Thank you to my PhD advisee, Susan Cossa, who took detailed notes on my behalf. Thanks to my research assistants, Beth Ann Card and Madi Wickett.

This book would not have become a reality without the faculty and publishers at the University of Michigan Press. Thank you Kelly Askew for organizing the African Perspectives series and for keeping it going. Deep gratitude goes to my commissioning editors, Dr. Elizabeth Demers, Dr. Katie LaPlant, Marcella Landri, and Delilah McCrea, who believed in the project. They were generous with their time when I needed an update. I extend my gratitude to Juliette Snyder and Danielle Coty-Fattal. Thanks to two anonymous reviewers. I am also grateful to Dr. Heather Martin, who provided excellent copyedits on the final manuscripts.

I am grateful to organizers of the African Studies Association annual meetings for giving me a chance to present my work at multiple conferences. Professor Howard Stein, along with Professors Faustin Maganga and Bayo Ijagbemi, provided excellent feedback on one of my chapters when I presented it in Philadelphia. The conversation went on long after our session ended. Thank you to Ricardo Soares de Oliveira, Claudia Gastrow, Sergio Calundungo, and Suzana Sousa, who I connected with through ASA. They each played a significant role in facilitating my research in Luanda.

I wish to extend my gratitude to Benjamin Selwyn and Adam Swallow. They believed in the project from the beginning and suggested avenues for publication. Professor Selwyn provided feedback that greatly improved the manuscript. Thanks also to my colleague Rachel Sigman, who assured me of the high quality of the African Perspectives series.

The evidence presented in the book would have been difficult to obtain without the excellent work of my data collection teams. In Nairobi, I benefitted from the experience of Samuel Balongo, Samuel Peru, Ben Obote, Rose Namanda, Nelly Caster, Kenneth Orango, Kate Nyoike, and Emily Atieno. In Cape Town, Bulelwa Nokwe and Thobani Ncapai were phenomenal. In Lusaka, gratitude goes to Nkatya Monde, Andsen Shawa, Sandra Ngosa, Elizabeth Nyirongo, Lisa Mwanza, Sepo Silishebo, and Mpatso Phiri. In Luanda, I thank Carlos Pacatolo, David Boio, Rosana Correia, and their team of 22 data collectors at Ovilongwa Consultants, who had to do my research immediately after administering the first wave of Afrobarometer in Angola.

At Yale, many thanks go to Professors Julia Adams, Cynthia Horan, and

Cheryl Doss. They gave me feedback on my presentations and chapters on Lusaka and Cape Town before the book was written. I also thank the Yale Fox Fellowship team, especially Julia Muravnik, Anne Kellet, the Fox Fellows who gave feedback on my presentations, and the Fox family for financial and moral support.

The project benefited massively from the unwavering support of my family. My wife and best friend, Abby, tolerated my absences, showed grace and love throughout the project, and provided feedback and criticism, even as she pursued her own academic career. My son Christian was very understanding, especially during what he calls my "nap phase"—a period when he would come to say goodnight in my home office and the next day find me in my office when he came to say good morning because I went to sleep late and woke up early to work on my manuscript. My father, Mr. Richard Muyeba, provided moral support, prayer, and encouragement throughout the project. Thank you, Aunty Mary Muyeba Sililo, Uncle Sililo, and family, who have always been there with moral and material support for my intellectual growth. Thank you, Dr. Bwembya Chikolwa and Mulenga Musambachime-Chikolwa, for allowing me to bounce off ideas, for your advice, and for keeping me grounded in reality. I also benefitted from the support of my brother and friend Mwape "Paki," Musambachime, his wife Chacha, and daughter Bella, who helped ensure that my project did not consume me, especially with their advice to not sleep with my computer next to my bed, and whose late-night conversations and phone calls left me laughing for weeks. I extend this gratitude to Bobby and Lachel Samakayi and their family. Thank you Kalumba and Cecilia Musambachime, Mwelwa Musambachime, Aunty Phoebe Musambachime, Aunty Ireen Kabaso-Kana, Uncle Ford and Aunty Chiko Matipa, Aunty Fannie Mubebo, Mrs. Reberiah Kabandula-Monde, Racheal Kabandula, and my mother-in-law Daina Kabandula. Thank you to my siblings Mulela Muyeba-Mazimba, Muziya Mazimba, Blessings Miti, Moses Miti, and their families, who bring joy and remind me that I do what I love to do to leave this world a better place for their generation and generations to come.

Finally, I am blessed to have friends who were there for me. Thank you to Dr. Isaac Chinyoka. I count myself fortunate to have a friend in you who is closer than a brother. Thank you, Dr. Sara Epstein, Chanza Sikazwe (SC), Dr. Mashekwa Maboshe, Dr. Madalitso Phiri, Dr. Mundia Kabinga, Dr. William Akoto, Dr. Isigi Kadagi, and your families. Thanks go to Kelvin Chibangula and the late Dr. Mutale Chileshe-Chibangula, Chipateni Nyirenda, Chrispine Maphenduka, Brian Mwanza, Simon Mwanza, and Lucy Mulesa-Mbewe. Your friendship, encouragement, and rooting for me, as well as your feedback helped me during presentations in Cape Town and fieldwork trips in Lusaka and Nairobi. There are many others, too numerous to mention by name, but please know that I am eternally grateful for your contributions. All faults and errors are my own.

CHAPTER 1

Poverty, Slum Conditions, and Homeownership

ZAWADI'S STORY

On a warm and dry August evening in 2019, we arrive at Canaan Estate. The compound contains 20 new high-rise towers built for the poor by the government of Kenya in Kibera, Nairobi. It is sunset. Zawadi sits outside the walls of her store. She is a beneficiary of a government-backed mortgage through the Kenya Slum Upgrading Program (KENSUP). A former member of the Sectoral Executive Committee warned Zawadi not to talk to us, but she invites us in anyway and closes the door. She wants to tell her story.

Zawadi grew up in the slum conditions of Kibera. It was not until she was in her thirties that she moved to a temporary settlement in Langata Decanting Site, where she waited for her new house to be built. Zawadi moved into her house in 2016. She tells us it has been three years since she was selected for ownership. Although she cannot borrow against her property, she reflects, "It was good I moved to a good house. I feel proud, but sometimes I'm worried because I am not affording to pay for that house. I was not paying rent [in the slum]." Although she feels more secure with her mortgage, she is afraid the government might one day take her house away. "I am afraid," she says, "sometimes they come, and they put our names on the wall where everyone can see." She is referring to a publicly displayed list of homeowners who are behind on their mortgage payments. Even so, Zawadi worries less about evictions than she used to in the slum. Since her move, she feels less stress, and her physical health has improved.

While Zawadi struggles to keep up with her mortgage payments, she notices that some of her neighbors can pay easily, and she does not recognize them from the old slum. She suspects that they circumvented the regular process of housing selection. Perhaps this is why the former SEC member warned her against talking to us.

Zawadi's story challenges the economic utility of freehold ownership of real property in urban areas among the poor. She struggles with the mortgage payment, and she cannot secure a loan using her property as leverage. At the same time, she worries less about potential eviction, and her health is better. In a context that values collective forms of tenure, the government of Kenya chose to provide Zawadi housing through individual ownership rights. In so doing, the government of Kenya contributed to the social production of tenure and reproduced the homeowner ideology.

MPHO'S STORY

Meanwhile, in Khayelitsha, it is gusty and cold. Mpho lives in a township in Cape Town's Cape Flats at the southern tip of Africa. The post-apartheid government in Cape Town built new houses for disenfranchised Black Africans. It is 2011, and Mpho is a housing subsidy beneficiary. With an air of confidence, she tells us that owning her house allowed her to become a "madam," suggesting a social status that commands respect. Black women housekeepers used "madam" to refer to white South African women for whom they worked in Cape Town's affluent southern suburbs. Mpho lived in a shack in Site C after moving to Cape Town from Eastern Cape Province in 1983. She labored as a domestic worker for the same madam for many years. "I used to look at my madam and never knew I could be like her," she recounts. "I used to watch her eating her breakfast, wearing her gown. I didn't know that I can be a madam. But today I do everything; I am happy."

Like Zawadi, Mpho cannot borrow against her house, but her housing subsidy came with a dwelling, ownership of the land, and housing under freehold tenure. With ownership, Mpho reports being treated with greater respect, decency, and dignity—especially compared to the dehumanizing experiences she faced as a Black woman in apartheid South Africa. She has pride in her house and neighborhood, and she reports greater life satisfaction and improved physical health. Her main concern is no longer survival. Instead, she worries about her family. Her teenage daughter got pregnant shortly after they moved into their new house.

Like Zawadi's, Mpho's story challenges the focus on economic benefits of freehold ownership, while shedding light on both the unintended consequences of property ownership and the non-economic dimensions of human welfare. Her story likewise reveals the government's role in the social production of tenure. Mpho became a homeowner through active and deliberate policy by the government of South Africa and the City of Cape Town. The purpose was to promote homeownership tenure through subsidizing urban areas in a context where 80 percent of the population lived in collective ownership. Mpho is proud of her house, and she is glad she is the owner.

MARY'S STORY

On a windy and dusty day in Matero in August 2011, we visit Mary. She benefited from the privatization of low-cost public rental housing in Lusaka. The initiative was part of Zambia's structural adjustment program (SAP), funded under the auspices of the IMF and World Bank in the mid-1990s. She likes her home, but she understands that it does not confer all the economic benefits she might have hoped for. She reflects that, in her life before homeownership, she thought that if she had "A house, I would be happy . . . that's what I would want." She now owns a house in Matero—a poor neighborhood in Lusaka. Understanding the role of property in wealth building, Mary wants a loan to purchase another house. However, the banks will not lend her money. She reports, "even when you have a house, we suffer." She considers the banker's question: "Where will you get the money to pay for another house?" Shaking her head, Mary questions, "How can I manage? There is no one who can help me find a way to get a loan. And if I [did] get a loan, I don't work, so how will I return it?" Working as a nurse, Mary's daughter supports her mother financially.

Mary used to run a small business selling Coca-Cola and other small items on her premises, but it collapsed. Although she is unable to obtain a loan or otherwise lift herself out of poverty, she says she is happy she has a house. She reflects, "As long as we manage to pay for electricity, we manage to pay for water, we manage to pay land [property taxes], as long as we manage, our hearts are at peace. We are seated at our home. It's different from when we were being forced [evicted]; now they are giving us papers respectably. . . . I am happy. I am free because the house is mine."

Mary's story challenges the conventional wisdom that ownership rights improve the economic chances of the urban poor, and that freedom comes from the economic utility of ownership title. Her story reveals the role of neoliberal ideology through privatization policy that influences the social production of homeownership tenure in a country context that maintains communal values. She is supported by her daughter, which reveals the role of family in the social production of tenure through intergenerational transfer of values about homeownership.

ROSANA'S STORY

On a hot and humid Saturday afternoon in mid-December 2019, Rosana is merrymaking and dancing to Kizomba music in Zango 1, a barrio of 3,000 houses built by the government of Angola to house people from a slum that was susceptible to natural disasters. Rosana grew up in Boa Vista, a *musseque* (informal settlement with slum conditions) located on a hill near the center of Luanda city. Her parents, along with millions of other Angolans, fled from rural areas to the city as a violent civil war was waged in the countryside from 1975 to 2002. Shortly before the end of the war, tragedy struck. In 2000 and again in 2001, mudslides destroyed houses and killed several people in the musseque. The government of Angola evicted residents and promised new and safer houses in Zango. Some residents of Boa Vista refused to move to Zango, moving instead to a musseque called Paraiso, which had accommodated returning civil war veterans since the early 1990s. Rosana and her family moved to Zango on the promise of a new house. Instead, they were housed in a shack in a temporary government relocation area for five long years. In 2006, Rosana finally received her new house. The house came with a document called a *guia de entrega*, explaining that the house was only to be used for habitation. She was prohibited from modifying the home, taking on additional tenants, or operating an at-home business. She could live there, but the land and house remained the property of the Angolan government.

Despite government restrictions, Rosana and her family converted the structure into a two-story home, painted it a new color, and built a wall around it. Indeed, few community members have kept the houses in their original form. Many opened businesses on the premises and rented out rooms. Rosana filled her house with durable goods, and she and her neighbors enjoy a higher income than those who moved to Paraiso. Although she does not own her house, Rosana is satisfied with her home and with her neighborhood, and she has a stronger sense of belonging and no intention to move. She has little fear of eviction, and her health is much improved since moving from Boa Vista.

Rosana's story teaches us that even without freehold or leasehold ownership, the poor can maximize economic and other forms of utility of low-income public housing under usufruct rights. What matters is that they think and believe they have security of tenure, which also solidifies the understanding that in a context where the ideological context leans left, the social production of urban tenure takes the form of social housing, which aligns with traditionally collective African societies.

Although the four stories challenge the economic utility of homeownership in African cities, they also show that homeownership emerges and remains the tenure of preference through social production processes involving the state, neoliberalism, and the family. Social production is driven by the pervasiveness of neoliberalism's homeowner ideology, the state's active support for homeownership, and the family's intergenerational transfer of a culture of homeownership.

In this book, I argue that claims about the economic utility of real property rights in African urban spaces are unsupported by the evidence, yet these claims persist due to social production processes that drive the homeowner ideology. Four secondary arguments support my claim. First, contrary to claims by market fundamentalist neoclassical economists, real property rights function as *structured idle capital* on the formal market in African cities. Next, the scholarly focus of market fundamentalist neoclassical economists on the economic effects of real property rights has obscured the evidence that ownership rights are associated with improvement in non-economic dimensions of human well-being. Third, the focus on the utility of real property rights obscures the evidence about the utility of usufruct forms of property rights. And, finally, the persistence of homeownership as the intervention of choice is explained by the social production of neoliberal ideology, the production and intergenerational transfer of homeownership culture within the family, and the state's deliberate and active support for homeownership tenure.

1.1. URBAN POVERTY AND THE CRISIS OF SLUMS IN AFRICA

While global poverty has declined since 1990, it remains widespread in sub-Saharan Africa. In a population of 1.2 billion, 35 percent (414 million people) saw extreme poverty in 2019 (World Bank 2022a)—a higher proportion than South Asia's 8.5 percent (161.5 million) and East Asia and the Pacific's 1.1 percent (26 million). In recent years, following decades-long declines in the poverty rate in sub-Saharan Africa, the COVID-19 pandemic threw almost 100 million people into extreme poverty (United Nations 2022b, 26). In 2022, over 750 million people lived in extreme poverty, existing on less than $2.15 a day (World Bank 2022b). Indeed, the World Bank (2022b) predicts that extreme poverty will continue to be concentrated within sub-Saharan Africa, and the region will not meet the Sustainable Development Goal of less than 3 percent by 2030 (United Nations 2022b). In addition, 70 percent of people in African cities earn their living hand-to-mouth in the informal sector. Sub-Saharan Africa faces extreme and rising income and wealth inequality, where the top-earning 10 percent receive over 50 percent of all income (Chancel et al. 2022). In terms of wealth inequality, the poorest 50 percent of Africans own just 2 percent of the wealth, with the top 10 percent owning 72 to 86 percent (Chancel et al. 2022, 37–40). Where inequality is high, those at the bottom experience extreme poverty even more severely (Ray 1998, 279–88).

Africa is the region with the highest proportion of the population living in slums. About a quarter of the 1 billion people living in slum conditions globally live in Africa (United Nations 2022b). Fifty-seven percent of the continent's city populations live in slums (United Nations 2022b, 48). The region has a housing backlog of 51 million houses (Bah, Faye, and Geh 2018, 7). Considering that average household sizes are between six and nine (UNDESA Population Division 2017), between 300 and 460 million people live in inhuman and undignified conditions. More than 234 million people who live in urban slums hope to someday own homes like Zawadi, Mpho, Mary, and Rosana (United Nations 2022b; World Bank 2018).

The housing crisis means indignity on a massive scale. Without formal services, scores of residents live near piles of garbage and have poor sanitation, without running water and adequate toilets and sewerage (Neuwirth 2006, 67–69). Dwellings are built from mud, cardboard, or steel or zinc sheets (Neuwirth 2006, 70). Slum conditions are frequent sites of city epidemics of cholera, dysentery, and diarrheal diseases such as norovirus, sapovirus, and astrovirus (Shioda et al. 2016). These diseases are a manifestation of conditions that are hazardous to physical health. In addition, living with the stress induced by fear of eviction via bulldozer leads to high stress and poor psychological health.

The crisis of slums is projected to worsen following population increases and the approaching urban tipping point. The urban tipping point is the point

Table 1.1. Percentage of Residences Under Ownership Tenure in 2021

Country	Total Residential Properties with a Title Deed	Households	Properties Under Ownership Tenure (%)
Angola	475,000	7,074,583	6.71
Benin	47,000	2,465,192	1.91
Burkina Faso	5,192	3,697,179	0.14
CAR	9,000	966,788	0.93
Chad	9,454	2,818,370	0.34
Egypt	3,450,000	26,436,963	13.05
Eswatini	315	289,534	0.11
Ethiopia	2,800,000	25,264,566	11.08
Gabon	23,307	565,159	4.12
Ghana	2,625,411	8,555,673	30.69
Guinea	557,504	2,088,862	26.69
Kenya	4,060,000	13,818,776	29.38
Lesotho	73,960	613,134	12.06
Madagascar	600,000	6,349,160	9.45
Malawi	241	4,565,870	0.01
Mali	250,000	3,717,465	6.73
Mauritania	27,000	785,564	3.44
Morocco	1,800,000	8,019,283	22.45
Mozambique	477,786	7,030,161	6.80
Namibia	274,897	597,885	45.98
Niger	2,419,116	4,200,947	57.59
Senegal	152,000	1,914,572	7.94
Seychelles	25,931	27,909	92.91
South Africa	6,738,520	18,480,534	36.46
South Sudan	10,000	1,777,836	0.56
Sudan	185,000	7,636,085	2.42
Tanzania	722,346	12,783,076	5.65
Togo	47,326	1,941,574	2.44
Tunisia	480,079	3,132,614	15.33
Zambia	200,000	3,840,102	5.21
Zimbabwe	256,780	3,958,527	6.49

Source: Data for residential properties with a title deed from Centre for Affordable Housing Finance in Africa (2022); data for households from United Nations (2022a).

at which 50 percent or more of a society's population lives in urban areas. By the year 2030, the majority of Africans will live in cities. Looking further ahead, by 2050 the region's population is projected to grow to 2.5 billion (see Bloom and Khanna 2007). A 1 percent increase in the urban population is associated with a 5 percent increase in the number of people living in African slum conditions (United Nations 2022b, 48). At the root of the urban crisis is that housing demand far surpasses housing supply (Potts 2020). Each year, 4.5 million people move into the slums of African cities (World Bank 2015), a rate of urbanization that far outpaces the capacity of governments to build houses. It can take up to nine years to supply housing for the annual increase in demand (Bah, Faye, and Geh 2018). It is also more affordable for the urban poor to access slum housing (Potts 2020). Of the 2.5 billion people who will be living in Africa in 2050, 1.2 billion of them will live in urban areas—most of them in slum conditions (World Bank 2015).

Moreover, Africa has the lowest homeownership rates by region, although data is hard to find. If we use the number of residential properties with the title deed complete and in hand, homeownership rates range from less than 1 percent in countries such as Burkina Faso, CAR, Chad, Eswatini, Malawi, and South Sudan, to those with high rates, such as Seychelles with 93 percent and Niger with 58 percent; the rest fall below 50 percent. Of 32 countries for which data is available, 19 have less than 10 percent ownership rates (see table 1.1). These data only provide a rough indication, however, as many title deed processes are incomplete (Albertus 2020) and the cadastral systems are out of date in most countries (Kohli et al. 2017).

1.2. REAL PROPERTY RIGHTS AND THE HOMEOWNER IDEOLOGY

In the field of development studies, mainstream thinking is dominated by market fundamentalist neoclassical economics. This economic school of thought posits that real property rights deliver enough economic utility to eradicate poverty in developing countries. Real property rights are defined legally as ownership of immovable property (land) and permanent developments on and under it, falling under a standardized set of rights, usually held in perpetuity (freehold) or tenancy (leasehold) for long periods of time, usually 99 years (Burn and Cartwright 2011, 5–6; Durand-Lasserve and Selod 2009, 106). Freehold entails formal documented private ownership with unrestricted and exclusive control and freedom to dispose or use as collateral

(Kalabamu 2019). Leasehold is practically lifetime ownership, with the power to bequeath to succeeding generations.

Ownership is a social fact and an idea agreed on by society (Bromley 2008). It is the evidence that a particular object or land belongs to a specific individual or group. The literature makes a distinction between possession and ownership (Bromley 1991, 2006, 2008). Ownership entails possession, but possession does not always entail ownership. Possession entails an empirical phenomenon involving regular use of property but does not always provide that the user is the owner (Bromley 2008). The tangible empirical evidence distinguishing ownership from possession is the title. Within a democratic context, title provides the possessor with protection from the state against eviction from other claimants (Bromley 1991, 21). Title provides real property rights (Durand-Lasserve and Selod 2009, 106). In slum conditions in informal settlements, slum dwellers are possessors, not owners, of real property.

Market fundamentalist neoclassical economists advance the libertarian philosophical idea that total and permanent ownership of real property gives the individual economic freedom to maximize economic utility (Anderson and Huggins 2009). They justify ownership as a natural human instinct and suggest that ownership reflects the utility of real property as a commodity (Robinson 2010; World Bank 2015). In general, market fundamentalist neoclassical economists proclaim that real property ownership increases security of tenure and property values; allows access to the capital market in general and the credit market in particular; leads the owner to make investments to maximize value; allows for accumulation of household wealth through durable goods; and leads to more household participation in the labor market. All this is postulated to translate into higher income, improvements in slum conditions, and overall poverty reduction (Buckley and Kalarickal 2006; Durand-Lasserve and Selod 2009; World Bank 2002, 2015). By extension, scholarship from institutional economics likewise asserts that poor property rights contribute to the failure of nations (see Acemoglu and Robinson, 2012). In short, market fundamentalist neoclassical thought focuses on economic utilitarian aspects of ownership of real property (Abrams 1966; Alchian and Demsetz 1973; Barzel 1997; de Soto 2003; Robinson 2010; World Bank 2002, 2015).

A belief in real property rights as an effective intervention against slum conditions in informal human settlements across the developing world is pervasive. Indeed, it is held up as the ideal in economic development, particularly through promotion by the most influential international development institution: the World Bank. Since the late 1970s, the World Bank has instituted ownership-based property rights as a sine qua non of their shelter lending to developing countries for interventions against slum conditions and housing poverty (Alexander 2012; Buckley and Kalarickal 2006; World Bank 1980, 1993, 2002, 2015). In the late 1970s, socialist ideologies were widespread, debts were high, and slum conditions proliferated across the developing world. Market fundamentalist neoclassical economists helped the World Bank craft structural adjustment programs (SAPs)—later known as Washington Consensus policies—to condition development financing. In 1980, the World Bank (1980) issued the influential report, *Shelter*, which advocated for slum-upgrading programs that involved transfer of ownership rights. In the 1990s, their publication *Enabling Markets to Work* (World Bank 1993) advocated that developing countries strengthen private ownership rights to achieve economic growth. Thereafter, the 2002 *World Development Report* emphasized strengthening of property rights institutions, with an emphasis on ownership rights to reduce poverty (World Bank 2002). Property rights were noted 87 times in this report, noting, "Without land-titling institutions that ensure property rights, poor people are unable to use valuable assets for investment and income growth" (World Bank 2002, III). Elevating real property rights as a central strategy for ending poverty persists in later publications, such as Buckley and Kalarickal (2006) and the World Bank (2015).

Development scholars know that the World Bank strongly favors private property ownership, and strongly discourages public ownership and the state's involvement in providing brick-and-mortar housing—even for the poorest of the poor. Instead, it promotes the strengthening of markets and private-sector firms. The World Bank advises governments to scale down the role of the state and establish the primacy of the market, which cannot exist without ownership. It has promoted the provision of real property rights and homeownership schemes by funding slum-upgrading programs and self-help housing schemes alike (Alexander 2012; Buckley and Kalarickal 2006). Even the United Nations Development Program (UNDP) promoted ownership rights as a means to eradicate poverty in its Legal Empowerment of the Poor program (United Nations 2009).

For decades, studies have challenged mainstream thinking about the economic superiority of real property ownership (Bromley 1991, 2008; Doebele 1978; Gilbert 2012; Jacobs 1992; Kemeny 1981, 2015; Konadu-Agyemang 2001; Obeng-Odoom 2020, 2021; Ronald 2008; Turner 1976; Turner and Fichter 1972). Such studies decry the mythology around ownership in Europe,

United States, and Australia (Kemeny 1981, 2015; Ronald 2008); challenge the standardization of evictions and bulldozing of slums; promote support for self-help housing across the developing world (Turner 1976; Turner and Fichter 1972); rebut the commodification of customary land through capitalist conversion to ownership under private property (Bromley 1991, 2008; Obeng-Odoom 2020, 2021); show how formal ownership titles introduce new forms of vulnerability (Choplin and Dessie 2017); and show that legal ownership title under a private property regime was neither a necessary nor a sufficient condition for tenure security and investments (Angel 1983, 136, as cited in Varley 1987). This vast body of literature also challenges the Washington Consensus policies that reinforce ownership policies as the right institutions (Chang 2002). De Soto's (2003) libertarian claims that a lack of legal ownership title has locked up trillions of dollars' worth of property that can be released through real property rights has been thoroughly debunked (Davies, Narsoo, and Tomlinson 2007; Gilbert 2012; Kingwill et al. 2006; Tomlinson 2007).

Particularly in Africa, claims about the effects of ownership rights on access to credit, land, housing investments, and poverty in general are unsupported by the evidence (Choplin and Dessie 2017; Davies, Narsoo, and Tomlinson 2007; Kingwill et al. 2006; Payne, Durand-Lasserve, and Rakodi 2009; Tomlinson 2007). Indeed, market fundamentalist neoclassical economists do recognize that formalization of land rights in Africa has often failed, but rather than considering more significant ideological flaws, they attribute the failure to tactical issues, such as incomplete land registries, derailed land registration processes, and costly land formalization approaches used by African governments (Ali, Deininger, and Goldstein 2014, 266). In their view, once the land registration system is modernized and structural transformation is complete, the regularized system will allow access to credit and investments and reduce poverty. Despite the complexity of the argument, it is overly simplistic when viewed as part of the modernization school of thought. Problematically, the view ignores the vast decolonization literature and the need to understand that African land tenure systems have their own unique formation that should be understood independently and not in analogy to the West (see Ayittey 2006; Mamdani 2018).

Two issues merit consideration with regard to the debate and the state of knowledge. The first issue pertains to the persistence of ownership models, despite the proliferation of contrarian voices. It is indeed puzzling that despite a long history of decrying, challenging, debunking, rebutting, and demystifying the apparent mysteries of real property ownership, the scholarly idea and accompanying policy practices of property rights as a panacea to poverty persist in urban Africa. While the concept has been interrogated by scholars with a focus on the nonpoor in industrialized countries, the urban poor in the African context have received less scholarly attention.

Several theories have been advanced to explain the persistence of real property rights as a means of eradicating poverty. One theory is the economic expansion thesis, which suggests that home ownership emerges as the dominant tenure preference as economies grow. The emphasis on owner occupation is explained as a function of the expansion of economic growth under globalization. A second theory is the cultural disposition thesis, which suggests that some societies are predisposed toward a particular housing tenure. For example, societies that highly value individualism are more likely to veer toward homeownership, while collectivist societies are oriented more toward social housing. A third theory is Kemeny's "homeownership ideology" thesis, which suggests that the persistence and push for homeownership can be explained by the classical Gramscian theories of hegemony and dominance by the political elite (Kemeny 1981, 2015). This thesis suggests that dominance by hegemonic elites who hold an ideology that favors a particular tenure type occurs through state control and political power. Thus, the push for homeownership tenure occurs when bourgeois elites who hold a libertarian ideology that favors homeownership gain political power and control coercive state apparatus. Note the subtle, but important, distinction made between "the homeownership ideology," which is about a structural determination of tenure, and "the homeowner ideology," which engages claims about the effects of homeownership (Ronald 2004, 49). A fourth theory pertains to the restructuring of the welfare state through a one-off transfer of an economic asset to the poor. In industrialized societies, the argument is made that homeownership has expanded due to restructuring of the welfare state by direct state provision of one-time assets—particularly housing—to poorer households (Ronald 2008). The restructuring is explained as a convenient policy for addressing the fiscal difficulties encountered by the shrinking state. A final theory is the social production of tenure thesis advanced by Poggio (2006) and further developed by Ronald (2007). This theory suggests that tenure is socially produced. Any emphasis on a particular tenure must be explained by the process of social production. Social production can take place through a combination of sources, including intergenerational production and transmission of ideas through family relationships, liberal market channels, and state support for homeownership. Ronald (2007) adds that the process of social production involves economic, cultural, and ideological elements.

These theories have not been empirically evaluated within developing countries, especially in the context of Africa. Thus, their applicability to developing country contexts is questionable.

The points of departure in both Kemeny (1981, 2015) and Ronald (2008) are already problematic for application in the African context. For example, political parties fall much more neatly into ideological orientations in industrialized countries. Ronald's point of departure is the welfare state, which exists in industrialized countries but has only shown recent incremental development in Africa (Seekings 2017). Nevertheless, the intriguing question for the present debate is whether these theories about the exercise of state powers—underpinned by dominant ideologies that intertwine with the social structure—can explain the persistence of ownership as interventions against poverty in cities in Africa.

The second issue pertains to the sources of evidence used by scholars from the two sides of the debate in the study of African contexts. The nature of the existing evidence and the absence of other forms of evidence may offer some insight into the debate and persistence of ownership-based policy interventions. Although evidence challenging mainstream thought within the context of Africa is rich and convincing, it is dominated by in-depth, qualitative, urban literature. These rich discursive works, such as those by Choplin and Dessie (2017), Konadu-Agyemang (1990), Neimark et al. (2018), Obeng-Odoom (2020, 2021), Parnell and Pieterse (2014), and Pieterse (2011), have advanced scholarship on ownership and the urban formation in Africa remarkably, but do not lend themselves easily to evidence-based policymaking in global development institutions. At the same time, there is a remarkable scarcity of quantitative scholarly works examining the causal effects of ownership rights to land and housing in urban Africa. Meanwhile, the market fundamentalist neoclassical literature is dominated by quantitative literature employing econometric modelling in conjunction with natural experiments, observational surveys, and other forms of control group designs that lend themselves well to evidence-based policymaking. These scholarly works speak directly to policy, from seminal works by Alchian and Demsetz (see Alchian 1965; Alchian and Demsetz 1973; Demsetz 1966) to the groundbreaking and Nobel prize–winning Cambridge series featuring works by Libecap (1989), Barzel (1997), North (1990), and Weimer (1997), to more recent works by Hailu et al. (2017) and Hailu and Rooks (2016), and World

Bank economists such as Deininger and Ali (2022; Ali, Deininger, and Goldstein 2014; Deininger 2003). Indeed, many of these scholars work at or have worked as research staff or consultants for the World Bank.

This book challenges mainstream scholarly thought and international development practice about real property rights and interrogates the persistence of claims about ownership tenure in Africa. Using advanced quantitative methods not used before in the study of real property rights in the African context, along with time-tested quantitative methods, I interrogate long-held beliefs, values, assumptions, and claims about permanent ownership rights in a new way.

1.3. THE (F)UTILITY OF REAL PROPERTY RIGHTS

While claims about ownership rights hold some truth among the nonpoor, I demonstrate that real property rights constitute structured idle capital among the urban poor. Idle capital is private property from which owners decide not to extract maximum value or to maximize returns (Weil 2013). Private owners can decide to utilize their capital for maximum gain, low-capacity gain, or no gain at all (Weil 2013, 283). The present book contributes to this idea through the addition of structured idle capital—that is, the structural constraints such as legal and lending conditions that constrain the agency of the poor in their use of their capital asset for gain.

Ownership rights add little economic value in the formal market among the poor living in slum conditions. Markets disincentivize capital investment by developers in low-cost or low-value property, such as land located near slums or former slums. Ownership rights fail to fulfil their promise of prosperity and freedom by way of increased access to credit, increased property values, labor market participation, investments, greater household wealth and income, and overall reduction in income poverty. In some cases, they even fail to secure tenure security. Ownership rights fail to overcome the potential perils of low returns for banks, other lending organizations, and property developers—given the conditions of low savings rates, poor credit, insufficient insurance markets, and widespread informal employment among the poor in former settlements and slums. In line with this thinking, some scholars have agreed that claims about the effects of real property are exaggerated (Reerink and van Gelder 2010, 84).

The second supporting argument suggests that the scholarly focus of neoclassical economics on the economic effects of real property rights has obscured evidence that ownership rights are associated with improvement in non-economic dimensions of human welfare. A single-minded focus on the economic utility of ownership rights has obscured the social reality of several non-economic effects of ownership. In focusing on the economy, market fundamentalists miss equally valuable benefits of ownership rights to human welfare—including social, human capital, and subjective well-being benefits. Often, market fundamentalists focus the research agenda on researching the social reality that aligns with market fundamentalism and the neoliberal ideology; this limits our understanding of objective social reality. In this way, market fundamentalist neoclassical economics ideas and the obsession with the economic utility of ownership rights pervade the scholarly research and policy, at the expense of objective reality. The full examination of claims in this book shows that real property rights improve physical and psychological health and engender subjective well-being in terms of sense of belonging, self-esteem, and pride in one's housing and neighborhood. In addition to empowering the poor with ownership and security of tenure, however, real property rights can lead to unintended outcomes for the poor such as teenage pregnancies and threats to tenure security.

The third supporting argument suggests that the focus on ownership obscures evidence on the utility of usufruct property rights. Contrary to dominant assumptions, where there is state recognition and administration of usufruct rights, the urban poor have tenure security, engage in trading, invest in their land and housing, and conduct informal businesses. Indeed, the focus on the utility of ownership obscures the social reality that documented ownership is neither a necessary nor sufficient condition for economic utility. What matters is perceived tenure security. With over 70 percent of countries lacking sufficiently developed cadastral systems, formal ownership documents are seldom used in property transactions (Kohli et al. 2017). What is more, the literature shows that in developing countries, those with usufruct rights, like Rosana, and even those living with untitled, de facto tenure rights engage in the informal market.

Finally, the persistence of theories and development policies about the economic paramountcy of ownership in the eradication of poverty can be explained through processes of social production of homeownership tenure. The social production of homeownership takes place through a combination of sources, including the family's intergenerational production and transmission of homeownership culture, liberal market channels, and state support for homeownership. The main social production element is the liberal market channel, which is informed by the homeowner ideology perpetuated by market fundamentalist neoclassical economists. The homeowner ideology is pervasive in urban Africa. Globally, the homeowner ideology developed over time through libertarian philosophers and market fundamentalists, and became a pervasive set of ideas in the late twentieth century with the promotion of private ownership in economic development through economists such as Milton Friedman, Harry Johnson, Bela Balassa, Lord Peter Bauer, Jagdish Bhagwati, Deepak Lal, Ian Little, and Anne Krueger, some of whom held influential positions at the World Bank, the IMF, and in leadership in developing countries (Todaro and Smith 2020). These scholars helped the World Bank and IMF develop SAPs at the end of the 1970s, with private property ownership being an essential part. Privatization of state-owned property, an essential part of the conditions for accessing World Bank and IMF aid, forced the dominance of these policies on the continent. Finally, the fall of the Soviet Union and the triumph of neoliberalism ensured the dominance of ownership and libertarian thinking. Thus, freehold and leasehold tenure were internalized and localized by developing countries as the tenure of preference for economic development. Importantly, the values of homeownership existed alongside usufruct, renting, and customary tenure during colonialism, the early post-independence years, and even during the adoption of socialist-oriented ideals in Africa, yet they became pervasive under ideological claims that emerged following the fall of the Soviet Union. At that point, it became the aspirational tenure among African families and urban policymakers alike.

In essence, the homeowner ideology refers to the libertarian philosophical system of beliefs, values, assumptions, and claims about the effects of permanent ownership of real property. While partially unsubstantiated and built on neoclassical assumptions about leasehold and freehold ownership titles in other contexts, the system remains pervasive in Africa.

1.4. ASSESSING THE EFFECTS OF REAL PROPERTY RIGHTS IN AFRICAN CITIES

The book utilizes over a decade of accumulated research and evidence about ownership and usufruct property rights in four Southern and East African cities. It examines about 20 hypotheses in each city. In three of the cities, governments provided freehold and leasehold property rights along with formal housing. Eight neighborhoods were researched. Altogether 2,418 data points were utilized—with 2,068 data points from original questionnaire survey research, and 350 data points from existing surveys. Ninety-three qualitative interviews were conducted. The study took advantage of a natural experiment in one case study and utilized control-group designs in the others. It applied propensity score matching models in three case studies—a recent application to urban studies on Africa—and difference-in-differences in another to address concerns about the difficulty in establishing causal inference in studies of the effect of real property rights (Rafael Di Tella, Galiani, and Schargrodsky 2012). The nuance from these methods provides a fresh perspective on the effects of real property rights.

The four cities were selected because of the different value they bring in interrogating homeowner ideologies in Africa: Nairobi and Cape Town are freehold ownership cases, Lusaka is a leasehold case, and Luanda is a city that transferred social housing under usufruct rights, thereby playing the role of a comparison case. In each of the three freehold and leasehold cities, the government employed a different way of delivering ownership rights to the poor and used implementation mechanisms that provided an opportunity for rigorous interrogation of the claims of the homeowner ideology. Nairobi was selected because the state used no-interest mortgages with the end goal of transferring freehold property rights to provide low-income housing to the poor in Kibera, a large slum. The Nairobi case used a phased-in approach such that there were three coexisting groups in the project: beneficiaries, potential beneficiaries in a temporary housing site, and nonbeneficiaries. These allowed for group comparisons using a natural experimental design. I selected Cape Town because, at the time of the study, the state was in the process of providing low-income housing subsidies accompanied by freehold property rights. The state used a phased-in approach to housing subsidy delivery, meaning that housing was delivered to groups of people in phases. At any one time, beneficiaries and nonbeneficiaries coexisted, allowing the study to make comparisons between them. Lusaka represents the privatization of publicly owned housing at low cost to poor beneficiaries, with the state's goal of delivering housing with leasehold ownership rights. Study of an upgraded slum where residents possessed usufruct rights, next to a neighborhood that received leasehold property rights, allowed comparison of freehold rights and usufruct rights. Finally, Luanda provided a contrast to freehold and leasehold rights. The government provided social housing under occupancy or usufruct rights to the poor who had been evacuated from Boa Vista—a slum destroyed by mudslides in 2000 and 2001. While many capitulated and moved to Zango, some residents moved to another slum, Paraiso, to remain close to economic opportunities. The case study is one of self-selection into usufruct rights and informal/untitled or no land and housing tenure rights.

Evidence supporting arguments in this book combines household surveys and in-depth interviews with beneficiaries, nonbeneficiaries, and key informants. In Nairobi, our team of nine researchers conducted a household survey in Kibera—one of the largest slums on the continent—from July to August of 2019. The sample comprised 815 households. Additionally, we conducted 18 in-depth, one-on-one qualitative interviews with key informants and residents from different beneficiary groups. In Cape Town, we analyzed existing panel survey data on 330 households that benefitted from the South African housing subsidy program. Complementary to survey data analysis, the research team conducted 37 in-depth interviews with heads of households (28 beneficiaries and 9 nonbeneficiaries) from June to August 2011. In Lusaka, from July to August of 2011, a team of 7 researchers and data collectors conducted a survey of 623 households. In addition, we conducted 35 qualitative interviews in Matero, a neighborhood that benefitted from the privatization of council housing, and George, a neighborhood that was part of the World Bank–funded slum-upgrading program where people held occupancy rights, providing a comparison case study. In Luanda, a study team of 22 researchers and data collectors conducted a household survey of 640 households during December 2019. Household heads were surveyed from two neighborhoods: Zango, where beneficiaries of social housing were settled by the government, and Paraiso, a musseque populated by nonbeneficiaries.

The analysis employed both experimental and non-experimental causal analysis methods, some of which are employed for the first time in the urban African context. The analysis in Kenya takes advantage of a phased-in natural experiment to housing delivery under the Kenya Slum Upgrading Program (KENSUP). At any one time, there were potential beneficiaries living in Kibera, potential beneficiaries living in a decanting site without freehold rights, and beneficiaries living in newly constructed housing. Quantitative data analysis methods were employed, including propensity score analysis (PSA) matching methods and logistic and ordinary least squares regression, analysis of variance (ANOVA), Kruskal-Wallis H-test, and thematic analysis for the qualitative data. In the analysis on Cape Town, the study employed quantitative analysis methods (multiple regression and difference-in-differences) and thematic analysis of qualitative evidence. In the case of Lusaka, multiple regression analysis and propensity score matching methods were used to overcome selection bias. A thematic analysis of qualitative evidence was also employed. In the case of Luanda, we employed propensity score matching methods.

The book has both theoretical and policy implications. It challenges decades of market fundamentalist development economics on the effect of freehold and leasehold property rights among the urban poor. The book demonstrates through both quantitative and qualitative approaches that the mainstream understanding that property ownership rights include powers to consume and obtain income from these assets through market exchange is more complex among the poor in urban sub-Saharan Africa. Since freehold and leasehold tenure fail to live up to the economic claims of the homeowner economic ideology, even engendering tenure insecurity for some, there is no justification for taxation and market-rate bills in the freehold and leasehold cities examined. Through evidence from the four cities, the book challenges ideological claims about the economic story of freehold and leasehold property rights, illustrates a richer narrative of the effects of property rights on non-economic dimensions of human welfare, and highlights the story of usufruct property rights. It is also an exploration of how property rights advance non-economic dimensions of human welfare, when we expand beyond a narrow economic and ideologically informed paradigm. Finally, it is a story of how freehold and leasehold rights are neither necessary nor sufficient to maximize utility.

The book does not suggest that freehold and leasehold ownership should be denied to the poor. Rather, it suggests a need to break from an ideologically informed view that ownership of real property among the poor is an economic capital asset. It proposes a paradigm shift from ideologically based claims in policymaking to greater awareness of the social production of tenure processes. Therefore, there is need to understand the process of social production of homeownership tenure—not simply focusing on the neoliberal ideology and policies informed by neoclassical economics, but on the role of intergenerational transfer of culture about homeownership in families, and the role of the state in re/producing a preference for homeownership through policy. Such a shift should involve not only recognizing the role of neoliberal ideology, the family, and the state in social production processes, but also developing an appreciation of social reality through empirical evidence.

1.5. ORGANIZATION OF THE BOOK

Following this introduction, chapter 2 introduces the conceptual and theoretical framework for understanding the homeowner ideology among the poor in African cities. The framework consists of the homeowner ideology and four main theses that support it. I introduce the homeowner economic ideology and further propose that the idea of economic utility of freehold and leasehold tenure is unsupported, explaining it through the idea of structured idle capital. The second thesis demonstrates that the economic utility of ownership rights is a pervasive concept in the scholarly and policy field of property rights. Furthermore, the concept obscures the social reality of several effects of real property rights on non-economic dimensions of human welfare, such as human capital and subjective well-being, among other unintended consequences. The third thesis advances that the pervasiveness of the homeowner ideology obscures the utility of usufruct property rights. Finally, the fourth thesis argues that the social production of tenure driven by the homeowner ideology explains the persistence of homeownership as the intervention of choice. Further, chapter 2 locates the knowledge gaps created by the homeowner economic ideology, highlighting the dearth of empirical studies investigating claims about the effects of real property rights for the urban poor in African cities.

Chapter 3 shows that the homeowner ideology is pervasive in Nairobi, Cape Town, and Lusaka, which can be contrasted with the case of Luanda where usufruct rights are more pervasive. The chapter introduces the country and city contexts where the women homeowners are from, and provides justification for the use of their cities in the interrogation of the homeowner ideology. The chapter provides an account of how the homeowner ideology became a pervasive idea in African countries, specifically through the neoliberal economic reforms of the late 1980s and through the 1990s. In this way, it introduces case studies of the cities of Nairobi, Cape Town, Lusaka, and Luanda, justifying their use in the interrogation of the homeowner ideology.

In Nairobi, liberalization in the 1990s entrenched owner ideologies that provided the basis for delivery of houses to the poor using freehold tenure. In Cape Town, the post-apartheid government's adoption of Washington Consensus policies laid the foundation for correcting apartheid injustices in the housing sector through delivery of subsidized housing using freehold tenure. In Lusaka, privatization and liberalization of the economy under SAPs provided the structural conditions for the sale of public rental housing to sitting tenants and for the transfer of derelict housing under leasehold tenure to the poor for free. In Luanda, the prevalence of state ownership and delivery of housing under usufruct rights provides a useful comparison case for examining ideological claims.

Chapter 4 narrows to the specific neighborhood contexts introduced in chapter 3. The chapter shows how in the case of Nairobi, freehold property rights for the poor were transferred through low-interest mortgages under the Kenya Slum Upgrading Program to residents from two sections with slum conditions, making the case that this constituted a natural experiment. In Cape Town, the government delivered freehold rights through subsidized housing to people in Khayelitsha who had been marginalized during apartheid. The phased delivery of real property rights provided conditions where both beneficiaries and nonbeneficiaries existed simultaneously, making the case for a control group design. Lusaka also makes a case for a control group design, where the government transferred ownership of leasehold property rights to the poor in Matero through privatization of derelict public rental housing, and adjacent to Matero is George Compound, where the government granted usufruct rights. This allowed the study of the effects of property rights based on differences in bundles of rights possessed—that is, between ownership and use rights. Finally, a case is made for a control group design in Luanda, where residents of Boa Vista moved to Zango and Paraiso after mudslides. The comparison case is for Zango residents, who possessed usufruct rights, and Paraiso residents, who were in an informal settlement with no documented rights, allowing observation of the effects of usufruct rights with informal condition as the control condition.

Building on the stage set in chapters 3 and 4, chapter 5 delves deeper into the Nairobi case. The chapter describes the novel methods employed to examine the provision of freehold property rights to the urban poor in Kibera through low-interest mortgages. The chapter shows that freehold real property rights are bundles of rights to structured idle capital, but they are also associated with other improvements in non-economic dimensions of human welfare. Property rights are not associated with access to credit, labor-market participation, income-generating activities, or income. However, they are associated with stronger tenure security, better physical and psychological health, and a sense of pride, self-esteem, and belonging. Differences in household income are attributed to corruption. Thus, ownership rights are not associated with economic well-being but with psychological, human capital, and subjective well-being.

Chapter 6 goes further into the case of Khayelitsha, arguing that freehold property rights delivered through housing subsidy programs produce structured idle capital among the poor, even as they are associated with improvements to non-economic dimensions of human welfare. There are no economic benefits. Housing subsidies are associated with better physical health and (counterintuitively) higher occurrence of teenage pregnancy, and potentially help with accumulation of household durable goods, attainment of higher status, and neighborhood satisfaction. These improvements are attributed to better housing quality and environment rather than directly to real property rights for the poor. This means that the effects of housing extend to human capital, which has been obscured by the focus on economic benefits. The chapter also shows that poverty is driven so strongly by factors such as unemployment that property rights make little overall difference to income poverty.

Using the case of privatization of low-cost low-income housing located in Matero Lusaka and self-built housing in a slum-upgraded neighborhood of George also in Lusaka, chapter 7 examines claims that leasehold tenure rights improve property values, credit access, employment, household income, and participation in income-generating activities among the poor. The chapter shows that residents of Matero living under leasehold rights are associated with significantly higher property values and with less participation in income-generating activities. However, these property values are not high enough to allow access to credit. There are also no significant differences in tenure security. In fact, those with stronger rights reported fears of losing their property because of difficulty paying taxes. However, those in George also engage in investments and businesses, even though they only have usufruct rights. This case shows that property rights are bundles of rights to structured idle capital and usufruct rights are just as strong as ownership rights among the poor.

Using the case of Luanda, chapter 8 shows that ownership rights are neither necessary nor sufficient for the poor to pursue the claimed benefits made in favor of ownership forms of tenure. Although beneficiaries are officially allocated usufruct bundles of rights to land and housing in Zango, they invest in the land and housing, and they engage in property transactions. Usufruct rights are just as strong as ownership rights in providing tenure security and other economic and non-economic benefits for human well-being.

Chapter 9 concludes the book. The chapter highlights that an emphasis on real property rights reflects the pervasiveness of the homeowner ideology in development thought and in international development policymaking. More research on other dimensions of effects of real property rights in Africa is needed to effectuate the paradigm shift from ideologically based claims in policymaking to the development of an awareness of the social production of tenure processes. Therefore, there is a need to understand the process of social production of homeownership tenure—not focusing just on the role of neoliberal ideology and policies informed by neoclassical economics, but also on the role of the intergenerational transfer of culture about homeownership and the role of the state in producing and reproducing preference for homeownership through policy support. Such a shift should involve recognizing the role of neoliberal ideology, the family, and the state in social production processes, but also developing an appreciation of social reality through empirical evidence.

The final chapter summarizes the findings, argument, and implications of the book. These findings include that (1) real property rights for the urban poor in sub-Saharan Africa are bundles of rights to idle capital and are not of sufficient economic utility to the poor; (2) empirical evidence examining the utility of ownership rights beyond economic dimensions demonstrates that there are benefits to human welfare that have been obscured by the focus on economic utility; (3) there are benefits to usufruct tenures; and (4) social production processes that take into account homeowner ideology explain the persistence of the preference for this intervention.

The implication is that real property rights matter less for eradication of slum conditions and poverty among the urban poor in the cities examined. Clearly, ownership rights have failed to eradicate poverty among the urban poor. The evidence for the current large and growing scale of slum conditions in sub-Saharan African cities is a powerful argument against the current focus on private ownership property rights. Several governments have transferred property rights to slum dwellers, yet slum conditions and poverty persist. This approach literally transfers of responsibility for building adequate housing from the state to the urban poor, who lack the financial resources to build adequate housing, let alone withstand the power of distress sales and gentrification, and in many cases are unable to withstand other new forms of vulnerability.

The alternative is to understand the social production of tenure processes in each city or country context through empirical and not ideological policy justifications. The solution to the low-cost, low-income housing crisis has always been and will always be low-cost, low-income housing with the type of tenure that suits the local context.

1.6. DELIMITATION

This book focuses on real property rights among the poor in urban areas. It does not focus on intellectual property rights, nor does it focus on property rights related to rural or agricultural purposes, even though some theoretical content interacts with that literature. Finally, the book does not interrogate the functioning of neoliberal free markets among the nonpoor.

1.7. CONCLUSION

Through the stories of Zawadi, Mpho, Mary, Rosana, and over 2,000 others, I argue that the economic utility of real property rights among the urban poor in sub-Saharan Africa is not supported by the evidence. Rather, the social production of homeownership through the state, family, and neoliberal homeowner ideology explains the persistence of these claims in scholarship and international development practice. The ensuing chapters demonstrate that real property rights among the urban poor in African cities are bundles of rights to structured idle capital. They also demonstrate that the concentration of research on economic outcomes has obscured effects of real property rights on non-economic dimensions of human welfare, as well as the benefits of usufruct tenure rights. It further explains the role of homeowner ideology in the persistence of the belief, in scholarship and international development policy, that ownership is an effective intervention in the eradication of poverty.

CHAPTER 2

Conceptualizing and Theorizing the Homeowner Ideology

With the larger goal of examining the role of home ownership in the lives of impoverished peoples, this chapter develops a conceptual and theoretical framework for understanding real property rights among urban poor in African cities. The framework interrogates the homeowner ideology and its four main theses. The first thesis dissects the homeowner economic ideology, locating economic utility of freehold and leasehold tenure as the central tenet of the ideology. The second thesis highlights the disconnect between this ideological belief and the economic realities of the poor. The third thesis proposes that assumptions contained within the homeowner economic ideology actually obfuscate the social reality of several effects of property rights on non-economic dimensions of human welfare. The final thesis explores the underexamined utility of usufruct property rights that is obscured by current conceptions of the homeowner ideology.

2.1. THE HOMEOWNER IDEOLOGY

Adapting Ronald's (2004, 2008) definition of the ideology of home ownership, the homeowner ideology here is conceptualized as the libertarian philosophical system of beliefs, values, assumptions, and claims about permanent ownership of real property rights. The salient component of the homeowner ideology is formal, lifetime ownership, with the power to bequeath to succeeding generations. The classical libertarian claim suggests that ownership of real property gives the owner freedom to do whatever they wish with the resource (Anderson and Huggins 2009). Other claims suggest that ownership is a natural preference of rational man (Ronald 2008), the norm, the most desirable tenure, and a symbol of status attainment (e.g., the American dream). Within this conception, it follows that ownership is best because it accompanies and incentivizes community investment, it contributes to satisfaction and achievement in life, and it is cheaper in the long run (Acolin 2020; Acolin, An, and Wachter 2022).

The homeowner ideology falls under the broader market fundamentalist neoliberal ideology, the religious belief in the power of neoliberalism, laissez-faire or free-market ideas in market self-regulation, and the notion that markets can handle all economic issues without state involvement (Block and Somers 2014, 3; Jo, Chester, and King 2012; Shaanan 2017; Stiglitz 2009). The religious underpinnings of market fundamentalism are reflected in a lack of economic science or historical evidence to support it (Stiglitz 2009). The belief in freehold and leasehold ownership as ideal tenure is likewise unsupported by empirical and historical evidence from industrialized countries (Kemeny 1981, 2015; Ronald 2008). Yet market fundamentalism rests on the premise that freehold property ownership is the most important institution in a world where property rights institutions are the backbone of economic transactions (Robinson 2010).

2.1.1. The Homeowner Economic Ideology

The homeowner economic ideology reflects a collection of not entirely substantiated claims pertaining to the economic utility of real property rights. Market fundamentalist neoclassical economists take as established facts that ownership rights are "superior institutions," central to freedom and prosperity. Economic prosperity and several individual freedoms such as geographic, social, and economic mobility have been linked to the rewards of property rights (Anderson and Huggins 2009). By contrast, lack of property rights has also been proposed as a reason why nations fail (Acemoglu and Robinson 2012). A widely cited idea is that legal titles that prove formal ownership are a mystery of capital that bring dead capital to life and unlock trillions of dollars trapped in the hands of the poor in slums of the developing world (de Soto 2003).

A major claim in the homeowner economic ideology is that property titling increases credit access (Besley 1995; Durand-Lasserve and Selod 2009; Feder and Noronha 1987). The mechanism is such that freehold and leasehold titleholders can use their property title as collateral to obtain credit. And, further, freehold and leasehold titleholders can improve the value of the house, in order to borrow against it. The association of ownership rights with credit access is based on three main assumptions: the investment capacity of untitled households is hindered by credit constraints; titleholders are willing to risk their property as collateral to finance their business; and financial institutions will provide credit to households in low-income settlements using real property as collateral (Durand-Lasserve and Selod 2009, 109).

Also claimed is that real property ownership can have several effects through the mechanism of strengthening tenure security. Homeowner ideologists claim that titling using freehold and leasehold property rights results in an increase in property value (Durand-Lasserve and Selod 2009; Lanjouw and Levy 2002). Freehold and leasehold formalization may result in an increase in tenure security, which may in turn result in several housing investments and improvements and further increase property value (Besley 1995; Durand-Lasserve and Selod 2009, 108).

Under conditions of tenure insecurity, occupants in informal settlements have no incentive to invest in their houses (Abrams 1966; Durand-Lasserve and Selod 2009, 108–9; Turner and Fichter 1972). Thus, freehold and leasehold ownership can lead to investments by increasing tenure security. Investments may be made in the housing stock or dwelling, which increases property value and savings; in improvements to the dwelling, which improves health because the living environment is better, and improves education because fewer days of school are missed and the learning environment is better; in producing positive externalities for neighbors and investment in community assets (social capital and property values); and in increasing the return on home businesses, thereby increasing or substituting home employment for external employment (Durand-Lasserve and Selod 2009, 108–9).

Three arguments on the effects of tenure security on household investments are often made (Besley 1995, 908). Initially posited by Demsetz (1966) and Alchian and Demsetz (1973), the security argument asserts that individuals underinvest if the fruits of their investments may be seized by others. The collateral-based view posits that freehold and leasehold ownership titles increase property value, reducing credit access constraints and making it easier to use land as collateral. In turn, this leads to more investments. The third argument presumes that gains are made from trade. This view holds that the possibilities of increased gains from trade not only increase property value, they make it easier for individuals to rent or sell all or part of their land at higher value (Besley 1995, 910).

Another claim is that conversion to freehold and leasehold tenure through property titling can influence labor-market outcomes among the poor via increases in tenure security. The main idea here is that untitled households devote much of their time to guarding their homes from eviction (Durand-Lasserve and Selod 2009, 108; Field 2007). This reduces their time available for work. Further, because home protection is best provided by adults, tenure insecurity may provide an incentive for child labor outside the home. In this regard, freehold and leasehold titling should lead to tenure security because it frees up this labor, so freehold and leasehold titling may lead to an increase in labor supply and a reduction in child labor (Durand-Lasserve and Selod 2009, 108; Galiani and Schargrodsky 2010). It may further lead to female employment, because women are more likely to stay home while men go to work.

Relatedly, it is claimed that freehold and leasehold tenure can empower vulnerable individuals (Durand-Lasserve and Selod 2009, 110). When granted to women or jointly to couples, ownership can increase women's bargaining power. Without freehold and leasehold rights, women lack such power. The evidence of increased bargaining power can be seen through reduced fertility because of women's stronger position in family decision-making. It can also be a mechanism for increased labor market participation among women.

Finally, the claim exists that freehold and leasehold tenure can change beliefs among holders to those that support the market. This change in beliefs can drive them to decide to make investments (Di Tella, Galiant, and Schargrodsky 2007).

2.1.2. The Pervasiveness of the Homeowner Economic Ideology

The economic utility of ownership tenure is a pervasive idea that has strongly influenced the courts, public policy, and political debate through market fundamentalism and neoclassical economics (Block and Somers 2014). After sweeping through the developing world in the late 1970s, ideas on the economic utility of real property ownership have become conventional wisdom in economics, politics, and social policy (Burgin 2012; Cassidy 2009; Jones 2012). As discussed in chapter 1, continued demand for owner-occupied housing has led to significant increases in housing prices in Western countries and building projects across the developing world (Ronald 2008).

While the homeowner ideology can be viewed simply as a pervasive idea, scholars following social theorist Gramsci advance homeownership as a dominant ideology (Kemeny 1981, 2015; Ronald 2008). Naming it as a dominant ideology suggests that it has become widely accepted to the extent that the social, economic, and political agenda-setting is structured by that ideology's own mode of discourse (Kemeny 2015, 96). An ideology becomes dominant when a competing interest group dominates the state. The strategic alliance that has attained hegemony in civil society will hold political power to the exclusion of other interests in society, reflecting classical political dominance (Kemeny 2015, 99). In this case, it results in political support for policies encouraging owner occupation (Kemeny 2015, 48). The notion of market fundamentalism transforming into a dominant ideology can be traced back to writings by Karl Polanyi (2001) in *The Great Transformation*, which lamented market dominance in all spheres.

Dominant ideologies literature sees market fundamentalist neoliberal ideology as central to claims calling for formal property ownership, even as these ideological claims are not supported by the evidence (Gurney 1999a, 1999b; Kemeny 1981, 2015; Potts 2020). In groundbreaking research during a historical moment defined by Reaganomics and Thatcherism, Kemeny (1981) investigated types of housing tenure in different industrialized countries. Using case studies of owner occupation in the United States and Australia, social housing in Sweden, and social housing and owner occupation in Britain, Kemeny (1981) found no significant differences in costs incurred to individuals using different tenure systems across the three countries. Findings suggested that the aggregate cost is more or less the same, as the cost was spread out over time for renters, and the cost was concentrated at a single point for buyers. Kemeny demonstrated that for industrialized countries, the relationship between ideology and social structure—mediated by the exercise of state powers through political dominance—is vital for understanding why societies develop characteristic social structures and emphasize particular tenure types. In a follow-up study, he demonstrated that social, economic, and political agenda-setting is structured by the parameters of an ideology's own mode of discourse (Kemeny 2015, 96). In essence, classical political dominance occurs when one of several competing interest groups with a particular ideology dominates the state to the exclusion of other societal interests (Kemeny 2015, 99; Kemeny, 1992, 99). He extends this notion to explain ownership in terms of political support for policies that encourage owner occupation (see Kemeny 2015, 48).

Ronald (2008) expanded Kemeny's work using case studies of the liberalization of welfare in Anglo-Saxon homeowner societies in the United States, Great Britain, and Australia, and East Asian societies of Japan, Hong Kong, and Singapore. Ronald (2008) questioned arguments about the expansion of economic development under globalization, arguing that the dramatic increase in emphasis on and commitment to homeownership revealed embedded ideological structures and power relations more than a natural evolution toward ownership. Thus, attributing economic development to homeowner occupancy is misguided (Ronald 2008, 6). Rather, socio-ideological forces are central to understanding the proliferation of homeownership in industrialized countries.

The dominant ideologies thesis has potential to explain why homeownership is promoted in African countries, as they have long been pressured to accept this ideology through conditional aid and Western propagation of neoliberal ideologies and neoclassical development models. For example, Washington Consensus policies promote ownership and real property rights as a primary avenue to the right policies. Recognizing the role of dominant ideologies allows the interrogation of existing claims through objective empirical examination.

Nevertheless, the idea of dominant ideology has certain inadequacies compared to the concept of a pervasive idea. The political economy literature has shown that African countries have controlled the process of liberalization during their economic stabilization and adjustment, often using it to their advantage (Chabal and Daloz 1999; Van de Walle 2001). While pervasive, the homeowner ideology is not dominant in African countries. Also, the idea of a dominant ideology assumes the inevitability of class consciousness among the dominated, which is difficult to find evidence for, where the existence of class is contentious. There is value in aligning with scholars such as Potts (2020), Lemanski (2011), and Payne et al. (2009), who take a critical view of the claims based on ideology and utilize an empirical approach to examine pervasive ideas.

Other competing explanations include those of neo-Marxists who contend that propagation of ownership tenure is part of a wider trend toward market fundamentalist neoliberal economic policies that commodify houses and integrate them into the world capitalist economy for the benefit of wealthy elites (Fauveaud 2020; Glynn 2009, 38–67; Mwingyine, Akaateba, and Laube 2020, 185–208). Such positions extend long-held views by Marxist scholars, who argue that once people become homeowners, they move from proletariat to bourgeoisie (Engels 2004). The argument follows that industrialized countries use international financial institutions such as the World Bank and International Monetary Fund (IMF) to promote policies that support private ownership of property (Glynn 2009). Examples include property titling and privatization. Local elites and multinational corporations create common cause to buy land and exploit the housing markets of developing countries in the interest of profit (Aldrich and Sandhu 1995, 24). The populations of developing countries become dependent on property-owning elites and multinational corporations for shelter and business operations. Because local elites and multinational corporations export their profits to more lucrative investments in industrialized countries, there is little benefit to poor countries (Aldrich and Sandhu 1995).

Specifically, the privatization of public rental housing in developing countries as well as some industrialized countries has come under criticism from neo-Marxists. Policies of privatization in many countries in Africa, Asia, South America, and Eastern Europe were part of structural adjustment programs (SAPs) advocated by the World Bank and IMF. In this school of thought, SAPs were interpreted as an expansion of exploitative economic relationships in developing countries (Glynn 2009). Neo-Marxists explain privatization as the accumulation of the international capitalist classes by dispossession of the poor (an application of Marx's term "primitive accumulation," which he used to describe the expropriation of the peasants from the land) (Glynn 2009, 45). Scholars note that the people most affected by housing privatization are poor, working-class people who do not have the resources to buy the houses. In turn, they end up being dispossessed by capitalist classes. Through gentrification, property ends up with the already well-to-do, who can afford to buy and develop it. As Glynn (2009, 86) argues, those who are unable to afford property are marginalized and thus absent from the public discourse, evidently forgotten. In sum, this view perceives the pervasiveness of ownership as a further development of the international capitalist system and continued exploitation of noncapitalist populations under the guise of market fundamentalist neoliberalism.

While somewhat convincing, neo-Marxist arguments are not comprehensive. For example, some housing programs have been implemented as social welfare to correct past injustices, as with the South African program under study here. Furthermore, ownership programs are also implemented in left-leaning societies with several restrictions on selling. Lastly, the poor do have agency under the law to decide if and when to sell their property.

2.2. FUTILITY OF THE HOMEOWNERSHIP ECONOMIC IDEOLOGY AMONG THE POOR

A dearth of evidence exists on the causal effects of freehold and leasehold rights in Africa, but extant research questions their measurable impact on the economic lives of the poor. I advance the idea that the bundles of rights that poor freeholders and leaseholders possess are rather challenging to use in formal markets. The idea of idle capital comes from the economic theory of capital utilization. In the theory of capital, a firm can decide to utilize capital stock at full capacity to yield maximum flows of profit, at low capacity, or not at all. Idle capital refers to an inefficient equilibrium whereby a firm does not employ or underemploys a resource or capital—that is, low-capacity utilization, or non-utilization (Weil 2013, 283). The decision not to utilize capital stock renders the capital asset idle. In this theory, the firm, specifically executives as actors on behalf of the firm, decide whether or not to utilize capital by strategic management of the resource, based on market conditions such as demand and supply and profit potential. Idle capital reflects capital that owners decided not to extract from or maximize.

Idle capital conceptions alone are insufficient to explain the circumstances of capital utilization among the freeholders and leaseholders discussed in this book. Hence, I offer further delineation of idle capital. *Unstructured idle capital* is real property over which an owner has the power to decide whether or not to utilize the capital asset. By contrast, *structured idle capital* is a capital asset over which the agent or owner may exercise only limited agency, due to structural constraints to utilization. Even as the agent is theoretically free to decide whether to utilize the asset, structural constraints outside of the agent's control limit agency. In this case, the agent's only definitive option is to alienate themselves from the resource. Structured idle capital means that the freeholder cannot extract maximum utility due to market or societal conditions, or institutions that place limits on its use. Beneficiaries of real property rights among the urban poor are unable to utilize their property to accumulate profit. In short, structured idle capital is idle not entirely by the choice of the property owners; rather, it is subject to external market and legal constraints.

Real property rights represent bundles of rights to idle capital among the urban poor, as little evidence suggests that freehold and leasehold rights increase credit access in Africa and the rest of the developing world. Such mechanisms for increased access to credit do not work in Africa and the rest of the world (Domeher and Abdulai 2012). The World Bank's view seems to be that developing countries do not place high priority on property registries (Deininger and Ali 2022). Access to formal credit has not increased more noticeably under freehold tenure in South Africa and Senegal than under other tenure regimes, nor is there significant evidence of poverty reduction

(Payne, Durand-Lasserve, and Rakodi 2009). Indeed, South African freeholders who benefitted from housing subsidies are often wary of the risk involved in using their property as collateral (Boudreaux 2006; Kingwill et al. 2006, 53–65; Lemanski 2011; Tomlinson 2007, 17–31). Despite providing a financially tradable asset, low transaction values of subsidized houses in Westlake Village in Cape Town mean they cannot be sold for sufficient value (Lemanski 2011). Poor freeholders are also reluctant to use Reconstruction and Development Program (RDP) houses as collateral for credit. In Langa, few freehold titleholders put their newly formalized rights to use as collateral for commercial loans (Boudreaux 2006). Likewise, banks argue that they cannot lend to the poor because they are not assured of repayment (Tomlinson 2007), and the houses have too low a value to allow the poor freeholder to access credit. In Joe Slovo Park in Cape Town and Ekuthuleni in KwaZulu-Natal, freehold titles do not increase lending to the poor (Kingwill et al. 2006). In summary, banks do not lend to the poor due to the high risk of nonrepayment, the low value of houses, and high transaction costs.

While freehold and leasehold titles do have positive and significant effects on housing investments through the mechanism of increasing tenure security, it is not a wealth-creating effect. In Ghana, Besley (1995) found that freehold facilitated investments in Wassa, while it did not in Anloga. In Langa, poor freeholders invested in improving their homes, which raised property values; however, the extent of these improvements is unclear, as is percentage increase in property values (Boudreaux 2006). Complicating matters, untitled households also make improvements. Freehold titling improved entrepreneurial activities in 18 South African townships of Johannesburg, Cape Town, Durban, and East Rand, but Rust (2007, 44–52) showed that these activities did not result in more wealth. Freehold requires a functioning secondary property market for the poor, sufficient housing stock, people's ability to afford repayments on housing finance, and mortgage lenders willing to move downmarket to the poor.

Findings are ambiguous and the evidence is scarce on the effects of freehold and leasehold ownership on participation in the labor market in African countries. In Senegal, for example, the impact of titling on the economy of families is "limited and barely measurable," suggesting that there is barely an effect on labor market outcomes, because some of the families are so poor that their only option is to sell the property (Payne, Durand-Lasserve, and Rakodi 2009, 455).

2.3. THE OBSCURITY OF NON-ECONOMIC DIMENSIONS OF HUMAN WELFARE

The pervasiveness of market fundamentalism and the economic focus on freehold economic utility obscures knowledge on the effects of real property rights on other dimensions of human welfare. As Berry (2014, 16) asserts:

> The worst consequences of the rule of market fundamentalism in economics are, as Galbraith argues, that it has "crowded out" alternative, more fruitful analytical models and approaches, both with respect to more realistic assumptions concerning human agency and the network effects that increasingly link agent behavior.

Several ideological claims about the effects of ownership on non-economic dimensions of human welfare are understudied. I discuss these in the following paragraphs.

Homeowner ideologists claim that ownership forms of tenure can empower vulnerable individuals (Durand-Lasserve and Selod 2009, 110). Particularly when granted to women or couples, they argue, it increases women's bargaining power. Increased bargaining power is visible through reduced fertility, a stronger position in family decision-making, and increased labor market participation. The argument suggests that when their name is on the title, ownership rights empower vulnerable individuals, giving them more say in their families and lives. However, a dearth of research exists on the empowerment effects of freehold in African cities, and little evidence seems to support this claim. While women do not know of the existence of co-titling in Dar es Salaam (Kongela and Didas 2021), there is promising evidence in sub-Saharan Africa that women who access property rights may boost their welfare (O'Sullivan 2017).

Homeowner ideologists further claim that ownership rights have a positive association with physical health. It is thought that homeowners generally maintain their housing conditions better than nonhomeowners (Rohe, van Zandt, and McCarthy 2013). Homeownership leads to ontological security, which is associated with better physical health (Saunders 2022). However, it is not clear whether real property rights or physical housing conditions are responsible for better physical health (Rohe, van Zandt, and McCarthy 2013, 9). Here again, causal analysis is scarce on the effects of real property rights on health in the African context.

A similar claim suggests that freehold improves psychological health. Scholars suggest that the social status and personal freedom associated with freehold provides feelings of self-esteem and perceived control over life and (Rohe, van Zandt, and McCarthy 2013, 4). Because owners are largely in control of the everyday happenings in their housing units, they gain a stronger perception of control over life events (Rohe and Stegman 1994). Not only are they no longer worried about the likelihood or possibility of eviction, owners have control over who enters the house, have the freedom to make modifications, and are independent of slumlords and landlords. In this way, scholars claim, homeownership yields higher self-esteem (Rohe, van Zandt, and McCarthy 2013, 5) because homeowners are afforded higher social status; they take their housing tenure as indicative of doing better than others, providing a favorable self-comparison; and they perceive owning a house as the achievement of a major life milestone. As with other claims, little causal evidence in Africa supports these indicators.

Another claim is that real property rights improve neighborhood outcomes. Real property rights are thought to lead to social stability, social/civic involvement, socially desirable behavior, and social attachment (Rohe, van Zandt, and McCarthy 2013, 19). Social stability improves when homeowners move less frequently than renters or untitled households. This happens through several mechanisms. First, owners invest more in human capital over time and through education and income because they anticipate staying longer in their neighborhood. This leads to their stability because human capital investments are long term. Owners have both use and exchange interest in their housing and land, which increases civic engagement. With a stake in their neighborhood, they form organizations to maintain stable property values and social conditions.

Second, they are thought to be better citizens. With a greater stake in their neighborhood, they are more invested in its development and sustainability. To this end, they are more likely to participate in voluntary and political actions because they see participation as a way to protect their homes (Blum and Kingston 1984). They are also thought to be more likely to vote in elections. Third, homeownership may impart socially desirable behavior to local youth (Rohe, van Zandt, and McCarthy 2013, 19). Because homeowners have a financial stake in their homes, they are more likely to be concerned about antisocial behavior of their own and other children. Further, because homeowners stay longer in the neighborhood, they become more effective monitors of children, and may use collective socialization and peer influences. Finally, homeownership leads to more local social interaction and attachment (Rohe and Stewart 1996, 54–55). Because homeowners stay longer in their neighborhood, they come to identify strongly with their homes. Such identification builds collective socio-psychological feelings of pride, which may foster social attachment and interaction.

Causal analysis is scarce, but the available qualitative literature suggests that homeowners espouse values of respectability, decency, dignity, and belonging as they forge their relationships in new neighborhoods in South Africa (Lee 2005; Ross 2005a, 2005b, 2021). These values contrast with the dehumanizing experiences of apartheid.

What we do know from the very few studies examining the effects of real property rights on neighborhood outcomes and on aspects of social capital in developing countries is that there is no effect or a negative effect. Contrary to ideological claims about freehold, it seems to break down social capital—although much of this research is qualitative and excludes long-term impacts. Meinzen-Dick and Mwangi (2009) looked at how freehold titling affects social capital in rural areas of Kenya. They examined the manifestations of the web of interests generated by real property rights and the role they play in livelihoods, social relations, and ecological functions. They found that freehold ownership created exclusive forms of ownership. Therefore, it cut preexisting webs of overlapping interests, implying a reduction in social capital. The literature also shows that efforts of freehold subsidy beneficiaries during community-making in South Africa were undermined by segregation (Lemanski 2011; Oldfield 2000, 2004; Seekings et al. 2010). However, there were signs of tolerance in new mixed neighborhoods (Muyeba and Seekings 2011).

Other factors that constrain community-making in South Africa include jealousy and gossip (Ashforth 1998; Bray et al. 2010, 108; Ross 2021, 160–63), social disorganization (Berg and Scharf 2004; Breetzke 2010; Emmet 2003; Nina 2000), witchcraft (Ashforth 1998, 2005), and violent crime and criminality (Gastrow and Shaw 2001; Jewkes and Abrahams 2002). Coping mechanisms include kinship support (Seekings 2008a), domestic fluidity in the sense of individuals moving between households and being members of multiple households at a time (Seekings 2008a; Spiegel, Watson, and Wilkinson 1996), and privacy (Muyeba and Seekings 2012; Ross 2005b, 633).

Further, the claim is often made that ownership leads to greater satisfaction with life and home. Scholars holding this view define satisfaction as a person's level of contentment with all aspects their life; residential satisfaction is one's level of contentment with one's housing and surrounding neighborhood (Rohe, van Zandt, and McCarthy 2013, 2). The logic is that owning a home is an important goal for many individuals; once the goal is attained, it must result in satisfaction. Moreover, satisfaction arises from housing maintenance and improvements (Saunders 2022). Also, customizing housing units to one's taste can result in satisfaction with one's living environment (Rohe, van Zandt, and McCarthy 2013, 3). Likewise, making financial investments in the house may result in a better financial position, which in turn can lead to satisfaction (Rohe, van Zandt, and McCarthy 2013, 3).

In summary, claims about ownership of real property that go beyond economic utility have been obscured by the market fundamentalist focus on the economic utility of ownership rights. These ideological claims include that homeownership is associated with social stability, psychological health, satisfaction with life, social status attainment, socially desirable youth behavior (in terms of reduced teenage pregnancies and school dropout rates), and neighborhood outcomes. The state of knowledge about the effects of freehold on non-economic aspects of human welfare is poor in African countries, because it is obscured by the focus on economic utility of real property rights. Appendix B shows a summary of the homeowner ideological claims and the state of knowledge in Africa.

2.4. THE UTILITY OF NONOWNERSHIP FORMS OF TENURE

The homeowner ideology's emphasis on the utility of real property rights obscures the social reality that the absence of ownership title does not imply the absence of tenure security and utility. In research in Senegal and South Africa, Payne et al. (2009) pointed out that we do not know whether ownership title is the only form of rights that can achieve the objective of increasing housing investments. Although ownership titles may achieve the objective of housing improvement and investment, they are by no means the only route to those objectives. In Lusaka and Cape Town, for example, simple binaries of owner and nonowner fail to capture resident lived experiences, as rights to houses are not embedded in legal title but are shaped by shifting economic social and cultural realities (Butcher and Oldfield 2009). Furthermore, lack of formal ownership title does not detract from the occurrence of transactions and investments. In Angola, 96 percent of transactions take place without formal documented ownership (Cain 2013).

Sometimes, the primary tenure system offers more security to dwellers than titling or upgrading. For example, in informal settlements built on customary land in Kenya, private title may not easily accommodate competing interests from extended relatives and group rights (Durand-Lasserve and Selod 2009; Lanjouw and Levy 2002; Meinzen-Dick and Mwangi 2009, 107–8).

Ownership title is a source of tenure security, but not the only one. Even though it is equated to tenure security, it is possible for households to have tenure security without title (Durand-Lasserve et al. 2007, 22). In sub-Saharan Africa, a 140-country survey done in 2020 found that formal title brings less additional security of tenure in Africa than in other parts of the world. Sub-Saharan Africans with formal ownership documentation perceived tenure security at 70 percent, while those without it scored 65 percent (Prindex 2019, 18; *The Economist* 2020).

In some contexts, titling using real property rights actually reduces tenure security (Payne, Durand-Lasserve, and Rakodi 2009). Titling programs are often used in informal settlements in countries or cities that already have some degree of de facto tenure security (Payne, Durand-Lasserve, and Rakodi 2009). For example, Rwanda and Egypt offer cases of market-driven displacements of titled households through gentrification. Tenure security can be achieved through several means other than titling, and titling may actually lead to an increase in tenure insecurity.

In sum, the findings from past empirical studies on the effects of titling on tenure security lean toward the affirmative, but are nevertheless ambiguous. Measures of tenure security are rarely included in existing surveys, and context seems to play an important role in the effects of titling on tenure security.

2.5. SCARCITY OF QUANTITATIVE KNOWLEDGE ON EFFECTS OF REAL PROPERTY RIGHTS IN AFRICAN CITIES

Although there is a rich body of qualitative work exploring various aspects of freeholders and their experiences with social capital, especially in new post-apartheid housing projects in South Africa (see Bray et al. 2010; Lemanski 2011; Muyeba and Seekings 2012; Oldfield 2000, 2004; Ross 2005a, 2005b, 2021; Seekings, 2008a, 2008b; Seekings et al., 2010), far fewer causal analyses test claims about real property rights.

Like South Africa, Zambia has a rich collection of qualitative studies on urban housing tenure concerned with the privatization of publicly owned housing from 1996 to the early 2000s (Adams 2003; Butcher and Oldfield 2009; Mususa 2010, 2012; Palmer 2000; Schlyter 1998). However, the empirical studies concerned with the privatization of public housing were framed within the international political economy literature in which the sale of publicly owned housing to sitting tenants was explained to be part of market liberalization and SAP designed to stimulate the housing market and increase investments in housing.

2.6. CONCLUSION

Despite its relative lack of nuance, the homeowner ideology is pervasive. Within the ideology, the presumption of freehold tenure's economic utility may be the strongest-held belief, yet it does not reflect the economic reality of the poor. In fact, homeowner economic ideology obscures the social reality of several effects of property rights on non-economic dimensions of human welfare. Indeed, the homeowner ideology obscures the social reality that documented ownership is not a necessary condition for economic benefit.

Despite the pervasiveness of the homeowner ideology, the present chapter revealed the dearth of studies testing homeowner ideology claims in Africa. Although a rich literature exists on land and housing in sub-Saharan Africa, it employs mainly qualitative approaches. Many studies are concentrated in South Africa as a response to de Soto (2000). This book offers a fresh examination of claims about real property rights using quantitative techniques such as natural experiments and matching methods—not heretofore employed in the African context. The next five chapters reexamine the homeowner ideology in Nairobi, Cape Town, Lusaka, and Luanda.

CHAPTER 3

Pervasiveness of the Homeowner Ideology in Three of Four Sub-Saharan African Cities

In chapter 1, I introduced four women experiencing urban poverty in different cities. Three of them lived in slum conditions before being granted real property rights. Zawadi is from Zone A of Soweto East Neighborhood in Kibera, Kenya. She moved to the Canaan neighborhood in Nairobi. Mpho is from Site C of Khayelitsha in Cape Town, South Africa. Mary is from Matero in Lusaka, Zambia. And Rosana was from a slum called Boa Vista in Luanda, Angola. She was resettled in Zango, where she experienced usufruct rights.

Even though the governments in Kenya, South Africa, and Zambia provided housing and property rights to beneficiaries like Zawadi, Mpho, and Mary without World Bank support, they pursued delivery using ownership tenure. By contrast, the Angolan government chose to pursue delivery using usufruct rights. The present chapter introduces the city and country contexts for each of the four women discussed, and provides justification for use of these four cities in interrogating the homeowner ideology. The chapter provides historical context for the homeowner ideology in sub-Saharan African countries, exposing state and ideological roles in the social production of homeownership tenure.

3.1. SHIFTING OWNER IDEOLOGIES AND THE TRIUMPH OF MARKET FUNDAMENTALIST NEOCLASSICAL ECONOMICS IN AFRICA

Ideologies governing ownership in urban Africa have shifted across time. While collective forms of tenure—such as customary tenure—existed in

African civilizations and rural areas, colonialism brought bifurcation (Mamdani 2018). Many countries favored private ownership models under capitalist ideologies during the colonial and immediate postcolonial era. And with independence, sub-Saharan African countries inherited existing capitalist economies (Moss and Resnick 2018, 75). In the 1970s and early 1980s, socialist-oriented ideologies influenced a shift toward collective ownership. Since the late 1980s, however, many countries have shifted back to private ownership under neoliberalism.

3.2. FIRST SHIFT: FROM CAPITALISM UNDER COLONIALISM TO SOCIALISM UNDER POLITICAL INDEPENDENCE

Chartered by their governments, private companies—including the British South Africa Company, the British East Africa Company, the Imperial British East Africa Company, the Dutch East India Company, and the French West India Company—were the leading edge of colonialism. Colonial governments closely protected these private companies and their investments. In later years, multinational corporations became the main avenue for exploiting natural resources for the benefit of the colonial government. To streamline governance, colonialists often created a bifurcation of state, such that ownership in urban areas was governed by civil law, while ownership in rural areas was governed by customary law (Mamdani 2018). In such bifurcated states, a civil, Westphalian state system in urban areas coexisted with a traditional, customary system in rural areas.

Within these systems, ownership approaches oscillated widely. In the first decade following independence, there was a notable shift from colonial capitalism to public ownership under socialism. After the first few years of independence, the national euphoria was interrupted by the realization that although they had achieved political independence, the new countries were still very much colonized in terms of economy, bureaucratic governance, culture, language, and appearance (Moss and Resnick 2018, 107–8). Indeed, multinational corporations and private firms operating in these regions were still owned by their former colonizers, who still occupied leading roles. These colonizers continued to influence civil service, universities, and public schools, and were often paid expatriate salaries.

Several nationalist leaders instituted African socialist philosophies and nationalized privately owned property (Friedman 2021). Kenneth Kaunda of Zambia developed the ideology of Zambian humanism and nationalized companies by expropriating 51 percent of ownership for the government under the Mulungushi reforms in 1968. Julius Nyerere adopted Ujamaa, and Leopold Sedar Senghor of Senegal adopted Negritude. Mobutu Sese Seko adopted Authenticité. Although maintaining a capitalist economic system, even Jomo Kenyatta adopted harambee, which emphasized a collective ideology. Nationalist leaders passed acts of legislation, presidential declarations, and policies of nationalization that allowed them to repossess capital from Western firms that had been taken during colonialism. African governments employed eminent domain, taking ownership of private property such as firms, land, mines, houses, and ports. The state created public entities or state-owned enterprises to take over these private entities, actively using them to engage in economic production. In many cases, the state gave the populace access to land, housing, jobs, healthcare, education, and sometimes food from the proceeds of these enterprises. All goods and services were publicly owned.

Several factors led nationalist leaders to adopt socialist ideologies and policies. At the time, Marxism was a popular theoretical view among political scientists, developmentalists, political economists, and policymakers (Moss and Resnick 2018, 107–8). Scholars at state universities associated themselves with the Marxist tradition and provided policy advice on that basis. What is more, Lenin's *Imperialism: The Highest Stage of Capitalism* was popular among intellectuals in Africa and much of the developing world. The book held the added appeal of direct applicability to the times. Dependency theory was also emerging as a leading theory through Raul Prebisch at the United Nations Economic Commission for Latin America (Moss and Resnick 2018; Todaro and Smith 2020, 122–26). In Africa, Walter Rodney had skillfully disseminated his dependency theory and its application to Africa while at the University of Dar es Salaam, later releasing *How Europe Underdeveloped Africa* in 1972 (Moss and Resnick 2018; Rodney et al. 2018). Independence movements across the continent had close relations with socialist and communist governments, since they had received support from them (Moss and Resnick 2018). The leading communist states of China and the Russian Federation were the most supportive of decolonization and provided notable support in the decades following independence. Several nationalist leaders were trained in these countries, including Kwame Nkrumah and Jomo Kenyatta. Further, socialist ideologies and policies were much more closely related to African traditional values of communalism and egalitarianism than to capitalism.

Several African customs and cultures emphasized collective ownership rather than individual ownership, entrusting resources to the traditional ruler and sharing resources equally. Socialism also emphasized collective ownership, entrusted resources to the state, and emphasized equal distribution of wealth. For African people, these principles were easier to relate to their own socialization than an emphasis on private property ownership, individualism, and the inequality of resource distribution associated with capitalism.

Moreover, Africans had rejected the institutions patterned after the Westphalian state system along with colonial rule (Fanon and Philcox 2004; Hydén 2013). Wounds from a 70-year reign of imperial violence, brutality, and colonial subjugation, with centuries of slavery preceding it, were still fresh. Colonial institutions were instruments of plunder, dispossession, and exploitation (Wallerstein 2020). To the African, Western institutions embodied the white supremacy and racial humiliation of Black Africans. They were symbols of genocide, brutality, and bodily trauma at the end of the baton and maiming at the blade of the machete. As Frantz Fanon declared in *Wretched of the Earth*, the institutionalization of colonialism was a violent process and therefore decolonization is a violent process (Fanon and Philcox 2004). Transplanted colonial institutions, especially constitutions, did not make sense in the common life of an African, yet Africans were punished for not conforming. Africans resorted to their community identity in response to threats posed initially by the slave trade and later by the colonial state (Hydén 2013, 65–66). Even today, few Africans maintain any loyalty to the civil institutions of the Westphalian state. Instead, they nurture their membership in a local community based on a primary social organization such as lineage, clan, or tribe (Hydén 2013).

In 1973, a global economic crisis threw Africa into a three-decade economic spiral that Van de Walle (2001) later called a permanent economic crisis, and Mkandawire and Meagher (2019) termed "Africa's great depression." In the decade following the start of the crisis, African governments accumulated unsustainable amounts of international debt. Market fundamentalist economists such as Milton Friedman, Harry Johnson, Bela Balassa, Lord Peter Bauer, Jagdish Bhagwati, Deepak Lal, Ian Little, and Anne Krueger diagnosed the involvement of the state in the economy as a major cause of the crisis (Todaro and Smith 2020, 127). With US presidents, British prime ministers, and IMF managing directors as his market fundamentalism disciples, Milton Friedman has been described as the most influential economist of the last half-century (Klein 2008, 7). The market fundamentalist prescription for the crisis was freer markets and a reduction in the state role. Reducing the role of the state entailed the transfer of capital assets from public hands to private ones through the process of privatization. The "shock therapy" treatment was to drive economic stabilization and adjustment policies (Klein 2008).

3.3. SECOND SHIFT: FROM SOCIALISM TO NEOLIBERAL FREE-MARKET CAPITALISM

When Washington Consensus policies were institutionalized to address the crisis, the pendulum swung in the other direction. As the market fundamentalist economists gained influence through positions at the World Bank, IMF, and leadership in developing countries, they defined international development finance policy. The same economists helped the World Bank craft structural adjustment programs (SAPs)—later known as Washington Consensus policies. SAPs were implemented as a condition for accessing monies to assist with stabilization and economic adjustment. SAPs were an imposition on developing countries, yet they needed financing and the Bretton Woods Institutions made financing conditional on implementation.

The homeowner ideology became a pervasive idea in sub-Saharan African countries through Washington Consensus policies after those policies supplanted socialist-oriented ideologies. Along with privatization, the international financial institutions developed policies to support individual private ownership. In the 1980s in their report *Shelter*, the World Bank (1980) advocated for slum-upgrading programs and ownership rights. In the early 1990s, the Bank's publication *Enabling Markets to Work* (World Bank 1993) advocated for the centrality of private property rights in enabling markets to work and achieve economic growth. Later, the *World Development Report* for 2002 mentioned property rights 87 times, with an emphasis on freehold ownership rights (World Bank 2002). The report stated, "Without land-titling institutions that ensure property rights, poor people are unable to use valuable assets for investment and income growth" (World Bank 2002, III). The idea of government-built and -provided housing went against conditionalities. States were required to downsize and limit their role to regulation and enforcement of the institutions that support markets.

Since the implementation of SAPs, governments in developing countries have struggled to provide housing and basic services. Indeed, conditionalities from international financial institutions constrain government involvement in the social and housing sector. Under such conditions, governments are confined to the role of arbiter, providing and enforcing housing regulations and standards, while encouraging private-sector-driven housing provision. However, the private sector keeps away from ventures involving financing of low-cost housing for low-income urban populations because it is not profitable (Potts 2020). The poor lack formal or adequate income, access to credit, and insurance, which makes it difficult to secure adequate housing through the private and formal market. Moreover, even if governments in Africa want to fund housing construction, many lack the economic resources to do so. Indeed, several factors militate against housing provision, including poor governance, corruption, unviable institutions, and insufficient community involvement. However, the economics of housing plays a critical role.

Even so, governments in Kenya, South Africa, and Zambia defied the odds and navigated market fundamentalism to provide housing to the poor. Angola's provision of housing using social housing policy is offered as a comparison case where the homeowner ideology is not pervasive. The following sections demonstrate how the homeowner ideology became a pervasive idea in three of the four cases under examination, highlighting how governments in these countries became directly involved in providing housing despite prohibitive conditionalities.

3.4. DEVELOPMENT OF THE HOMEOWNER IDEOLOGY AND HOUSING POLICY IN KENYA

As in many African countries, the development of urban land and housing policy in Kenya is intertwined with its colonial history (Mamdani 2018). When the Imperial British East Africa Company (IBEACO) arrived in precolonial Kenya in 1888, they observed large tracts of unoccupied land, some of which were buffer areas located between mutually hostile tribal lands (McGregor 2014). Ethnic groups occupied the most fertile and choicest land. Kikuyu and Maasai land stood out. While the Kikuyu cultivated their entire land and used small patches for grazing (a total of just over 100 miles by 18 miles of land for grazing), the Maasai kept vast areas unoccupied and without tillage (McGregor 2014, 41–42).

The IBEACO annexed the unoccupied lands for the British Empire and turned over its governance to the British government in 1895. The colonial administration called it the East Africa Protectorate and later the Colony and

Protectorate of Kenya. The IBEACO had respected the rights of the natives to their land. However, two years later the commissioner and colonial administrator issued government notices that "certain evil disposed" colonial settlers were taking advantage of the ignorance of natives about the value of their land. These evilly disposed buyers acquired prime land, particularly from women, at low prices (McGregor 2014, 44).

While the colonial administration set up a land tenure system where it offered freehold title deeds to settlers, it neglected to issue titles for the native lands—even though the topic came up several times in official communication. In effect, this created a bifurcated system consisting of a civil land tenure system with public and freehold tenure, and a customary rights land system with communal tenure. Bifurcation created a system where the land under the British was highly valuable, even though the land in the hands of the natives was the "choicest." Gradually, the colonial administration encroached on and incorporated native land into the civil law system, through legal means and outright dispossession. The administration required that all land transactions, including those involving natives, be conducted with consent from the commissioner. They also alienated vast amounts of native land for European settlement.

The development of the city of Nairobi involved the colonial government's creation of Crown land and freehold private property rights over land dispossessed from the Maasai and the Kikuyu, the latter being the largest tribe in Kenya (McGregor 2014, 43). Present-day Nairobi is located close to Kikuyuland. It was actually the Maasai who called it Nairobi, meaning "cold water," their name for the river that flowed out of the forests and into the plains (McGregor 2014, 43). Nairobi rests on the southern edge of Kikuyuland. To the north and northeast, Kikuyuland was surrounded by the White Mountains, present-day Mount Kenya. For the British, Nairobi was a railway settlement. From 1895 to 1902, the colonial administration built a railway line—the Uganda-Kenya railway—from the port of Mombasa through Nairobi to Nyanza on Lake Victoria, and expropriated land within one mile of the line. The colonial administration decided to move the capital of the British East Africa Protectorate to Nairobi when railway construction reached there in 1899. In 1914, official communication involving a committee of three recommended that the colonial administration reduce Kikuyuland to 10 percent (McGregor 2014, 48). The colonial administration alienated more than 100 square miles of Kikuyuland in the vicinity of Nairobi (Meredith 2011, 80). The Kikuyu had a deep attachment to their land, such that it was deeply

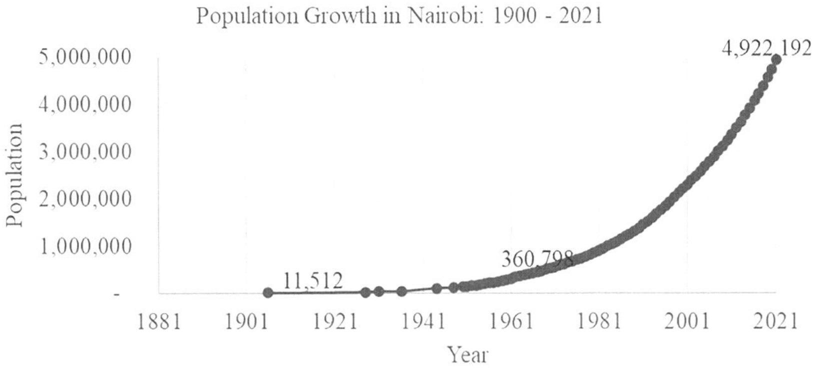

Fig. 3.1. Population Growth in Nairobi, 1900–2021

painful to see it taken away. This was such a constant source of grievance for the Kikuyu that it birthed the brutal Mau Mau rebellion and bore the seeds of an independent Kenya (Meredith 2011, 80).

The creation of freehold and public land in Nairobi created conditions for the development of slums for natives. After the colonial government moved the capital to Nairobi, a large urban settlement developed. However, it excluded the Black population, confining them to areas lacking legal ownership rights. From 1900, Nairobi grew into a business hub for the colonial administration as well as a segregated settlement for Europeans and Indians (Mitullah 2003, 2). The Indian population was employed as laborers on the railway construction. The colonial administration did not build formal settlements for Africans.

In addition to their policy of segregation based on race, the colonial government's refusal to build formal settlements or assign property rights the native population contributed to development of slums in Nairobi. Colonial urban planning and policy divided Nairobi into four areas (Mitullah 2003, 10). The administration allocated the north and west to the European population; parts of the north, east, and southeast to the Asian population; and parts of the east and southeast to Africans. The administration did not allocate enough resources to build housing and provide services in the African part of the city. As figure 3.1 shows, Nairobi experienced rapid population increases from 1901. While the colonial administration built insufficient housing for the African population, they migrated to the area surrounding the city in large numbers. As in other colonies, the colonial administration required that every married person pays a hut tax, every worker pay a poll tax, and every person carry an identification card proving they were a worker permitted to be in the city. Since Africans in rural areas could not afford to pay the taxes without a job, the segregated part of the city grew rapidly with rural-urban migrations, and without appropriate increases in housing and services.

Unlike most African states, Kenya maintained and pursued a capitalist economic development model following independence in 1963, though it saw decline and economic reforms like other African states. Kenya underwent SAPs in the late 1980s and 1990s, which expanded neoliberal policies. Public enterprises and assets were privatized, and the economy was liberalized—both of which were key policies for private ownership.

3.5. LAND AND HOUSING POLICY IN SOUTH AFRICA

Land and housing policy in South Africa is the story of dispossession and marginalization under racial segregation. It also tells a story of post-Apartheid attempts at land empowerment, desegregation, and correction of historical injustices. Land policy in South Africa has a long history, but a useful place to begin is June 19, 1913, three years after the Union of South Africa was established. On that day, the government of Louis Botha published the Natives' Land Act in the government gazette. This law restricted the purchase, lease, ownership, and occupation of land by natives. To this point, South Africa had practiced a policy of segregation by race. The Natives' Land Act restricted Blacks and other nonwhite persons to owning land in certain rural areas where land was of less value. The act was also the premise for evictions of natives from areas designated as white-only—effectively dispossessing Blacks of valuable land for decades to come.

The policy of excluding Africans from urban areas and containing them on the periphery of cities created poorly serviced spaces and slum conditions. From the 1920s to late Apartheid, South African state policy primarily concentrated on the "native question" or the "Bantu problem"—alluding to the challenges of urbanization and urban housing for a majority of the African population (Mamdani 2018). The "Bantu problem" was about keeping Blacks from freehold ownership of valuable urban land. The government allowed nonwhites to hold land through freehold in segregated territories across South Africa. It did so without creating economic opportunities.

In the 1950s and 1960s, the government built housing in sprawling urban fringe townships for "pass-holding" African people to use under public usufruct or tenancy agreements (Porteous 2005, 34). In Cape Town, the first townships were constructed at Nyanga and Gugulethu (Wilkinson 2000, 197). These houses were not sufficient to address the housing shortage. Indeed, the situation created conditions for political unrest. Moreover, the government could not contain the proliferation of squatting. Meanwhile, those with expired or nonexistent passes ("illegals") did not return to their places of origin, mostly in the Eastern Cape. Moreover, the Provincial Government in Cape Town established the Colored Labor Preference Act in 1956. This act established Cape Town as a labor preference area for the colored population (a term that continues to be in common parlance in South Africa, referring to mixed-heritage), allowing coloreds to work and live in neighborhoods dubbed "colored-designated areas." The act excluded Blacks and Indians from living and working in Cape Town. Thus, "illegals" settled on the fringes of urban areas and squatted in formal African townships. Informal settlements multiplied. The government estimated that as of June 1982, the population of Africans in Cape Town was 226,000. Only half could be accommodated in the formal townships (Cook 1986, 58). The government estimated a shortage of 10,000 housing units (Seekings, Graaff, and Joubert 1990, 8). In addition, an estimated 76,000 "illegal" immigrants violated the terms of the policy of influx control (Cook 1986, 58). Some Africans were squatting in the formal townships of Langa, Nyanga, Gugulethu, and Old and New Crossroads, so the population of informal settlers increased. The rise in informal settlements both indicated the rise in housing demand and created urban land undesirable for future land markets (Wilkinson 2000, 197).

Moreover, in 1970 the Apartheid government passed the Bantu Homelands Citizenship Act, dispossessing Black South Africans of their citizenship rights and sealing their fate of only owning land in parts of the country where the natural resources and land were of little value. The act established territories based on ethnicity called Bantustans where Blacks were citizens. The act created ten homelands: the Transkei, Bophuthatswana, Ciskei, Venda, Gazankulu, KaNgwane, KwaNdebele, KwaZulu, Lebowa, and QwaQwa. Each ethnic group was designated a specific homeland. The rest of South Africa was called white South Africa. The homelands had underdeveloped economies dependent on the white South African economy and a poorly developed agriculture sector. In the homelands, Blacks owned the lowest-value land in South Africa.

The government's policy response on the Bantu question and housing on the fringes of urban areas was to deliberately build insufficient housing and make the area undesirable. Indeed, the demand for housing among Blacks was deliberately not met, even for those who were in Cape Town legally. Rather, there were forced evictions from illegal settlements and squatter areas. Because of this housing shortage, many people legally allowed in the city lived in shacks with no formal security of tenure. Eventually, Africans were allowed to apply for permits that enabled them to work in the city but live outside it. This policy produced overcrowded conditions. By the beginning of the 1980s, the issue was so severe that the Apartheid state finally agreed to build more houses to address this shortage—about 30 years too late.

With the impending dissolution of Apartheid, a great many Africans in rural areas looked forward to migrating to Cape Town. However, only slum conditions awaited them (Western 2002, 713). In 1986, the pass laws were repealed, and the Colored Labor Preference Area was dropped in 1988 (Western 2002, 713). Rural-to-urban migration into Cape Town increased significantly. Migrants came largely from the Eastern Cape Province, sustaining one of the largest waves of migration in Cape Town history. This influx worsened an already acute shortage of housing, which multiplied the population living in slum conditions. The population growth of the city before and during this period is shown in figure 3.2. Between 1980 and 1996, the city's population experienced one of its fastest rates of growth. The population doubled in 15 years; the previous doubling had taken 30 years.

The Apartheid government began to build new low-cost houses on city outskirts to accommodate Black South Africans toward the end of Apartheid in the mid-1980s. The move was designed to mitigate fears that Blacks living in nearby squalid conditions might rise in rebellion. In the post-apartheid era, the central feature of the housing policy was providing urban housing under freehold tenure to the previously disadvantaged. The majority of recipients were Africans, as the number of colored, Indians, and whites who live in poverty is a significant minority (Wilkinson 2000).

The post-apartheid government's low-income housing policy has focused on construction and transfer of ownership of publicly owned housing under freehold tenure. The 1994 White Paper on Housing, which became the Housing Act of 1997, in clause 4.2 committed the state to the establishing viable socially and economically integrated communities. Meanwhile, in 1996, the government implemented market reforms with the growth, employment, and redistribution (GEAR) strategy with the involvement of the IMF and World Bank. It saw implementation of Washington Consensus policies, especially

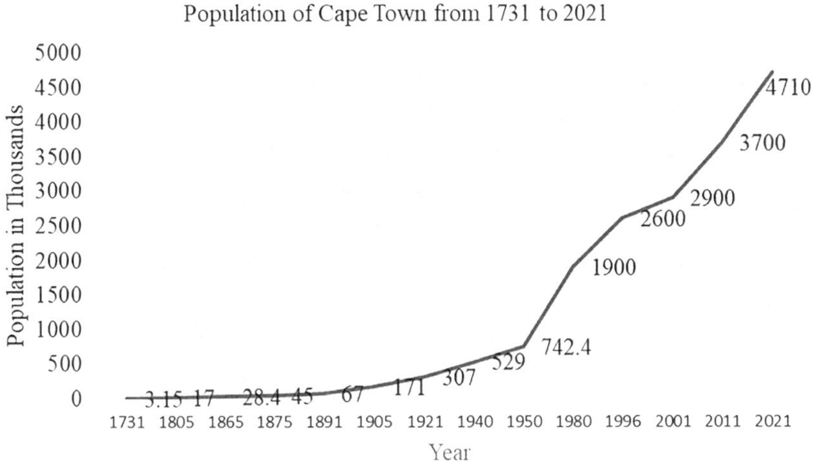

Fig. 3.2. Population Growth in Cape Town, 1731–2021

privatization of government property, including housing (Republic of South Africa 1996). The 2004 housing policy known as Breaking New Ground reiterated this position.

The post-apartheid state instituted the housing subsidy program, providing freehold title for new houses mainly through upgrading in or near areas where informal settlements were located. The program was a conscious effort to correct apartheid injustices and attempted to address the large informal settlement population that evolved after influx control was removed. It greatly expanded the policy of providing low-cost housing on the fringes of the city. The post-apartheid state built over 3.6 million houses nationwide and claims to have benefitted more than 10 million people (Republic of South Africa 2013). However, these settlements are located far from economic opportunities.

With a large and growing housing backlog in slums on the outskirts of the city, many potential beneficiaries of housing subsidies are poised to join the pool. Despite building many houses, the demand for adequate housing continues to be higher than the rate of production. The provincial government of the Western Cape reported in March 2020 that the backlog is more than 550,000 households—the number of applicants on the Housing Demand Database. Of these, more than 300,000 are applicants from the Cape metro area, and over 225,000 from outside the metro area (Gontsana 2020). It seems that the new housing units are accommodating a number equal to the new inflow, while the overall backlog remains stagnant. Statistics South Africa in 2011 reported that of the total population of 3.5 million people, 16 percent, or nearly 600,000, live in informal settlements. Between 1994 and 2013, the state built 323,000 housing units and provided 140,200 serviced sites (plots with electricity, water, sewerage, and other municipal services) in Cape Town (Republic of South Africa 2013). The state built 10,212 housing units in 2017, another 7,828 in 2018, and 8,028 in 2019. At this rate, it will take more than 30 years to build enough units to meet the demand from metro area applicants alone (Gontsana 2020).

3.6. LAND AND HOUSING POLICY IN ZAMBIA

Zambia's land policy explicitly included homeownership for the first time in 1995. Zambia's property rights system is governed by the 1995 Land Act, the 2020–2024 national housing policy, and the 2021 national land policy. The Land Act is the culmination of several attempts at land reform that began during the colonial era (1884–1964). As in other places, the colonial administration created a bifurcation and a two-tier system of property rights. As codified under the Northern Rhodesian constitution in the early 1900s, areas under colonial administration were subject to a formal property rights system under British common law with freehold tenure, while the rest of the country fell under customary law.

Following independence from colonial rule in 1964, the new nationalist government headed by President Kenneth Kaunda initially continued the two-tier system. However, it later implemented reforms that abolished freehold and introduced leasehold ownership. Between 1964 and 1975, much of the land and the country's resources were still in the hands of the British. Citizens of the new country expressed discontent that they had won political freedom but were still economically colonized. Citizens applied political pressure on the government. In 1975, the government instituted nationalist policies, including passing the Land Act of 1975. Under this act, the government implemented sector-wide nationalization reforms. The government exercised eminent domain in a process of expropriation without compensation. Consequently, all property rights fell into the hands of the state. Customary tenure persisted, while freehold tenure was abolished and turned into 99-year leasehold tenure. The government retained ownership under this state planning model and provided all housing opportunities through employment until 1991.

Shortly after implementation of SAPs that restructured the economy from a socialist-oriented and nationalist ideology to neoliberalism, the government passed the Land Act of 1995. The act stated that all land is vested in the republican president and is held by him in perpetuity on behalf of the people of Zambia. However, the act also removed presidential and state approval in transactions involving land, and provided for state compensation in cases of eminent domain.

In 1996, the Ministry of Local Government and Housing published the Zambian housing policy during a period of aggressive privatization and liberalization. The policy provided for multiple tenure systems aimed at expanding the free market in land markets. The policy clearly outlines its commitment to homeownership, noting that it "strongly supports the principle of homeownership as a means of providing security, stability, and economic power to the family unit and as a basis for the development of economically strong and motivated communities" (Government of the Republic of Zambia 1996b, 18).

The 1996, the housing policy was a government endorsement of market fundamentalism and freehold ideology within the housing sector. As the quote above demonstrates, the government saw (and today sees) homeownership as both tenure security and economic power within the family and wider community. This view aligns with the homeowner ideology. In addition, the government removed the policy of rent control under the housing policy, because "[r]emoval of rent control stimulates investment in housing. Rent control is not necessary in a free market economy" (Government of the Republic of Zambia 1996b). The government provides 99-year leasehold rights. Every new transaction that changes ownership means 99 years for the new owner.

Following a more recent housing deficit among the low-income population, a new housing policy was developed for 2020–2024, focusing on providing affordable and decent housing for all Zambians. The policy responded to high levels of income and wealth inequality and bias in the market, whereby private-sector housing investments targeted the middle- and high-income portions of the population with little investment and supply for low-income populations (Government of the Republic of Zambia 2020). The bias and deficit in supply of low-income housing has increased demand for housing in lower-income groups and increased the growth and expansion of informal settlements. This is a symptom of wider growth in economic inequality, where the poorest 50 percent of the population hold just 7 percent of the national income (World Bank Group 2016). The policy aims to upgrade existing informal settlements, effectively manage urbanization, promote equitable access to land for housing development, and facilitate increased access to housing finance. The policy does not commit the government to building new housing. Instead, it commits to strengthen land-use planning, regularize informal settlements, prioritize financing for informal settlement upgrading, promote participation in the upgrading process, and promote partnerships among traditional authorities, government agencies, and private developers to provide serviced land. The policy seeks to strengthen and promote market-oriented policies, engaging private developers in the housing sector, even though private-sector investment in low-income housing has historically been low.

In addition to legal and institutional frameworks such as these, presidential directives may be issued to circumvent housing policy. Essentially, a presidential directive can privatize with the stroke of a pen. For example, the privatization of council housing was not provided for in the constitution, but via a presidential directive. From the middle of 1996, the government "privatized" 150,000 publicly owned houses countrywide (Free Library 1997). Of the 150,000, 7,000 were low-cost houses transferred to low-income households as a redistributive and developmental strategy. Until that point, the state had pursued a state-rental housing policy inherited from the colonial government. The new democratic and neoliberal-oriented government under President Frederick Chiluba could not sustain a policy of providing public rental housing, because the rapid urbanization that occurred immediately after independence exacerbated an already acute housing shortage and swelled the number of people living in informal settlements.

3.7. HOUSING DEFICITS, SLUM CONDITIONS, AND OWNERSHIP IN LUSAKA CITY

With a population of 3.2 million in 2020, and with 85 percent of its population living in urban areas, Lusaka city has the largest urban population in Zambia (Central Statistics Office Zambia 2015). Zambia's share of people living in urban areas is 41 percent, with the urban tipping point projected for 2030. Lusaka's annual population growth rate is high at 4 percent in 2020, although the trend has been falling gradually from almost 14 percent following inde-

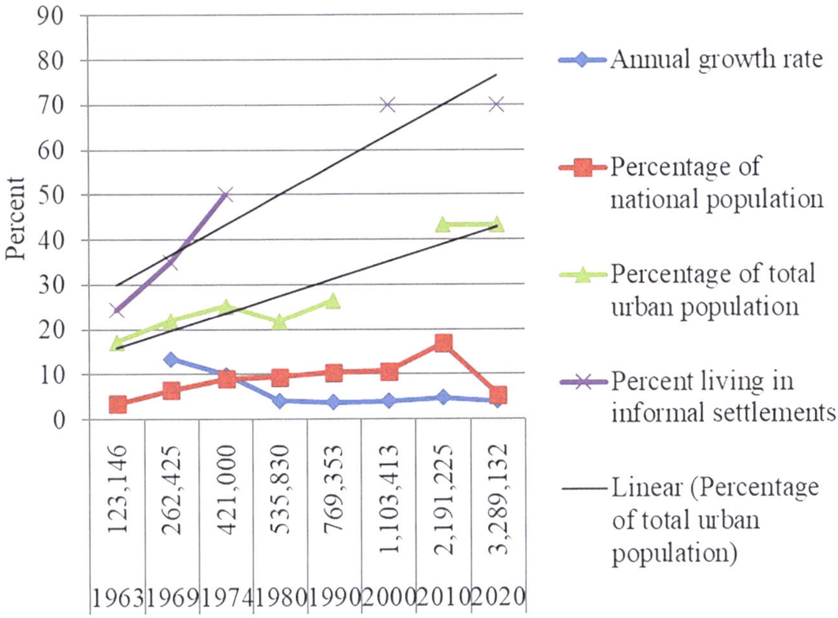

Fig. 3.3. Population Growth in Lusaka, 1963–2020

pendence (World Bank 2015). At the time of independence in 1964, about 30,000 people were living in informal settlements in Lusaka. With independence came the lifting of restrictions on Africans living in urban areas, which accelerated urbanization. Since housing in urban areas was disproportionally built to accommodate the small colonial population, a shortage of housing for urban migrants led to the proliferation of informal settlements (Mulenga 2003, 3–4). The population growth rate of Lusaka is shown in figure 3.3.

A year before independence in 1963, Lusaka had an African population of 110,000. Half the population lived in municipal townships, a quarter lived in slum conditions, and the rest lived in private or government compounds or servant quarters in European areas. However, from independence to 1970, the share of people living in informal settlements increased to more than one-third of the city's population (Hansen 1982). Informal settlements jumped from just 9 to 32, and three years later in 1973, half of the people were living in informal settlements. Lusaka's overall population doubled from 123,146 in 1963 to 262,425 in 1969 (Mulenga 2003, 3). It doubled again to 421,000 in 1974, again two decades later in the 1990s, and once more by 2020.

To address the housing needs of the growing African population of workers, the colonial government built hostels and huts outside the city. Later, in 1959, the state built stronger brick-and-mortar houses in four areas: Matero, Chilenje, Lilanda, and Kabwata. Workers were required to pay a poll tax if living without their families and a hut tax if living with their families in urban housing. Informal settlements and slum conditions emerged in Lusaka partly because of poll and hut taxes; those who could not afford the taxes occupied municipal and private farmland on the city outskirts (Hansen 1982, 118). Some of those who went to live in informal settlements did so because there was not enough housing for workers.

Following independence in the late 1970s and early '80s, the new government upgraded some of the squatter settlements with the support of the World Bank. The settlements were placed under the Lusaka Urban District Council. However, informal settlements continued to grow and accommodated a large part of the population by the time housing privatization began in 1996.

3.8. PRIVATIZATION OF PUBLIC HOUSING

The shift between socialist ideology and market dispensations that occurred in 1991 provided the institutional framework for transfer of ownership of property rights from the state to private individuals under leasehold tenure. The government drew up a housing policy in 1996 based on the principles outlined in the World Bank's *Enabling Markets to Work Strategy* (World Bank 1993). Although the housing policy allowed for recognition of private property rights and emphasized homeownership, it did not allow for privatization of public houses. In response, President Frederick Chiluba signed a presidential directive to sanction the sale of publicly owned houses to the poor (Schlyter 2004, 5). The president went as far as determining the prices of some of the houses on the spot during a visit to affected areas (Free Library 1997). Political commentators have held that the president privatized houses as a political maneuver aimed at assuring him reelection in the same year.

Nevertheless, when the government privatized publicly owned houses, it allowed individuals who occupied the houses to benefit. This is not to suggest that all employees were offered the houses they occupied. Most employees residing in squatter settlements were not offered houses because they fell in the backlog. Since the government and private companies did not have houses of their own, they paid the workers a housing allowance. Unemployed people were also among the nonbeneficiaries.

The abridged process of transfer of ownership, as recorded in circular number 2 of 1996 of the Ministry of Local Government and Housing titled "Revised Procedures for Sale of Council Houses" was as follows. First, the government valuation department evaluated the property. The department considered the age and physical condition of the property, supply and demand forces, and a maintenance and repair discount. The government sold low-cost houses with a discount determined by the age of the property. The government sold houses it built or purchased between 1991 and 1996 with no discount; those it purchased or built between 1981 and 1990 had a 20 percent discount; and so on, up to a 100 percent discount for houses the colonial government purchased before 1959 or built during colonial times.

3.9. LAND AND HOUSING POLICY IN ANGOLA

Angola is a postconflict society under a one-party authoritarian state. It's housing crisis can be traced to colonialism, prolonged conflict, and authoritarian rule. Although the Portuguese made contact with Luanda as early as the 15th century (Soares de Oliveira 2015, 6), Portuguese colonialism began in 1910, instituting racial segregation and policies of forced cultivation and labor. Segregation created indigenous neighborhoods on the outskirts of Luanda and other major urban centers. Indigenous people who had lived in urban centers for centuries were pushed out. The governor-general of Luanda established conditions for determining citizenship for the indigenous population in urban centers based on what they determined to be the extent of European civilization exhibited by the individual (Croese 2013, 66). In 1926, the government in Portugal fell and António de Oliveira Salazar's dictatorial regime rose, passing the Colonial Act of 1930, which bifurcated the colonial government in Angola with a civil system under which whites automatically acquired citizenship, and a customary system under which Blacks and indigenous people were to be ruled. Blacks and the indigenous population were to apply for citizenship from these areas if they felt that they were civilized enough to live in urban areas (Croese 2013, 67).

Protracted conflict began in 1960 with the war for independence from the colonial regime, followed by the civil war between the Popular Movement for the Liberation of Angola (MPLA) and the National Union for the Total Independence of Angola (UNITA) that started in 1975 and ended in 2002, compounding the impact of segregationist policies on the housing crisis. By 1960, the urban population in and around Luanda had grown so much that it caused housing shortages in the city periphery. The shortages instigated the anticolonial and independence movement (Croese 2013, 67) as residents of the musseques (neighborhoods with slum conditions) were dissatisfied with both land alienation and the forced labor system. Three anticolonial groups arose across the country. The MPLA consisted of the *mestiços* (people of a mix of Portuguese and indigenous African heritage) and arose from the musseques of Luanda. The União dos Povos de Angola (UPA), later called the National Liberation Front of Angola (FLNA), was a guerrilla movement made up of the Bakongo people. And UNITA was an offshoot of the UPA founded by Jonas Savimbi. The war of independence ended in 1975 after Salazar's government was deposed in a coup in Portugal. The Portuguese abruptly departed without preparing Angolans for independence. Shortly after independence, the different movements decided to form a coalition, but the alliance between Neto's MPLA and Savimbi's UNITA did not hold. Each party wanted to maintain control of the capital, where MPLA was strongest. The new independent nation fell into civil war. In the conflict, MPLA controlled the oil-rich capital from which it drew its war financing. UNITA controlled the diamond-rich interior, receiving support from the United States until 1992 and from the apartheid government in South Africa.

The conflict had an immediate effect on the urban population and housing. The battlefront was concentrated in rural areas, driving four million people to urban areas over 27 years of civil war (Cain 2004). The war-induced urbanization created overcrowding and stress in Luanda (Jenkins, Robson, and Cain 2002). As figure 3.4 shows, Luanda's population increased from 599,000 in 1975 to 3.2 million people in 2002 (Jenkins, Robson, and Cain 2002, 144). Many of the rural-urban migrants settled in the musseques, and some established new ones. Making matters worse, the civil war caused extensive destruction to infrastructure and land registration, further limiting services and urban housing options. When the war ended with the death of Jonas Savimbi, the government faced the challenges of a war-induced housing crisis, a large slum population, and a rapidly growing urban population that stressed the limited resources. The population of Luanda doubled in the first 10 years after the conflict ended. In 2015, the percentage of the population living in urban agglomerations with over one million people in Angola was 24 percent (World Bank 2015). In 2020, the population was more than halfway to doubling in the second decade following the war, standing at 8.6 million in 2020.

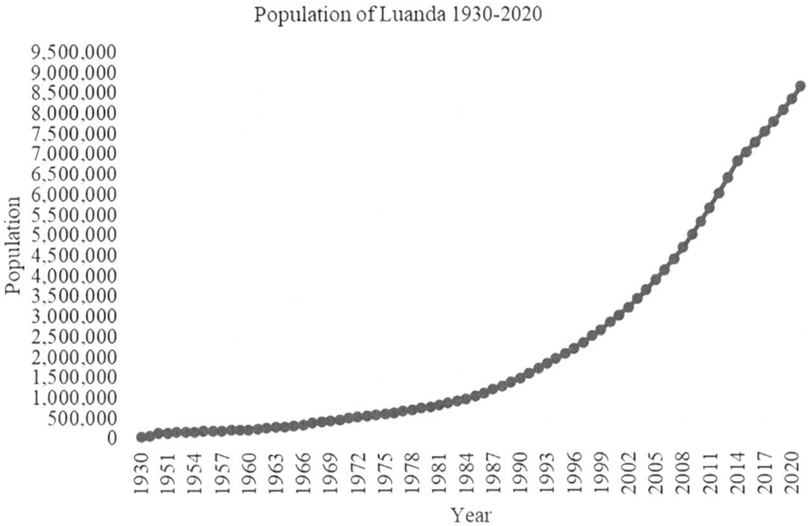

Fig. 3.4. Population Growth in Luanda, 1930–2020

Angola emerged from the conflict with both an urban housing crisis and an authoritarian president. President Jose Eduardo Dos Santos took power after the untimely death from cancer of Dr. Agostinho Neto in 1979. He ruled until 2017, when he handed over power to Joao Laurenco. In 2008, President Dos Santos promised to build one million houses by the 2012 election (Cain 2013, 12). The president could make such ambitious promises because at the time Angola's economy had been enjoying large revenues from high oil prices for six consecutive years. The country signed a construction deal with China, often referred to as the oil-for-housing deal. The government built several cities using the deal. Kilamba City comprised 1,500 houses in high-rise buildings resembling those found in Beijing. The challenges of rapid urbanization continued to increase.

As of 2021, Angola was governed by the 2004 Land Law. Angola's land tenure system and provincial and municipal administrations have little capacity to administer land (Cain 2013, 15). Approximately 75 percent of land in Luanda is held outside of the formal system of property ownership and management (Cain 2013, 20). Ninety-three percent of transactions take place informally. There are often no formal records of the transaction and no registration of ownership (Cain 2004, 14). Many poor people live on unserviced land on the city periphery. Lands the state has designated as "housing reserves" continue to be occupied by newly arriving rural-urban migrants. Cain (2013) refers to these areas as "marginal locations of low value, difficult-to-service, and inconvenient-to-access centers of employment. The poor . . . are unable to generate wealth on the periphery of the city" (14).

What is more, in the postconflict era, the poor lack security of tenure since the MPLA government adopted a policy of evicting residents from areas marked for development. Most of the poor who live in musseques located closer to the city have been evicted and moved to peripheral areas to make way for construction of hotels and office buildings (Watson 2014). The poor in areas marked for urban development live with the real threat of eviction every day. Evictions have also taken place to move people living in areas of high risk of natural disasters to safer locations, mainly on the periphery of Luanda (Croese 2010, 2013). This was the case of people who were moved from Boa Vista to Zango 1.

3.10. CONCLUSION

Ideologies have shaped housing tenure in the four African cities examined in this chapter. In general, ideologies governing ownership in most of urban Africa shifted between private ownership under free-market capitalism during the colonial and immediate postcolonial era, to public ownership under socialist-oriented ideologies during the 1970s and 1980s, and then back to private ownership under free-market capitalism from the late 1980s to the present. South Africa is the exception, as it moved from divisive apartheid-era economic policies to Washington Consensus policies under GEAR in 1996. At independence, sub-Saharan African countries inherited market-oriented economies instituted under colonialism. The first shift from colonial free-market capitalism to public ownership under socialism occurred in the first decade following independence. However, the 1973 global economic crisis occurred, and African economies fell into a three-decade crisis that Van de Walle (2001) came to call a "permanent economic crisis" and Mkandawire (Meagher 2019) named "Africa's great depression." The second shift from socialist to market fundamentalist ideology took place when Washington Consensus policies in the form of structural adjustment policies were institutionalized to address the crisis.

The homeowner economic ideology became pervasive in sub-Saharan African countries through SAPs and Washington Consensus policies, which conditioned funding to address the debt crisis and implement economic stabilization and adjustment policies. Since the implementation of SAPs, governments in developing countries have struggled to provide housing, let alone basic services, thus leaving it to the market. Conditionalities for support from international financial institutions constrain government involvement in the social sector. Meanwhile, because it is not profitable, the private sector avoided ventures involving investments in low-cost housing for low-income urban populations. Kenyan, South African, and Zambian governments addressed this market failure and navigated the pervasiveness of market fundamentalism through direct and deliberate involvement in housing the poor under ownership forms of tenure. By contrast, Angola provided housing using the social-housing approach in a context where the owner ideology is not a pervasive idea. The next chapter details the contexts where the present research was conducted.

CHAPTER 4

Kibera, Khayelitsha, Matero, and Zango

The four case studies provide a rare opportunity to study ideological claims about real property rights in African cities and ideological, state, and familial processes in the social production of homeownership tenure. Opportunities to investigate the effects of real property rights in African contexts are rare; few African governments can afford such large-scale projects following structural adjustment programs that reduced state capacity. Likewise, few private-sector firms are willing to invest in low-income housing targeted at the poor. This chapter introduces the four neighborhoods in the study. In Kibera, Nairobi, freehold property rights for the poor were transferred to residents living in slum conditions through low-interest mortgages under the Kenya Slum Upgrading Program. In Cape Town, the government delivered freehold rights to marginalized groups in Khayelitsha through subsidized housing. In Lusaka, the government privatized derelict public rental housing and transferred ownership of leasehold property rights to the poor in Matero. Adjacent to Matero, the government granted usufruct rights to those living in George Compound. Finally, I compare Zango, where residents possessed usufruct rights, to Paraiso, where residents lived in an informal settlement. In each case, deliberate action by governments in creating these housing projects reveals the social production of homeownership and forms of social housing tenure.

4.1. KIBERA

Under the colonial administration in Kenya, leaders neglected to assign formal property title in areas of Nairobi where natives settled. Kibera was the quintessential case of such neglect. As far back as 1912, the colonial administration allowed the settlement to develop, but neglected to formalize ownership of the land for African settlers. The result was one of the most densely populated informal settlements in 20th- and 21st-century Africa.

With a long history of informal operations, Kibera is located about two miles west of the Nairobi Central Business District. In 1912, the colonial administration gave the portion of land now known as Kibera to retired Nubian soldiers of the King's African Rifles without formal land title (Schramm 2017, 119). The soldiers named the area Kibera—the Nubian word for jungle. Kibera's population grew rapidly as a housing settlement occupied by those migrating in search of work. The colonial administration withheld formal land rights from residents, regarding Kibera as a temporary settlement even as its population swelled. In 1945, Commissioner for Local Government, Lands and Settlement Sergeant C. E. Mortimer remarked that while the policy adopted toward Kibera assumed it would disappear in a relatively short time, he feared that it would probably exist for another twenty-five years (Meredith and MacDonald 2017, 2). The settlement existed for more than seven decades after Mortimer's remarks, and the colonial administration never did provide services.

It was not until 1969—six years after Kenya's independence in 1963—that the new postcolonial government declared Kibera government land (Meredith and MacDonald 2017). By that time, nearly 6,000 people lived on 550 acres in Kibera. With no formal ownership title among the Nubians or many Kenyans on the land, the government denied Nubian ownership claims and denied usufruct or ownership rights to the Kenyans.

The new Government of Kenya (GoK) continued colonial-era government policies, failing to provide services or formally recognize Kibera as a settlement. By 1980, the settlement population had swelled to 60,000 (Schramm 2017, 119). Under the pressure of these increasing population numbers, environmental conditions in Kibera worsened. Much like the colonial administration before it, the GoK wished to alienate the land for its own purposes. Whereas the colonial government attempted to build a golf course and middle-class housing in 1930, the GoK just attempted to build middle-class housing. A few of these attempts were successful, such as the Nyayo Highrise Estate project led by President Daniel Arap Moi, marketed as a slum upgrading project. With the loss of land, settlement population density increased. By 1999, Kibera had an estimated 826 people per hectare (Mitullah 2003, 4). Between the 1970s and 2010, Kibera's land size had shrunk from 550 to 300 acres (Huchzermeyer 2008, 21; Mitullah 2003, 4).

Kibera was not the only Nairobi settlement whose land value was deteri-

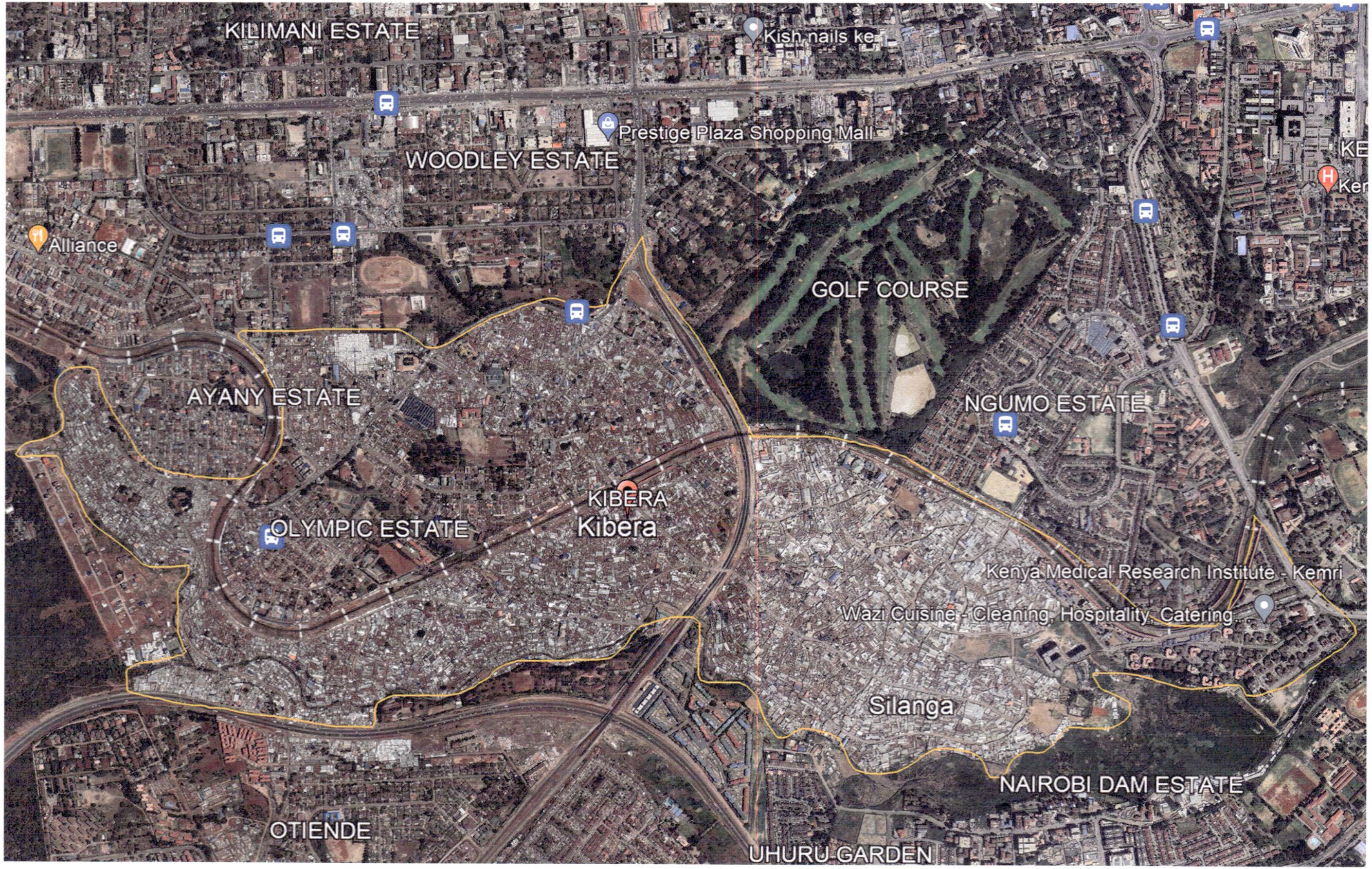

Fig. 4.1. Location of Kibera in Nairobi

orating. With 134 slums accommodating 60 percent of Nairobi's population by 1995 (Mitullah 2003, 11), settlements near urban centers lacked access to clean water, waste disposal, adequate housing, and other infrastructural services. At the turn of the new millennium, Kenya's housing and slum situation reached a crisis point, with Kibera as the quintessential example. Kenya's housing backlog was considerable, with two million households needing adequate dwellings (Bah, Faye, and Geh 2018). With an urban population growth rate of approximately 4.4 percent per year, Kenya was one of the most rapidly urbanizing countries in sub-Saharan Africa (Bah, Faye, and Geh, 2018). UN-Habitat estimated that 60 to 80 percent of the population lived in slums in Kenya, depending on the city (Syrjanen 2008).

4.2. KENYA SLUM UPGRADING PROGRAM

Despite the international pressures of neoliberal market fundamentalism, the GoK decided to provide freehold rights and build new low-cost, low-income, and affordable adequate housing. The result was the Kenya Slum Upgrading Program (KENSUP).

Under President Daniel Arap Moi in 2000, the GoK initiated KENSUP through an agreement with UN-Habitat (Huchzermeyer 2008, 21). The idea for a government-funded slum-upgrading program was born during celebration of World Habitat Day in Nairobi in 2001.[1] In the MOU, the GoK committed to systematically upgrade urban slums by 2020 in compliance with Millennium Development Goal 7. The administration initiated the KENSUP pilot in Soweto East Village, in the southeast corner of the Kibera settlement, with a population of 60,000 (Huchzermeyer 2008, 21). The National Rainbow Coalition led by President Mwayi Kibaki renewed the MOU in January 2003 and President Kibaki became the patron of the program. The GoK and UN-Habitat launched KENSUP during the 2004 World Habitat Day celebrations. The GoK made a graphic media presentation on upgrading the slum to privately owned two-bedroom apartments in several rows of apartment blocks (Huchzermeyer 2008, 21). In a market-oriented economy, the plan was to provide the housing under freehold tenure.

1. Unless cited otherwise, information in this section was obtained through a key informant interview conducted at the Ministry of Land, Housing and Urban Development. The official wished to remain anonymous.

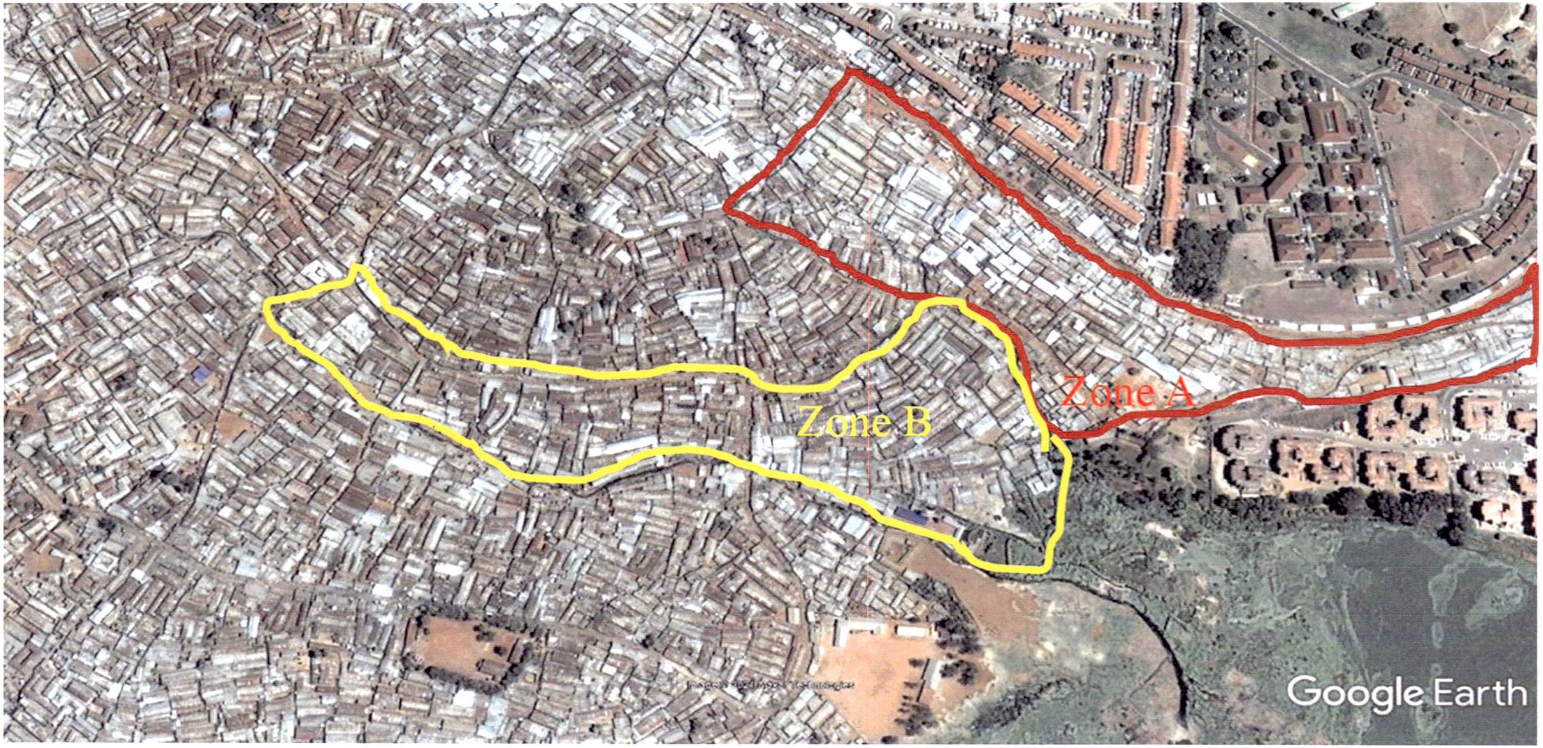

Fig. 4.2. Zones A and B in Kibera's Soweto East Neighborhood 2001

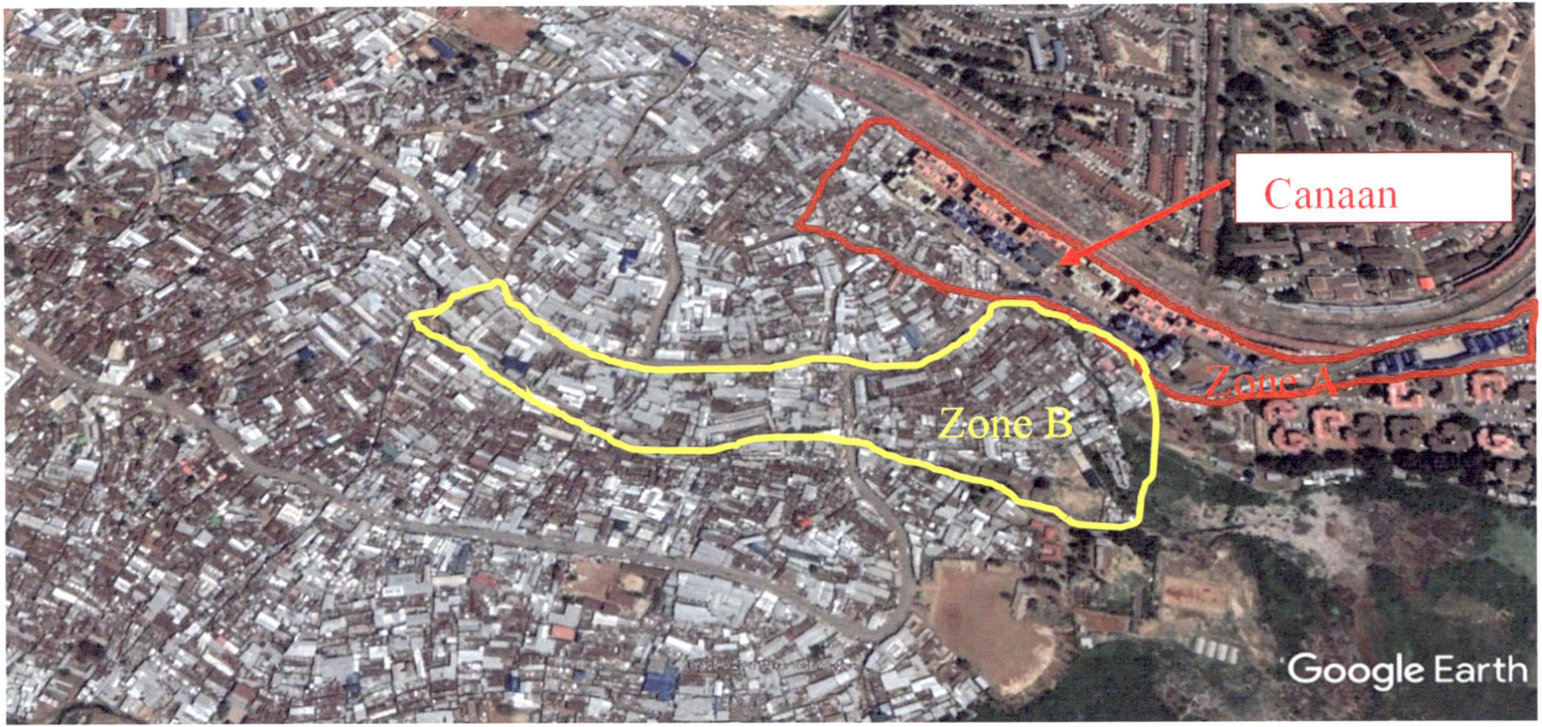

Fig. 4.3. Zones A and B and Canaan Estate in Kibera's Soweto East Neighborhood in 2019

The goal of KENSUP was to improve the livelihoods of people living and working in slums and informal settlements in urban Kenya by promoting and facilitating the provision of secure tenure; improving housing, income generation, and physical and social infrastructure; and addressing the impacts of HIV/AIDS (Syrjanen 2008, 15). It also aimed to promote and facilitate broad-based partnerships utilizing consensus building and consultation among stakeholders. KENSUP targeted four cities, including Nairobi, Mombasa, Kisumu, and Mavoko.

The goal of the Kibera Soweto East Neighborhood pilot project was to rehabilitate the neighborhood for KENSUP's construction of permanent supportive housing and service provision (Flores-Fernandez and Calas 2011, 3). The project divided the neighborhood into four zones: A, B, C, and D (Kenya National Commission on Human Rights 2015). Of interest in this chapter are Zones A and B, depicted in figures 4.2 and 4.3.

In 2004, the GoK conducted a socioeconomic survey to enumerate potential beneficiaries. The survey revealed that Soweto East neighborhood had a total population of 19,318. Tenant households were provided with allocation letters and issued identification cards to signify potential beneficiary status. To the northeast, Zone A accounted for 37 percent of houses in Soweto East, housing 6,376 tenants. To the southeast, Zone B accommodated 3,004 people. Zone C had 4,361 residents and Zone D 3,989. Of the total population, 16,899 were tenants and 2,419 were structure owners. Tenants rented their housing, while structure owners leased their structures. Many structure owners owned several slum properties and investments, collecting monthly rent from afar (Flores-Fernandez and Calas 2011, 2). The dwellings are informal—that is, they are not legally recognized housing structures.

As part of the KENSUP project infrastructure, the Ministry of Lands and Housing created the Settlement Executive Committee (SEC) to build support in the community (Meredith and MacDonald 2017, 3). Potential housing beneficiaries were elected to serve on the SEC, as representatives of stakeholders and community members. The Ministry of Lands and Housing defined the role of the SEC broadly:

a. Mobilizing and facilitating community and settlement stakeholders for active participation in the decision making, planning, and implementation process to ensure ownership projects.
b. Sensitizing the community, disseminating information, and soliciting views and perspectives on [KENSUP] and project-related issues

through regular meetings and sessions with settlement representatives and residents.

c. Working with the community in determining and prioritizing the needs of the community.
d. Marshalling community support and facilitating mobilization of community and stakeholder resources for investment in the upgrading process.
e. Representing community interests and linking community and institutional partners, including facilitating smooth, efficient, and adequate flow of information.
f. Providing the Programme Secretariat with accurate and timely reports on the situation on the ground at all times.
g. Creating unity among slum dwellers and stakeholders to ensure that valid and reasonable views of the slum dwellers are addressed through the project phases. (Meredith and MacDonald 2017, 3)

The SECs were comprised of 17 members from each zone (Flores-Fernandez and Calas 2011). Since the Soweto East Project began in Zone A, the first SEC was made up of potential beneficiaries from Zone A. A new SEC was elected for Zone B in 2018 as the project commenced. Setting it apart from other projects, the SECs succeeded in engaging the community in a bottom-up approach to communicating and addressing beneficiary needs.

The Soweto East project is an in situ upgrading project, in which new housing is built where potential beneficiaries currently live. To make way for construction, KENSUP proposed temporary resident relocation. Initially, the GoK arranged with the government of Finland to move residents into new flats built 23 km (14 miles) away (Flores-Fernandez and Calas 2011, 3). However, residents were wary of government attempts to take Kibera land and give it to middle-class residents. They complained to Kibera's representative member of parliament, Prime Minister Raila Odinga, who intervened on behalf of the residents. KENSUP complied, and chose Langata for relocation. KENSUP obtained land belonging to the Kenya Prison Service with the agreement that once the project was complete, KENSUP would give the apartment blocks to the Prison Service.

In 2009, KENSUP completed construction of 600 apartments in 17 apartment blocks, each with five floors. On September 16, KENSUP relocated 5,000 residents out of Soweto East Zone A. Only 1,200 families were allocated apartments at Langata, some of which were shared residences (Flores-Fernandez

Fig. 4.4. Housing Conditions in Zone B

and Calas 2011, 131). Residents were required to pay rent of Sh.2,000 (approximately US$18), with Sh.1,000 (US$9) going to garbage disposal, cleaning, and other services for the apartment blocks. However, 1,288 families refused to move because they did not want to pay more rent than they were paying in Zone A. The project relocated them to Zones B, C, and D. Others moved to other slums to wait for building to be complete.

The government organized potential beneficiaries into housing cooperatives in 2007. Established by the Ministry of Cooperatives, they were the primary means through which potential beneficiaries would save for a down payment valued at 10 percent of house value. Potential beneficiaries had three housing options: a one-room (studio) apartment, valued at Sh.600,000 (US$5,600), with a down payment of Sh.60,000 (US$560); a one-bedroom apartment, valued at Sh.1 million (US$9,350), with a down payment of Sh.100,000 (US$935); and a two-bedroom apartment, valued at Sh.1.35 million(US$12,625), with a down payment of Sh.135,000 (US$1,260). Potential beneficiaries were to make their deposits at the Cooperative Bank of Kenya.

Fig. 4.5. Housing Conditions in Langata Decanting Site

Qualitative interviews conducted with a key informant at KENSUP and residents at Langata reveal that the down payment was more acceptable to some potential beneficiaries than others. While some felt that 10 years was sufficient to save up their payment, others felt that potential beneficiaries were too poor to save anything. Living in a Zone B cooperative, Odhiambo was pessimistic:

> If I start saving for the house, the government said I am supposed to save like 130,000 for me to be able to get two rooms. Now, you see, I have children; I cannot stay in a one room with my three children. I am supposed to save for two rooms, so now that comes too much for me. So, now my challenge is, my worry is that I will not be able to save that KSh60,000 or even that KSh6,000 to save will be very difficult for me.

Indeed, KENSUP did not provide accommodations for widows, orphans, and vulnerable individuals who depended on formal or informal welfare. The assumption was that everyone living in Kibera could raise the required amount. A structure owner in Zone B, Gakuru knew that vulnerable people would not be able to afford it:

> My concern is the orphans, the widows, the old people. They have people 90 years of age down there. I worry where will the government take these people? When the day of demolition comes, where will they go from there? Because most of them do not have jobs. They just survive from handouts. When they move from here, where will they be taken too? How will they survive in the new environment? I am concerned that if the government really wanted to help them, the government should build houses and let them pay 1,000 shillings instead of asking them to save, yet you cannot find food for yourself. How can you save 130,000 when you cannot afford a vegetable that goes for 5 shillings? That is my most concern.

The government began construction in March 2012, completing the first phase of Canaan Estate apartment blocks in 2014. Only 824 apartments in 21 blocks were constructed, comprising 108 studios, 570 one-bedroom apartments, and 144 two-bedroom apartments. With fewer units than beneficiaries, potential beneficiaries were asked to submit applications. Applicants needed to reside in Zone A of Kibera, to save the required amount through the cooperative, and to show cleared rent arrears at Langata. The government received 1,590 applications.

From the start of KENSUP, the role of structure owners was complex. Many structure owners informally rented out multiple structures. Yet under law, owner structures were built on public land; thus, the GoK registered everyone as a potential beneficiary and provided one home—regardless of whether they were a structure owner or a tenant. Structure owners demanded that the government allocate more houses or compensate them for loss of land and income. Complicating matters, many structure owners lived offsite in wealthier parts of Nairobi.

When KENSUP decided to move residents to Langata, structure owners took the matter to court, delaying beneficiary selection for two years. The court ruled that tenants should move, but that the structures should remain (Flores-Fernandez and Calas 2011). Later, in March 2012, the court injunction was dismissed, structures were demolished, and construction of apartments at Canaan began (Mitra et al. 2017, 111). As Chitundu, a structure owner in Zone B, reports: "There was no compensation. The only thing they were given is that the government allowed them to transfer their goods from this point

Fig. 4.6. Housing Conditions in Canaan Estate

[Zone A] to Decanting [Langata]. Just once, the government transferred their goods to the Decanting Site." Structure owners were trying to hold on to their extralegal source of livelihood. Gakuru, a structure owner who participated in the negotiations, describe what happened:

> So, we were asked to come back to the villages [at the time residents were to move to Langata] and value our houses. Each house would cost how much? Remember, a person said they have three types of houses: the mud, the iron sheet, and the wooden. For our valuing, a mud house would sell at 25,000, an iron sheet house would sell at 30,000 shillings, and a wooden house would cost 50,000 shillings. We took the report to UN-Habitat, and then, they took this to the government. Since we got this report of the value of the houses given to the government, the government has never gotten back to us.

Once residents moved to Langata, structure owners had no leverage over the government, hence the lack of compensation. Gakuru believes that the GoK caused a lot of pain for structure owners:

> Because of disruption, some of them died. Most people died because of stress and others because of the disruption of life. Most people who are living here when they left, they got poorer than they were here. They have been suffering; it's like the government threw them out. . . . When they were moved, the government should have given us compensation. The government should have given them a program of how to survive. Like we would have been given, a way of how to start a business so that we may sustain ourselves because of that disruption. They have suffered a lot, those who went there. Now, I have a fear that Zone B would have the same. So, with the move from here to those places, how will we live? How will we live from the slum? Our life will be disrupted. That is the fear that I have.

Losses incurred by structure owners, including machinery in a factory destroyed by bulldozers during the eviction, stems from the fact that the GoK did not designate Kibera as a formal area. The structures owned by structure owners did not formally exist on government maps. Like Gakura, Chitundu fears that the same fate that befell owners in Zone A awaits her in Zone B:

> I have ten rooms. That's where I collect my rent; that's where I get money to feed my family. Once the government tears it down, I no longer have a place to live or a place to collect my rent, so I can feed my family. I have no job. Where does the government want me to go?

The position from the project side was equally convincing, as the GoK felt that structure owners were unreasonable in their requests. As SEC member Barasa explains:

> they [structure owners] were given a proposal. They were told that they should propose how their transition should be facilitated. Each one of the structure owners for example, owning ten rooms. They gave a proposal of KSh.50,000 per room for ten years. For us, that is quite difficult. You know the ministry cannot afford KSh500,000 for ten years. That's like, our government is giving you land. The government assumes that they are not compensating, they are facilitating because someone who is being compensated is being asked to move to another place and not to come back again. But someone who is facilitated, facilitated to save so that he can buy the house [in Canaan]. So, the structure owners gave their proposal back. We proposed to the ministry that the structure owners should be facilitated in the same way as tenants. If a

tenant is given an amount for a room, that's what the structure owner should be given for ten rooms. That would be easier for the ministry.

After the structure owners took the matter to court, the Kenya National Commission on Human Rights (KNCHR) presided over the case and resolved that the process and facilitation amount were fair. Structure owners responded by evicting poorer tenants from Zone B and bringing in wealthier ones in deals that would allow them to own the structure by proxy. This is the new issue that the Zone B SEC was trying to address. As Barasa notes of Zone B, "we have dealt with issues of infiltration . . . individuals who were supposed to benefit from the next project, their houses were being sold to other individuals, like the structure owners." Essentially, Barasa notes, structure owners sold houses out from underneath tenants "in order to benefit from the highest bidder."

In 2016, housing at Canaan was allocated to 824 households through a random-allocation process. Applicants gathered at Nyaya Stadium for a balloting process. Most applicants applied for two-bedroom units, and they were selected based on unit type. Since there were fewer two-bedroom units, some applicants were allocated one-bedroom and studio apartments instead. In July 2016, beneficiaries finally moved into Canaan.

Each beneficiary signed a 25-year mortgage. Although the GoK provided ownership documents, it did not provide title deeds. Residents could obtain title after making monthly payments for 25 years. Since they did not have title deeds, they could not use the house as collateral. The GoK provided insurance for mortgages since most residents were poor and could not afford it. If a mortgage holder died, the GoK paid off the house for the surviving family and delivered the title. Until the house was paid off, beneficiaries enjoyed all the rights of ownership except credit and sale.

The second phase began after Canaan was completed. By August of 2019, the government completed 4,789 households in Soweto Zone B and allocated beneficiary identity cards. The potential beneficiaries in Soweto Zone B were still living in the area where the new housing was going to be built because all the apartments in Langata were already occupied—the apartments left vacant by Canaan beneficiaries were occupied by other households from Zone A who had been living in the slum during the first phase. In December 2021, Zone B residents had been moved to Langata and other locations. The project was about to begin construction. The COVID-19 pandemic caused a delay.

4.3. KENSUP'S PROBLEMS WITH CORRUPTION AND FRAUD

The Zone A pilot project had many shortcomings pointed out by Amnesty International and observed by my study team during fieldwork and data collection. Corruption and abuse of power were rampant, especially in the SEC and the slum-upgrading department in the Ministry of Land and Housing. Several interviewees reported that beneficiaries obtained their Canaan houses fraudulently through SEC members. They reported further that SEC members bought beneficiary cards from other potential beneficiaries to buy multiple houses. People from middle-class Nairobi were offering a minimum of KSh5,000 (US$45) for the cards. Many of the potential beneficiaries had not seen such amounts of money before. As Odhiambo notes:

> First you want to pay rent and then the government is saying you need to save. The only cash you are able to get is like, per month, most are getting KSh4,000. So, you tell that guy to save 130,000 to be able to get two rooms. That guy will say the only option I have is to sell the ID to those people who are able to afford it. The government is not saving anyone. The government is not thinking of the youth. . . . The youths with what they can do, they cannot raise the money. Often what they do, the ID Card, they would rather sell the ID card to those who can afford and raise the money.

Odhiambo further explained the way the sale of ID cards was taking place. According to Odhiambo, it was with the involvement of the enumerators who were appointed to provide the ID cards following the survey in 2005:

> Someone will be given a job, like this one, to come and do registration of beneficiaries. The same guy because he's the one with you on the ground, he knows you are in financial trouble; he is like, "okay I will give you this ID," and then he starts giving another option, in mind. He said "you know, maybe I can give someone to buy this ID for KSh60,000 or maybe just KSh5,000. So, I can sell that ID for that, okay?"

Odhiambo continues, describing both the impulse to sell the ID and the way the system was abused:

> He is giving you the commission of your life. You have never ever had KSh5,000 cash. . . . Most of them are youth. They have all sold their IDs . . .

> people living in Canaan 95% of them are strangers. Those people can afford to live in those houses. They already bought the houses [fully paid the mortgage]. . . . Most of them are outsiders. Most people work for the government. The same people who issued our card, they come and tell their brothers, you have cash, you can buy this card from this guy; this guy doesn't have anything. So, if you give him KSh50,000 he would sell for you, this ID. . . . If the government comes here, everyone will be taken out because they are not the rightful owner of those houses. The government should come to the ground. They must make sure that the people who . . . registered for the project, are the real beneficiaries.

Similarly, people living in Langata Decanting Site were not all from Zone A and B. Zawadi lived in Langata for seven years and did not recognize many new neighbors from Zone A:

> They sell their cards. . . . I know some people, who acted as brokers. So, they come to you, and they can't manage to pay this rent, so you just sell your house for KSh100,000. Most people are not here and that is because they sold their ID to other people. . . . The person that you sold the ID to will be the one that is going to occupy the house in Canaan. When you go to Canaan actually and you see the people living in the two bedrooms and also the one bedroom, you just judge by their appearance and maybe the equipment in the house, this person has money. Most of them are in Canaan. Ninety percent of people in Canaan are there because they bought the house. Some of them, they sold their card at a very low price; I know of a person who sold her card for KSh40,000, in exchange for your house in Canaan. That's quite a disappointment.

Members of the Zone A SEC even went so far as to help state officials and other people from outside Soweto acquire cards and buy themselves into the project's housing units (Schramm 2017, 122). Flores-Fernandez and Calas (2011) reported that employees in the slum-upgrading department admitted that middle-class people and even students at the University of Nairobi were investing in the Langata apartments.

We found similar corruption. When conducting the pilot portion of my research, several beneficiaries ran away from us the moment we asked how they came to obtain their house. Others warned us that we were asking dangerous questions. A short while later, two members of the dissolved Zone

A SEC confronted our research team. Since the election of the new SEC in 2018, these members and their entire SEC refused to recognize the new SEC and refused to vacate their offices. My conversation with Barasa revealed that there were more issues involving the SEC:

> [P]olitics is always around. The outgoing officials are not happy with us, in the offices. There are always scoundrels here and there. The relationship we are maintaining is the one with the community, a good relationship with the community. Because they are relying on us for the next two years, until the project is fully implemented. We maintain our relationship with the community and the government, the community because we are representing them and the government because the government is the one providing the resources. We don't communicate with them mostly unless there is an issue that is affecting the community. . . . So, the government gave us the mandate to be with the community and represent them. So, the current outgoing has just been politics.

Barasa shared with me that the corrupt SEC members unsuccessfully attempted to incite the community against the new SEC on numerous occasions. They failed because the new SEC had dealt with the community well and according to procedure. The only complaints have been received from former structure owners and residents that did not benefit from the new housing opportunities. The SEC forwarded the complaints to the ministry.

The two former SEC members took us to the chief whose office was located at the UN-Habitat satellite office in Kibera. The chief referred us to the new SEC, who verified our research documents and allowed us to proceed with our interviews. Later, we found out that the two men were telling occupants of Canaan, including Zawadi, not to participate in our study. Out of 824 apartments and a target of 250 interviews, we secured 210, with many refusing. Several structure owners were part of the SEC. Since the project did not recognize their ownership rights, structure owners stood to lose their sources of income due to the project. Structure owners fought the project at every stage. They raised their concerns about losing their source of livelihood and asked for multiple houses to be given to them as compensation. Structure owners officially lost out, but found other sources of access to multiple houses and compensation.

A 2021 study on the politics of property rights formalization in Kenya shows that the allocation of property rights to land and housing occurs in a hybrid neopatrimonial system, rather than a purely patronage one in which changes in politics can alter how a government distributes resources (Dyzenhaus 2021). The political economy literature has shown how Kenya politics is highly influenced by neopatrimonialism and corruption. In such an environment, corruption in allocation of housing is highly probable.

Substantive space has been devoted to discussing corruption under KENSUP because it had very strong implications for the selection of beneficiaries and for evaluations of the effects of freehold property rights.

4.4. KHAYELITSHA

Khayelitsha (meaning "new home" in isiXhosa) is a township ranked on the Habitat for Humanity and World Economic Forum's list of the five biggest slums in the world. It was planned by the apartheid state to accommodate Africans who were legally in Cape Town and those who were squatting in the formal African townships (Cook 1992, 125). The minister of cooperation and development in the apartheid government, Piet Koornhof, announced development of Khayelitsha in 1983 in response to a severe shortage of housing for Africans in the Western Cape (Seekings, Graaff, and Joubert 1990, 8). The government cleared 3,220 hectares of land around Driftsands/Swartklip, 35 km from central Cape Town and to the east of Mitchells Plain. Squatters from formal settlements were temporarily housed in 14.4-square-meter Flexicraft tin huts (Cook 1992; Seekings, Graaff, and Joubert 1990, 10).

Construction started in 1984, and the first core houses were completed in October 1984. Forty of the 270 families living in the huts were allowed to rent the houses (Cook 1986, 60). House construction in Khayelitsha was completed in March 1985 and 1,740 families moved to the town. Earlier, in September 1984, it was officially announced that the Colored Labor preference policy would be abolished, and 99-year-leasehold tenure would be allowed only for Africans living in Khayelitsha. Hence, those who were given houses in 1985 were provided with leasehold tenure.

In November 1984, the government announced that African people who were not legally in Cape Town would be allowed to build shacks on site-and-service plots in Site C, Khayelitsha, near the N2 highway (Cook 1986, 60; 1992, 125). Their status became that of squatters with usufruct rights and temporary protection against eviction. Minister of Community Development Dr. Gerrit Viljoen affirmed that the apartheid government's intention to house the "ille-

Fig. 4.7. Khayelitsha in Cape Town, Western Cape

gals" on temporary site-and-service plots was to keep them there pending their redirection to rural areas (Cleminshaw 1985, 14). Site C was therefore established as a transit camp (Cook 1992). Forty-two families who came from the shack settlements of Old Crossroads were the first to resettle in Site C (Mdewu 2004). Soon after, 8,300 squatter families occupied 4,150 site-and-service plots. One water tap was provided for each four sites, and one bucket toilet for every two sites. However, adjacent land with no services was also occupied. Continued urbanization led to dense clusters of shacks on unserviced sites in Site C and other areas of Khayelitsha. By mid-1989, an estimated 13,000 families were squatting on unserviced sites. The population exploded from 1989 to 1991, increasing from 189,000 to 305,323 between 1988 and 1989, and growing by another 150,000 people by late 1990. Of the 450,000, 36 percent (162,000) lived in shacks on unserviced sites in Site C, Site B, Town Two, and other areas of Khayelitsha (Cook 1992, 125–30).

In 1991, the state built serviced sites in Makhaza and Site B, where some "illegal" families were moved based on a housing wait list. It is unclear how many people were moved, but the number of squatters remained high, with over 5,000 households on the waiting list before the government housing subsidy was implemented in 1994 (Cook 1992, 130).

In 1994, the new post-apartheid state developed a targeted one-off subsidy in the form of a grant to low-income households, which provided eligible households with freehold ownership of a newly built, fully serviced, one-bedroom house with real property rights. Individuals allocated property first registered on the housing waiting list at the Cape Town municipal housing office. The office then entered their information on the Housing Demand Database. A project plan was drafted by the municipality for approval by the provincial government of the Western Cape. Once the plan was approved, the municipality applied selection criteria. To be eligible, applicants were required to show proof that they were South African citizens with a household size of four or more, and to provide dependent birth certificates and spouse or partner ID books, if applicable. Application forms were processed through the Housing Subsidy System, an operational system that tracked housing subsidy applications and allocations on a national scale. To be allocated a subsidy, applicants had to have a maximum monthly household income of R3,500 with proof of income provided by pay slip (Republic of South Africa 1994). Joint spouses who earned R800 and below would get a capital subsidy worth R15,000, and those who earned between R801 and R1,500 would get a capital subsidy worth R12,500. Following this, the municipality publicized the list of beneficiaries. Beneficiaries contributed R2,479 so that they would have an economic stake in their asset (Tomlinson 2007). Once houses were completed, the project manager handed houses over to beneficiaries (Republic of South Africa 2013), who moved into their houses from 1997 under freehold tenure. Table 4.1 shows the timeline of events.

Several problems plagued the allocation process. First, the wait list did not work on a first-come, first-served basis. Indeed, many waiting lists were drawn up during the apartheid years, and some people were on multiple lists in different locations. Attempts by municipalities and the province to merge

Table 4.1. Timeline of Events: Residents' Access to Housing in Khayelitsha

1983	Khayelitsha established. "Legals" are housed in Flexicraft huts. Site C is established as a transit camp for "illegal" migrants. "Illegals" build shacks on site-and-services plots and other available spaces.
1990	High population growth leads to overcrowding in Site C, with 162,000 individuals living on unserviced land in shacks.
1994	Commencement of the phased rollout of government housing subsidies.
2002	Cape Area Panel Survey Wave 1 Conducted
2003–4	Some residents on serviced and unserviced sites receive housing subsidies and move into RDP housing. Overcrowding in Site C in Khayelitsha continues; there is a backlog of people on serviced and unserviced sites.
2004	Cape Area Panel Survey Wave 3 Conducted
2006	Cape Area Panel Survey Wave 4 Conducted
2009	Cape Area Panel Survey Wave 5 Conducted

lists failed (Tissington et al. 2013, 25). Although the Cape Town municipality kept a waiting list, they used a system based on the allocation to communities in catchment areas of specific building projects alongside the waiting list. Housing subsidies were allocated according to quotas for each community under a specific housing project. Communities established project committees to allocate houses to their members (Seekings et al. 2010, 4–6; Tissington et al. 2013, 26). Through this system, people of Khayelitsha were called to register during a given period of up to two weeks at a time to apply for a house if they wished. It did not matter how long an individual had lived in the community.

Second, some applicants came from communities as from the Eastern Cape and were awarded subsidies.[2] Meanwhile, others received their subsidies through the housing waiting list. Finally, as in Nairobi, fraud and corruption persisted, with some beneficiaries receiving more than one subsidy. Some people who had not been allocated subsidies invaded houses and were allowed to stay (Seekings et al. 2010, 4–6; Tissington et al. 2013, 26; Seekings et al. 2010, 4–6; Tissington et al. 2013, 26).

2. One of my interviewees registered a week after coming from the Eastern Cape and received a housing subsidy six months later. Another used ID books of other family members to obtain two houses.

Fig. 4.8. The Location of George and Matero in Lusaka City

4.5. MATERO AND GEORGE NEIGHBORHOODS

4.5.1. The Case of Matero

Matero developed during colonial times as a state public rental project for African workers. Initially under the administrative jurisdiction of the Lusaka Urban District Council and then the Lusaka City Council after independence, Matero emerged in response to demand for housing among African workers (Mulenga 2003, 6; Schlyter 2004, 7), following the enactment of the African Urban Housing Ordinance. This ordinance required employers and local authorities to provide housing for African employees and their wives (Mulenga 2003). From 1948 through to 1959, 5,097 houses were constructed and occupied by municipal workers in Matero (Mulenga 2003, 7).

In 1996, sitting tenants living in public housing in Matero were offered real property rights to their houses and land through leasehold titling under the presidential directive. At the time of privatization, Matero was a poor working-class area, where workers paid rent to the council. Many houses were dilapidated and had no electricity, with external water sources and pit latrines. Houses in Matero were privatized at almost no cost. Tenants paid a transfer fee of K10,500 (US$8) and a surveying fee of K60,000 (US$50). Those who paid the fees and the cost of the house received their title deed within 30 days (Schlyter 2004, 6). There were no restrictions, and the title deed gave new homeowners ownership rights for 99 years.

The primary beneficiaries of the privatization of housing in Matero were the occupants of rental housing at the time of offer. They included general workers in various government departments and private companies, as well as retired people and others who could pay the modest rent the council charged up to that point.

4.5.2. The Case of George

By contrast, to the southwest, George developed as an informal settlement originally intended to be demolished following independence. For political reasons, the state decided to upgrade it and began to provide services from 1978 to 1981. In 1981, the Lusaka Urban District Council issued occupancy licenses to residents of George, officially recognizing their occupancy. George compound was one of the neighborhoods where residents did not benefit from the state transfer of public rental housing or land to tenants. It was already the largest settlement in Lusaka, with a population of 120,000 people by 1996 (130,000 according to UNDP [2006]). George compound

Table 4.2. Timeline of Events in Matero

1948–59	Building in Matero, under a program established by the Lusaka Municipal Council of the colonial government to house African workers.
1951	Matero residents begin to take up residence. They pay rent to the Lusaka Urban District Council.
1996	Sitting tenants are offered leasehold title for a transfer fee.
2011	Survey and qualitative interviews are conducted.

Table 4.3. Timeline of Events in George

1968	George Hadjipetrou bequeaths his farmland to his workers. Squatters begin to settle on the land.
1974	George is formalized into a legal settlement under the Housing (Statutory and Improvement Areas) Act.
1978–81	George is upgraded and transferred to the Lusaka Urban District Council. Administrative recognition is provided through occupancy licenses.
1996	George residents are not offered the land on which their houses are built. They continue to occupy their houses under occupancy licenses.
2011	Survey and qualitative interviews are conducted.

began during colonial times when spouses and families of urban workers, unemployed urban migrants, and "illegal" workers whose contracts expired settled on an English settler's farm. The farmer, George Hadjipetrou, developed a business of making bricks, most of which were used to build Matero. As he employed more workers, he allowed them to build houses on his land. Hadjipetrou bequeathed his land to his workers (de facto and not freehold) as a gift in 1968 when he moved to Lusaka city to foster his growing business empire. In Hadjipetrou's honor, his workers called the area George's compound. George was typically the first place where rural-urban migrants established their households in Lusaka.

In the early 1970s, the post-independence government declared George compound to be an illegal settlement. The government decided to demolish all illegal settlements, including George, but President Kaunda changed his mind on account of political ramifications and earmarked it for upgrading. The government formally recognized George as a legal settlement following the state's decision to upgrade some squatter settlements under the Second National Development Plan for 1972–1976. The government obtained a loan from the World Bank to cover half the cost. The other half was to be paid for by the government. The Slum Upgrading Program commenced from 1978 to 1981. Upgrading involved servicing the existing 6,200 houses, and financial assistance for individuals to build or improve their houses (Rakodi and Schlyter 1981, 9–10). Servicing involved providing potable water through communal water taps at various locations, grading gravel roads, and constructing a primary school and a health clinic. The government also prepared 4,400 plots in a new extension of George to accommodate those who had to give way to the building of roads and other essential infrastructure. The government further provided households living in dwellings made of unconventional building materials with building specifications and encouraged (but did not force) them to replace their houses with those made from conventional materials. George was placed under the responsibility of the Lusaka City Council. This responsibility included collecting a service fee and providing municipal services.

In 1981, the government recognized residents as legal occupants by providing 30-year occupancy licenses. Residents received licenses allowing them to occupy council land; essentially, they owned the dwelling but not the land, with usufruct rights. Occupants were to apply for renewal in 2011. Following the upgrade, occupants of George began to pay a monthly service charge for use of the land. The Lusaka City Council (2010) referred to this service fee as "ground rent," defined as a "charge paid for a piece of land where a structure is built on council land . . . as a stopgap measure between those paying property rates and those not paying anything." Residents paid separately for water at communal taps and sewerage services.

Although residents were guaranteed tenure security with an occupancy license, they were subject to several conditions under the terms of occupancy:

(1) Occupants were limited to immediate families only. They were expected to obtain the consent of the council should they take in a lodger or other occupant.
(2) Occupants were not allowed to use the premises for purposes other than permitted use. Should they want to do so, they must apply for a business license from the council.
(3) Occupants were not allowed to sublicense or assign the benefit or part of the benefit of their occupancy license within the right granted. They could not rent to another person.
(4) If the occupant did not pay the service fee for three calendar months, they would have to address the situation or vacate the land. The coun-

cil would then remove any buildings and restore the land to its former state and condition.

(5) The license was not transferable and could not be used in any financial transactions.

(6) The council retained possession of the premises and had the right to inspect the premises at any time. The council had the right to erect any works thereon that the council deemed were in the general interest of the area. If the premises were declared unfit for human habitation by a medical officer of health, the officer could serve notice on the occupant and the occupant would have to make alterations accordingly, including demolition if that was the prescription.

As the above list of conditions shows, the occupancy license does not confer the same rights to the occupant as a leasehold title. Residents in Matero are allowed to sell their land, while those in George are not, because the land still belongs to the council (Lusaka City Council 2010). George residents are not allowed to rent out their houses or conduct business on their premises, though unofficial transactions take place despite restrictions. Indeed, many of these terms are openly disregarded, as I will show in chapter 7.

4.5.3. Comparability of Matero and George

While Matero residents were offered real property rights, George residents were not offered the public land on which their houses were built. Occupancy rights gave residents of George tenure security and access to services, but little control over the use of property. Matero residents had access to the full bundle of rights. Residents in Matero were allowed to sell their land, while those in George were not (Lusaka City Council 2010). Moreover, George residents were not allowed to rent out their houses or conduct any business on the premises.

The two neighborhoods are similar, particularly with respect to demographics and municipal services. Yet they differ in terms of legal status. Geographically, the two neighborhoods are adjacent and fall under the same electoral constituency, but their historical development is different. Residents in both neighborhoods had similar occupations, but those in Matero have more earners in the public sector. They had similar socioeconomic status: they were poor with working-class jobs, earning similar levels of income. Initially, all Matero residents were employees paid for by their employers, while those in George were a mix of employed and unemployed. However, from 1976, the government allowed people who were not working to continue living in the council house as long as they could pay the rent. Indeed, among occupants of Matero were people who had been laid off, who were retired or unemployed, or widowers who had been allowed to stay on after their husbands had died. In fact, during privatization, the council allowed transfer of rental tenure from the council to sons and widow(er)s of registered renters (Schlyter 2004, 3). Among 60,000 people who lost jobs in Lusaka from 1991 to 1997 under SAP, and those who were retrenched (laid off in order to reduce costs) from the council and government stayed on in the houses in Matero (Schlyter 2002, 17). But not every council employee was accommodated. Those on the long waiting list and living in squatter compounds like George were entitled to a housing allowance. The housing backlog in Lusaka was estimated to be over 850,000 (Schlyter 1998, 263). In 2018 it was estimated to have grown to two million (Bah, Faye, and Geh 2018).

Both areas had similar municipal services. Neither had electricity, and both areas had outdoor toilets prior to 1996. Matero had better access to a water supply, in that residents had a tap inside the yard, while those in George had to draw water from communal taps or wells that served whole neighborhoods. In 1993, the communal water supply in George was improved under a Japanese International Cooperation Agency (JICA)-funded program.

Another potential issue is that, due to their proximity, people in Matero and George may have mixed, because homeowners rented out houses in one area and moved to the other. But the percentage of such cases is likely to be insignificant.

4.6. ZANGO

After a heavy downpour in September 2000, mudslides swept over houses built on a hill in Boa Vista, an old musseque located between the port of Luanda and a luxury residential suburb (Amnesty International 2003). Several people died, including three children. That year, the government announced they would move residents to a safer location. In April and May of the following year, Boa Vista experienced more mudslides and more deaths. This time, the government decided to evict people from this hazardous musseque. In early June 2001, the vice governor of Luanda Province announced that families who lived in houses at risk would be moved and their houses demolished (Amnesty International 2003, 6).

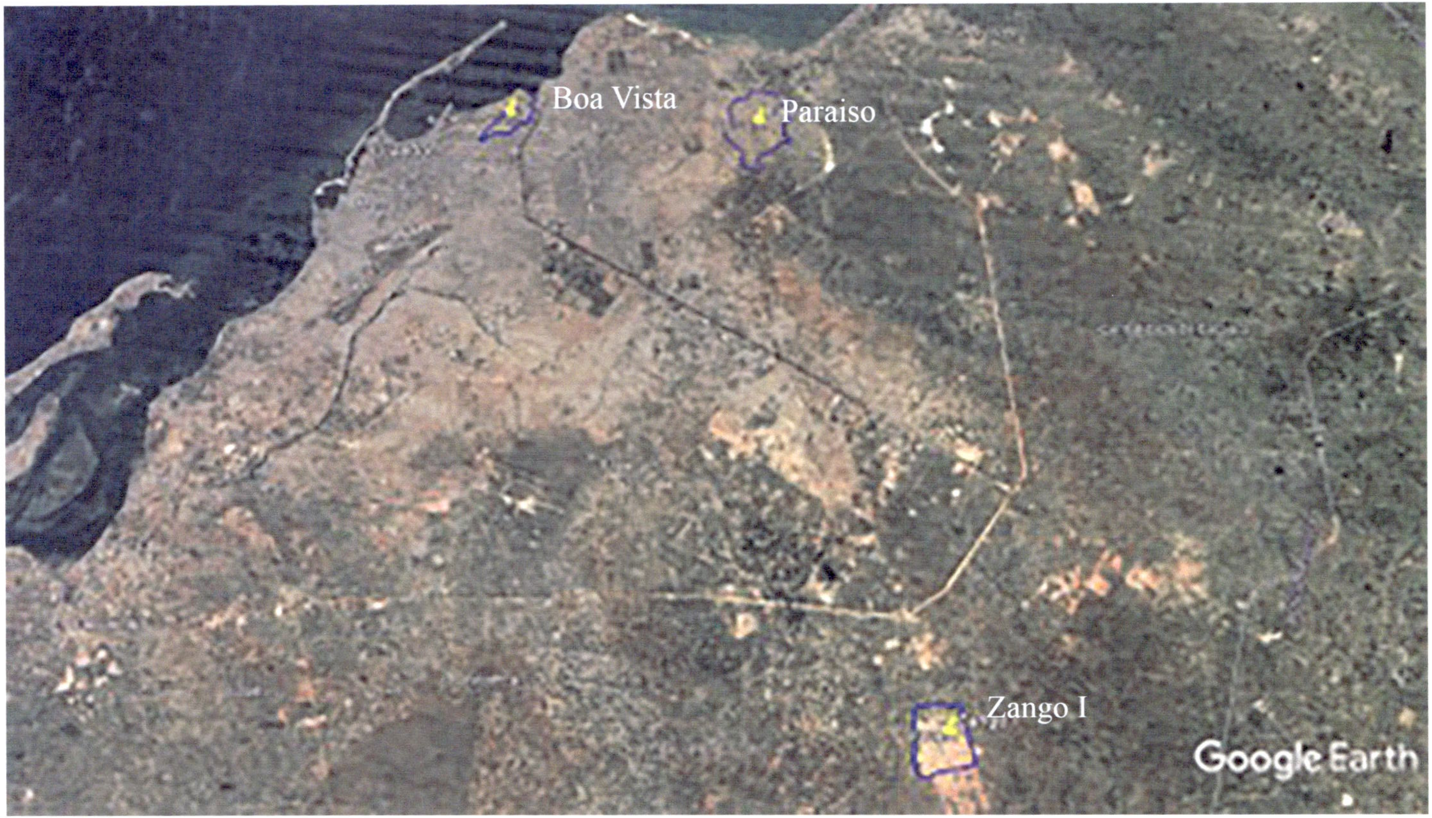

Fig. 4.9. Location of Boa Vista, Zango, and Paraiso in Luanda, Angola

Fig. 4.10. Boa Vista in January 2000 Following the Floods

Fig. 4.11. Zango in May 2008

Fig. 4.12. Boa Vista in 2019

In the early hours of Sunday, July 1, 2001, police surrounded Boa Vista and began forcibly and violently evicting residents. Two residents died and several were injured. Police returned the following week and demolished 117 houses (Amnesty International 2003, 7). Between June and September of that year, the government moved over 4,000 families from Boa Vista to Zango in Viana municipality, about 25 miles southeast of Luanda. Families in other musseques were also moved to Zango under similar conditions.

Evictees started from scratch in Zango, installing tents and shacks as they waited for houses to be built. It took three to four months for one house to be completed (Croese 2013, 97). When the issue of forced evictions and the deplorable conditions in which evictees were living caught international attention, President Dos Santos visited evictees in Zango in October 2001. In response, he moved organizational and human resources, including from his own foundation, to expedite the construction of houses. In fact, President Dos Santos placed the project under the charge of the president of his foundation, the José Eduardo dos Santos Foundation (FESA) (Croese 2013, 98). He decided to construct 3,000 houses and deliver them to the evictees free

Fig. 4.13. Shacks Where Former Residents of Hazardous Musseques Live While Awaiting Housing in Zango

of charge, to compensate households for the demolition of registered houses located in areas of risk or areas targeted for urban redevelopment (Croese 2010; Gastrow 2017a, 2017b). Two years later, the 3,000 houses had been built and delivered. In 2005, FESA contracted Dar-al-Handasah, a Lebanese firm, to draw up a master plan for the development of Zango (Croese 2013, 99). The approved design divided Zango into four areas: Zango 1, 2, 3, and 4. By 2012, over 36,000 houses had been built in these areas (Gastrow 2012). The houses all have the same semi-detached design, with three bedrooms, a kitchen, a lounge, and a bathroom (Gastrow 2013).

On delivery of houses, the government provided Zango residents with a document called the *guia de entrega*, translated as "delivery guide." The *guia de entrega* worked as a receipt for the beneficiary (Croese 2013, 106), though it did not transfer ownership to the beneficiary. Houses were delivered as social housing and remained the property of the state. The document also stipulated that selling, renting, or abandoning the house "without a justifiable reason and advance communication" was prohibited. The document also provided

Fig. 4.14. New Housing in Zango

that residents had usufruct rights: they could only use the house for residency. Violation of these conditions would result in loss of the house to the state. However, the government permitted residents to do basic work, such as "plastering and painting the interior of the house, laying tiles, installing burglar bars on doors and windows as well as ceilings without prior authorization" (Croese 2013, 106). They could not make any alterations or do other extensive work. Beyond the *guia de entrega*, there was no formal title. To date, no formal land or property registry exists for Zango or in Luanda in general, despite the ongoing delivery of houses and land for self-help building.

While the government was moving families from Boa Vista to Zango, some evictees moved to other musseques, such as Paraiso (meaning "paradise"), that were closer to economic opportunities or to their jobs. Paraiso is a musseque located on the outskirts of Luanda in Cacuaco municipality to the east of Boa Vista (Strønen and Nangacovie 2016). The area where Paraiso is now located used to be informal farmland in the early 1980s. In 1992, the area received a large wave of internally displaced persons who had been affected

Fig. 4.15. Paraiso in 2019

by the war in Huambo, Bié, Benguela, Kuando Kubango, and Uíge (Tvedten et al. 2018). Later, soldiers were also settled there. It was known more as a refugee camp during this time. In 2000, the provincial governor, Aníbal Rocha, closed down the camp. He then authorized people to build houses, and called it Paraiso. However, it is not clear whether this was a decision backed by the government, because the government did not provide any services. The houses are owner-built, mainly out of brick and mortar, giving credence to the idea that the poor in informal settlements in Luanda build houses out of brick and mortar to legitimize their tenure because they believe that such houses are more acceptable by the government (Gastrow 2017b).

Paraiso is the most populated musseque in Luanda, with a population of 120,000 in 2018 (Tvedten et al. 2018). Although the land is still officially in the hands of the government, residents feel that they own it. A study carried out by Cain (2013) in Paraiso found that 96 percent of residents paid for and therefore own their houses (the land is owned by the government), even though these were informal transactions. Paraiso is characterized by violent crime, which makes personal security a challenge for residents. Although the government allowed residents to settle there, it does not provide any services. Paraiso residents can live on the land because the government does not enforce evictions. Officially, they cannot sell their land or rent out or carry out business, but there is no regulation or enforcement.

4.7. CONCLUSION

Each of these four neighborhoods provides a rare and unique opportunity to understand the effects of real property rights in African cities and the social production of ownership tenure. Despite the large and increasing population of people living in slum conditions, there are few recent cases of public projects to transfer ownership rights as well as usufruct rights under the less popular social housing model. Thus, the four cases provide a scholarly opportunity to interrogate the homeowner ideology in urban Africa. The next four chapters examine claims about ownership by testing the effects of real and usufruct property rights in each of the neighborhoods from each city.

CHAPTER 5

The Homeowner Ideology and Freehold through Mortgages in Nairobi

Introduced in chapters 1 and 3, Zawadi is a beneficiary of KENSUP's Canaan Estate. Her 15-year journey from living in slum conditions in Zone A to Canaan Estate via Langata took a lot of patience, endurance, and tenacity. No wonder she told her story, despite stern warnings that she should not. The stories of Zawadi and others who endured the same journey effectively challenge the economic utility of real property rights, while revealing that secure tenure can produce important improvements to health and other non-economic dimensions of human welfare. Such cases show that the social production and reproduction of ownership tenure explains the persistence of homeownership as a tenure of preference.

Through quantitative and qualitative evidence from Kibera, this chapter demonstrates that freehold ideological claims about the economic utility of real property rights are ambiguous and obscure in social reality. Even though some economic benefits are documented, property rights to land and housing among the urban poor in Kibera are bundles of rights to idle capital on the formal market. A limited focus on economic outcomes has obscured evidence that property rights are associated with improved non-economic dimensions of human welfare, which this chapter shows for Kibera. The chapter also highlights the social production processes of ownership tenure in the context of Kibera.

5.1. MEASURING THE EFFECTS OF FREEHOLD TENURE IN KIBERA, NAIROBI

5.1.1. A Natural Experiment

The objective of the 2004 launch of KENSUP was to improve the lives and livelihoods of people living in slums through various initiatives and interventions. Home to slightly over 6,000 households, Kibera's Soweto East neighborhood was selected for intervention. A key goal was to provide housing to residents using low-interest, long-term mortgages. Eligible households were identified in 2004, and 824 households were randomly selected in 2016.

To isolate the causal effects of real property rights, the present study took advantage of the Kibera selection and delivery of housing as a natural experiment. Kibera was an ideal location as a natural experiment, in which naturally occurring circumstances in subsets of a defined population produce different levels of exposure to a supposed causal factor, in a situation resembling an actual experiment (Last 2001). Researchers often use natural experiments to study social phenomena where it is not practical or ethical for a researcher to expose subjects to a causal factor (Messer 2008).

The KENSUP project was a phased-in natural experiment. KENSUP delivered housing through three phases, corresponding to three sites. The three sites correspond to exposure of residents to different bundles of property rights. Kibera-Soweto Zones A and B represented the first phase. Zones A and B had been under slum conditions existing since 1912, and residents had no formal property rights. This group of potential beneficiaries represents the control condition. In the second phase in 2009, the government relocated a subset of residents from Zone A to a temporary housing area known as Langata Decanting Site (Langata). In Langata, the government constructed houses to the specifications of the promised permanent housing and allocated occupancy rights to potential beneficiaries. This is the first exposure to a bundle of rights in which the government allowed only usufruct rights. In the third phase, the government randomly selected a subset of those it had moved to Langata and allocated new permanent housing under freehold through low-cost mortgages in Canaan Estate (Canaan) in 2016. Canaan represents full exposure to the full bundle of freehold property rights.

Since not everyone was moved along the three phases at the same time, there were potential beneficiaries still living in Kibera Zone B, potential beneficiaries living in Langata, and beneficiaries living in Canaan. Hence, the different exposure to different bundles of property rights represents naturally occurring circumstances for a phased-in natural experiment that provides an opportunity to isolate the effects of freehold tenure.

The study employed two probability-based sampling methods, depending on the site. In Zone B of Soweto Kibera, systematic sampling with a random start was used; this approach has the property of ensuring that every person in the study population has an equal and random chance of being selected. Czaja et al.'s (2014) formula was employed to arrive at a representative sample size of 350. Google Earth images were obtained to identify clusters of houses and a random start for each of seven data collectors.

In Langata and Canaan, a probability-proportional-to-size sampling method was employed. Apartment blocks in each of the sites were of different sizes. Blocks were made up of studio apartments, one-bedroom apartments, and three-bedroom apartments. The target sample was 250 from both Langata and Canaan—500 total. This sample size was determined based on the highest number of households suitable for employing propensity score matching methods during analysis given available funding. The sampled Langata households made up 40 percent of all households at that site. At Canaan, the sampled households made up 30 percent of all households. The sample sizes were more than enough to represent each site.

The target sample was 850 households, while the realized sample was 820—representing 96.5 percent of the target. The realized sample was 350 (100 percent) for Zone B, 255 (102 percent) for the Decanting Site, and 215 (86 percent) for Canaan. Ultimately, Zone B accounted for 42.7, Langata 31.1, and Canaan 26.2 percent of the combined sample.

Once households were identified using the abovementioned sampling methods, six data collectors deployed a structured questionnaire survey instrument developed in English and translated into Kiswahili. Respondents were invited to choose their preferred survey language. Prior to fieldwork, data collectors participated in a two-day training on survey administration, using data collection devices, and ethics in human subject research. Table 5.1 presents the outcome variables.

5.1.2. Analysis

The analysis aimed to examine whether real property rights are associated with various outcomes (see table 5.1). Muyeba (2016) showed that distinguishing the effects of improved housing from property rights is challenging when they are simultaneously delivered to beneficiaries. By comparing households in Zone B and Langata, Zone B and Canaan, and Langata and

Table 5.1. Variable Descriptions

Variable	Description
Tenure Security	
a. Fear of eviction	Looking back to the time you have lived in this house and neighborhood, to what extent does the possibility of an eviction worry you? Scale of 0 to 10, 0 = Does not worry at all, 10 = Worry very much.
b. Possibility of eviction	To what extent would you agree with the statement that "The possibility that we get evicted from this neighborhood is always present?" Scale of 0 to 10, 0 = Does not agree at all, 10 = Agree very much.
Adult Health	
a. Self-reported health	On a scale from 0 to 10, how would you say your health is in general? 0 = Worst, 10 = Best.
b. Physical pain	On a scale from 0 to 10, how much physical pain have you felt in the past two weeks as a result of ill health? 0 = No pain, 10 = A lot of pain.
c. BMI	Computed from two anthropometric questions on height and weight: 1. What is your height in centimeters? (Converted to meters). 2. What is your weight in kgs? (Formula for BMI = Weight/Height^2)
d. Psychological health	Six-item scale with a possible score of 25: 1. On a scale from 0 to 10, how much distress/sorrow have you felt in the past two weeks including today? 0 = no distress/sorrow, 10 = a lot. 2. Over the past 2 weeks, how often have you felt anxious, nervous, or on edge? 0 = Not at all, 1 = Several days, 2 = More days than not, 3 = Nearly every day. [Also use this scale for questions 3 to 6.] 3. Over the past 2 weeks, how often were you worried? 4. Over the past 2 weeks, how often were you able to control your worrying? 5. Over the past 2 weeks, how often have you felt down, depressed, or hopeless? 6. Over the past 2 weeks, how often have you felt little interest or pleasure in doing things?

Children's Health	
a. Children's BMI	Computed from two anthropometric questions on height and weight: 1. What is Child 1's height in centimeters? (Converted to meters) 2. What is Child 1's weight in kgs?
Economic Utility	
Credit	Have you ever used this house as collateral to get loans or credit? (Interviewer: If the answer is no, go to question E.1)
Employment status	Employment status of the head of household: 1. Employed; 2. Unemployed; 3. Unemployed and job searching in the last 4 weeks; 4. Unemployed, but not actively seeking work. Changed to binary variable—1 = employed, 2 = unemployed
Income-generating activities	Has the house been used for some income-generating activity? 1 = Yes, 2 = No
Household income	What is the total monthly income for this family? (Interviewer: If the respondent cannot remember, use the following table of income categories). What is the total monthly income for this family?
Household assets/wealth	Does anyone in your home own the asset listed below in working/running conditions?
Social Capital	
Membership in associations	You are a member of . . .
Bonding social capital	In this neighborhood there are several people I trust to help solve my problems. (Type 1 to strongly agree; 2. Agree; 3. Neither agrees nor disagrees; 4. Disagree; or 5. Strongly disagrees) In this neighborhood there is someone I can turn to for advice on how to make very important decisions. In this neighborhood there's someone I feel comfortable talking about intimate personal problems. In this neighborhood when I'm lonely, there are a lot of people I can talk to. In this neighborhood if I need an emergency loan from Kz. 20,000, I know someone I can turn to. In this neighborhood, the people I interact with would put their reputation at risk for me. In this neighborhood, the people I interact with would be good work references for me. In this neighborhood, the people I interact with would share their last secret with me. In this neighborhood I know a lot of people to get them to do important things. In this neighborhood, the people I interact with would help me fight an injustice.

Bridging social capital	Interacting with people makes me take an interest in things that happen outside the home or neighborhood. Interacting with people here makes me want to try new things. Interacting with people makes me take an interest in what people different from me are thinking. Talking to people makes me curious about other places in the world. Interacting with people makes me feel like I'm part of a larger community. Interacting with people makes me feel connected to a bigger picture. Interacting with people reminds me that everyone in the world is connected. I am willing to spend time to support the activities of the community at large. Interacting with people gives me new people to talk to. In this neighborhood I interact with new people all the time.

Self-esteem, Sense of Belonging, and Satisfaction with the Dwelling, the Neighborhood, and Life in General

Self-esteem	On a scale of 0 to 10, how much do you feel that you are worthy of respect from others?
Satisfaction with the dwelling	On a scale of 0 to 10, how satisfied are you with your home?
Satisfaction with the neighborhood	On a scale of 0 to 10, how satisfied are you with your neighborhood?
Satisfaction with life in general	On a scale of 0 to 10, how satisfied are you with life in general?
Likelihood of moving	On a scale of 0 to 10, what's the likelihood of you leaving this neighborhood?

Matching Variables for Propensity Score Analysis

Age	Age of the head of household
Sex	Sex of the head of household
Education	Highest level of education of the head of household
Marital Status	Marital status of the head of household
Duration in Dwelling	How long have you lived in the residence? (Restricted to households that moved in before 2015)

Canaan, this analysis distinguishes the effects of improved housing conditions from those of property rights. Furthermore, the comparison between Langata and Canaan clarifies the distinction between housing and property rights effects, as Langata and Canaan residents experienced similar housing quality and conditions, with different ownership rights.

To estimate differences in outcomes between the three groups, analysis of variance (ANOVA) was first employed where the parametric assumption of equal variances was satisfied. Where the parametric assumption was not satisfied, a Kruskal-Wallis H-test was employed. Bartlett's test was employed to determine equal variances. Tukey's test was used as a post hoc test to identify significant differences where the omnibus test showed statistical significance.

Ordinary least squares regression analysis was employed to estimate the effects of real property rights on all outcome variables and to control for other factors. In this case, the independent variable is real property rights, that is, capturing variation from lack of property rights to occupancy rights to freehold rights. The equation to make the regression estimates is as follows:

$$Y_i = \alpha + \gamma \textit{property rights}_i + \beta Xi + \varepsilon_i$$

Y_i is any of the outcome measures for observation i. γ is the coefficient that provides an indication of the size of effect of the "property rights" measure. In the equation, "property rights" is a variable that equals 1 for households without formal property rights (Zone B Soweto), 2 for households with occupancy rights (Langata), and 3 for households with freehold property rights (Canaan). X is any of the covariates mainly controlled for demographic characteristics, including age, gender, number of years of education, father's number of years of education, mother's number of years of education, employment status, household size, and marital status. Marital status is a series of dummy variables with "single" as the reference category. Finally, ε is the error term, which represents the amount of variation in the outcome variables that is unexplained by the regression model. For each of the outcome variables, three models are estimated. Model A reflects a simple regression of property rights and the outcome variable. Model B includes demographic characteristics. Model C adds other controls, and in the process, a parsimonious model is developed as a final model.

ESTIMATING PROPENSITY SCORES

Propensity score analysis was employed in comparing Soweto East Zone B, Langata, and Canaan households. Unlike randomized control trials, observational studies do not eliminate selection bias in allocation of a causal factor. Following Rosenbaum and Rubin (1984), I employed nearest neighbor, radius, kernel, and stratification propensity score matching methods to eliminate selection bias and achieve comparability of Soweto East and Langata, and Soweto East and Canaan households. In other words, Canaan households differ from Langata households for reasons other than their beneficiary status—reasons that may determine differences in outcomes. The propensity score balances scores between the two groups on observed characteristics, thereby eliminating selection bias and making the two pairs of groups comparable on baseline characteristics. This means that conditional on their propensity scores, participants from both groups will have the same distribution of measured or observed baseline covariates. A note on observed characteristics: there was no measure of corruption in the questionnaire. The closest measure was a variable from a question that asked respondents to say the extent to which they agreed with the statement that they depend on the rule of law in their community.

An initial propensity score model was estimated using five variables as shown in table 5.1. To estimate the propensity score, a probit regression model was used in which treatment status (mortgage vs. occupancy rights and mortgage vs. untitled) was regressed on baseline characteristics (Rosenbaum and Rubin 1984). Rosenbaum and Rubin (1984) and Austin et al. (2007) recommend that models estimating propensity scores include those variables that affect the outcome or that affect both treatment selection and the outcome. The variables used are plausible predictors of tenure security and various outcomes with stronger tenure rights. Because of the need to ensure balance on variables that are predictive of these outcomes, the variables were included in the propensity score model.

MATCHING ON PROPENSITY SCORES

Household heads from Canaan were matched based on similar propensity scores with those from Zone B and with those from Langata. More participants were from Langata (255) than from Canaan (215), and thus there were more untreated than treated participants for each comparison. This distribution is ideal because there are more participants from the pool of the untreated group, which increases the likelihood of each treated household head being matched to one in the untreated group. However, inferences were only made in the region of common support—the space where propensity score distributions overlap. The objective was to match a treated participant to each participant who did not receive a mortgage. Participants were matched on propensity scores using nearest neighbor, radius with calipers of width equal to 0.1, and kernel matching. No specific matching technique is superior to another in estimation of treatment outcomes. However, use of multiple methods provides a good sense of the range in the average treatment effect on the treated.

STRATIFICATION AND BALANCE ON PROPENSITY SCORES

The region of common support ranged from 0.01 to 0.98 for Zone B vs. Canaan; and 0.24 to 0.75 for Langata vs. Canaan. Participants in the overall study sample were stratified into five equal-sized groups. The distribution of scores across groups is shown in figures 5.1 and 5.2. Results of the tests of equality of means in propensity scores within each block are not significant, showing that the means are equal.

ESTIMATING TREATMENT EFFECTS FROM PROPENSITY SCORE MATCHING METHODS

Propensity score matching allows one to estimate the average treatment effect for the treated (ATT) that is the average response to treatment for individuals who were assigned the treatment—freehold rights. The ATT are estimated for matched samples derived using nearest neighbor, radius, and kernel matching techniques. The models do not control for unobserved or unknown factors that may drive observed variation in outcomes. The assumption of the propensity score models in using observed characteristics is that there are no unobserved factors correlated with the outcome.

5.2. (F)UTILITY OF FREEHOLD IN THE SOWETO EAST PILOT PROJECT

Using the analysis methods discussed above, what are the effects of freehold tenure among the poor who benefited from the Soweto East Pilot Project? Each outcome variable is examined and the results are reported in the tables that follow. In each analysis, the first table is a comparison of Zone B (untitled) vs. Canaan (freehold) and the second Langata (usufruct) vs. Canaan.

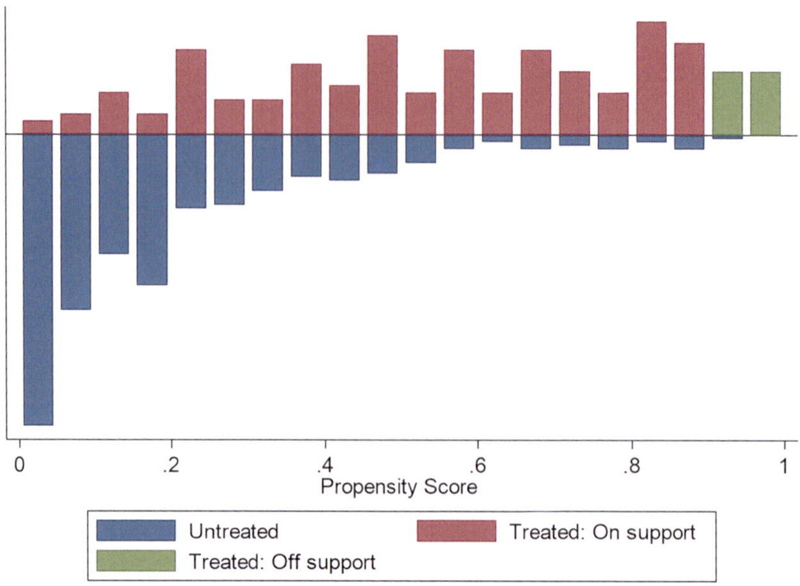

Fig. 5.1. The Region of Common Support in the Propensity Score Model for Zone B vs. Canaan

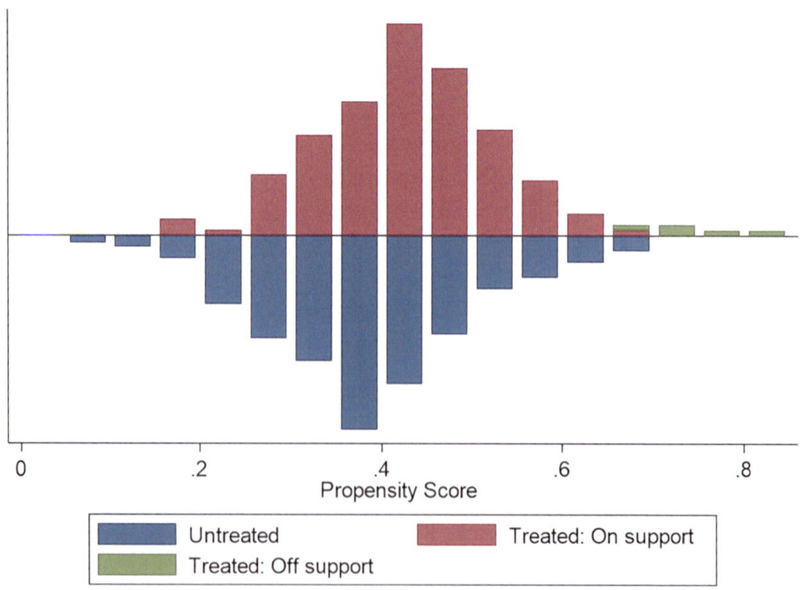

Fig. 5.2. The Region of Common Support in the Propensity Score Model for Langata vs. Canaan

5.2.1. Tenure Security

The propensity score models displayed in table 5.2 tell us that freehold owners have much lower fear of eviction and think that there is a much lower possibility of eviction compared to untitled residents of Zone B. On a scale ranging from 0 to 10, freeholders in Canaan score from 6.48 to 7.25 points lower on the fear of eviction scale and 6.38 to 6.81 lower on the possibility of eviction scale than untitled households in Zone B. Considering that untitled household heads witnessed evictions and structure owner struggles in Zone A, the fear of eviction is much higher.

Residents of Soweto East had stronger tenure security following their move from Zone A to Canaan via Langata. Compared to those living in Langata (and Zone B), residents of Canaan had significantly less fear of eviction and thought the possibility of being evicted was almost nonexistent compared to those in Langata. As table 5.3 shows, matching using different matching techniques yields an ATT of −4.05 to −4.16 in fear of eviction scores. This means that participants from Canaan reported an average 4.05 to 4.16 points lower on the fear of eviction scale than those in Langata. Scores on the possibility of eviction scale were an average of 3.85 to 4.05 lower for Canaan respondents. Resident beneficiaries no longer feared eviction or expected to be evicted, because they had the full bundle of property rights and the backing of the state. Although they feared losing their houses if they failed to make payments, no one had been evicted for missing payments.

Table 5.2. Average Treatment Effect on the Treated (ATT) for Tenure Security Using Nearest Neighbor, Radius, Kernel, and Stratification Matching

Zone B (Untitled) vs. Canaan (Freehold)

	Matching Method			
Outcome Variable	Nearest Neighbor	Radius	Kernel	Stratification
Fear of Eviction	−7.25***	−6.48***	−6.57***	−6.58***
	(0.46)	(0.37)	(0.32)	(0.39)
Possibility of Eviction	−6.81***	−6.38***	−6.44***	−6.43***
	(0.32)	(0.34)	(0.27)	(0.33)

Note: Standard errors in parentheses; *** $p < 0.01$, ** $p < 0.05$, * $p < 0.1$.

Table 5.3. Average Treatment Effect on the Treated (ATT) for Tenure Security Using Nearest Neighbor, Radius, Kernel, and Stratification Matching

Langata (Usufruct) vs. Canaan (Freehold)

	Matching Method			
Outcome Variable	Nearest Neighbor	Radius	Kernel	Stratification
Fear of Eviction	−4.16***	−4.05***	−4.11***	−4.08***
	(0.53)	(0.28)	(0.26)	(0.26)
Possibility of Eviction	−4.05***	−3.85***	−3.94***	−3.90***
	(0.50)	(0.27)	(0.29)	(0.34)

Note: Standard errors in parentheses; *** $p < 0.01$, ** $p < 0.05$, * $p < 0.1$.

5.2.2. Economic Utility of Freehold Tenure

Economic outcomes, as shown in table 5.1, included access to credit; labor market participation, as measured by employment status; participation in income-generating activities; household income; and wealth through durable household goods. Note that durable goods are often used as a substitute measure for household income where the income variable is not reliable. In this case, both measures were used for comprehensiveness and robustness. Mechanisms by which property rights increase income were many. Owners can use the title as collateral to obtain credit, which may in turn be used for investments. Increases in tenure security can likewise free up people to work rather than guard against eviction, leading to increased labor market participation. In addition, having a title and tenure security can lead to participation in income-generating activities by allowing owners to rent out rooms on the property. All these mechanisms can lead to higher income.

Freehold households in Canaan have significantly fewer income-generating activities, but, surprisingly, more household income and household durable goods than untitled households. It is surprising because there are no significant differences in credit access and employment status. In addition, with more income-generating activities, there should be higher income among the untitled. However, Canaan residents report about KSh8,000 (US$70) more. I explain this finding below.

Residents of Canaan had more income and durable household goods than residents in Langata. Table 5.5 demonstrates that Canaan residents had

Table 5.4. Average Treatment Effect on the Treated (ATT) for Household Economic Indicators Using Nearest Neighbor, Radius, Kernel, and Stratification Propensity Score Matching

Zone B (Untitled) vs. Canaan (Freehold)

	Matching Method			
Outcome Variable	Nearest Neighbor	Radius	Kernel	Stratification
Credit	0	0	0	0
Employment Status	−0.02	−0.05	−0.03	−0.02
	(0.04)	(0.04)	(0.03)	(0.03)
Income-Generating Activities	−0.08	−0.09**	−0.10*	−0.11*
	(0.06)	(0.03)	(0.05)	(0.05)
Household Income	7984.92***	8155.71***	8206.50***	1214.47
	(1202.82)	(1201.32)	(1117.15)	(1390.28)
Household Durables	1.92***	2.12***	2.04***	1.95***
	(0.38)	(0.32)	(0.40)	(0.42)

Note: Standard errors in parentheses; *** $p < 0.01$, ** $p < 0.05$, * $p < 0.1$.

household incomes between KSh4,078.79 and KSh5,508.79 more, and had an average of 1.38 to 1.79 (an average of 1 to 2) more household durable goods than Langata residents.

However, no evidence supports the differences in income or durable goods. None of the mechanisms described above accounted for any differences with residents of Langata. There were no significant differences in access to credit. Only three residents out of 810 reported using their house as collateral to obtain credit, meaning that obtaining credit was almost impossible. There was no expectation for anyone to report access to credit, since the government had held on to the title deed. There were no differences in employment rates and participation in income-generating activities between the two groups. In fact, among those who participated in income-generating activities, those in Langata reported more income on average than those in Canaan. The project included market stores alongside the wall of Canaan Estate and opposite Kibera market. No one occupied the market stores opposite the market. As Barasa describes, "the market stores are mainly for those who have businesses in the project-affected area. Anyone can benefit. So, you also have to save for the market store." Several market stores were vacant.

Since there were significant differences in income, yet the mechanisms

Table 5.5. Average Treatment Effect on the Treated (ATT) for Household Economic Indicators Using Nearest Neighbor, Radius, Kernel, and Stratification Propensity Score Matching

Langata (Usufruct) vs. Canaan (Freehold)

	Matching Method			
Outcome Variable	Nearest Neighbor	Radius	Kernel	Stratification
Credit	0	0	0	0
Employment Status	0.06	−0.00	−0.00	−0.01
	(0.06)	(0.03)	(0.04)	(−0.04)
Income-Generating Activities	0.03	−0.01	0.00	0.01
	(0.04)	(0.03)	(0.03)	(0.02)
Household Income	5508.79***	4620.14***	4238.84***	4078.79***
	(1772.20)	(1419.55)	(1286.50)	(1628.94)
Household Durables	1.79***	1.44***	1.41***	1.38***
	(0.34)	(0.25)	(0.27)	(0.22)

Note: Standard errors in parentheses; *** $p < 0.01$, ** $p < 0.05$, * $p < 0.1$.

by which we should see increases in income were not working as expected, I sought unobserved factors to explain higher levels of income among beneficiaries. The unobserved factor raised in the literature and in interviews is fraud and corruption, which led to bias in the selection of beneficiaries and bias in the natural experiment. Indeed, when the analysis controlled for whether a respondent relied on the rule of law in their community, the closest variable to a measure of corruption, income lost significance in the calculation employing nearest neighbor matching and had a reduction in its level of significance in the other three matching methods. A second factor was that while at Langata, some beneficiaries were eliminated for rent nonpayment. Indeed, several residents who had fallen behind on the monthly KSh2,100 were evicted. Zawadi called them "nice evictions":

> Sometimes, most people [in Langata] do not pay their rent. . . . Even if the government decides that they are building Zone B for them, there is no way they can go to that place, most of them, because they don't pay their rent. They don't even save. . . . My mom used to go to that stress when she was here. It is not good. . . . They evicted people, but it was a nice eviction. They came and they spoke to people, and they asked how you can clear this kind of amount. To be honest, some people are paying 2,100 per month so that

balance piling up to 105,000. The government is also losing 105,000 and its one person so imagine like 50 of them. . . . On our block, they evicted four.

Four households were evicted on Zawadi's block alone, which may suggest that evictions led to greater elimination of poorer households from the selection process. This meant that those who entered Canaan were probably already making more income than those who did not. A third source of unobserved variation may have come from the failure of the project to plan for orphans, widows, and older people, and how they might be included without meeting the minimum savings required, and without having to make rental payments in Langata and mortgage payments after selection.

5.2.3. Physical and Psychological Health

Freeholders reported better physical health than untitled households. However, physical health improves based on improvements in the living environment rather than because of freehold ownership. Freeholders improve their living environment through investment in their dwelling when they have less fear of eviction. Controlling for how long residents have lived in their house, freeholders also have fewer children, and freeholders scored lower on the anxiety disorder scale than untitled households.

Considering that the difference between Canaan and Langata was freehold tenure—not housing—it is unsurprising that freehold tenure was not linked to better physical health for adults or children in the Soweto East project. The estimated treatment effects on the treated for self-reported physical health and pain scales shown in table 5.7 indicate no significant difference between the two groups. Property rights are not associated with better physical health. A multiple regression model that included Zone B as part of the variation in property rights before the propensity score model showed positive and significant effects of property rights on these measures of health. The effects observed in the regression models suggest that the regression estimate was capturing the difference between those in Zone B who scored lower and both treatment groups. The observed difference between Zone B residents and residents in Langata and Canaan is quality of the dwelling.

In comparing the two sites, there was an issue of overweight health conditions in both locations, which is consistent with Vogl's (2007) work in Peru. Because they are poor communities, it is probably a case of poor nutrition. However, although respondents scored in the overweight category of BMI, there were no significant differences among the three treatment conditions.

The findings on children's BMI are at the same time somewhat consistent

Table 5.6. Average Treatment Effect on the Treated (ATT) for Health Indicators Using Nearest Neighbor, Radius, Kernel, and Stratification Propensity Score Matching

Zone B (Untitled) vs. Canaan (Freehold)

	Matching Method			
Outcome Variable	Nearest Neighbor	Radius	Kernel	Stratification
Self-Report Physical Health	0.77*	1.07***	0.78***	0.75***
	(0.39)	(0.22)	(0.25)	(0.22)
Physical Pain	−0.60	−0.61	−0.39	−0.36
	(0.47)	(0.26)	(0.31)	(0.31)
Adult BMI	0.52	0.22	0.41	0.56
	(0.59)	(0.46)	(0.59)	(0.64)
Child BMI	−1.09	−0.12	0.36	0.48
	(1.09)	(1.03)	(0.84)	(0.74)
Fertility	−0.43***	−0.43***	−0.44***	−0.43***
	(0.10)	(0.08)	(0.08)	(0.07)
Anxiety Disorder	−4.51***	−4.36***	−4.56***	−4.55***
	(0.75)	(0.72)	(0.52)	(0.59)

Note: Standard errors in parentheses; *** $p < 0.01$, ** $p < 0.05$, * $p < 0.1$.

Table 5.7. Average Treatment Effect on the Treated (ATT) for Health Indicators Using Nearest Neighbor, Radius, Kernel, and Stratification Propensity Score Matching

Langata (Usufruct) vs. Canaan (Freehold)

	Matching Method			
Outcome Variable	Nearest Neighbor	Radius	Kernel	Stratification
Self-Report Physical Health	0.46	0.31	0.12	0.02
	(0.24)	(0.22)	(0.21)	(0.22)
Physical Pain	0.25	−0.19	−0.02	0.10
	(0.40)	(0.27)	(0.27)	(0.33)
Adult BMI	−0.26	−0.54	−0.54	−0.46
	(0.61)	(0.44)	(0.43)	(0.46)
Child BMI	−2.18	−1.52	−1.44	−1.40
	(1.16)	(0.67)	(0.66)	(0.81)
Fertility	−0.27***	−0.18***	−0.20***	−0.21***
	(0.09)	(0.06)	(0.06)	(0.06)
Anxiety Disorder	−2.86***	−2.62***	−2.77***	−2.56***
	(0.83)	(0.55)	(0.40)	(0.53)

Note: Standard errors in parentheses; *** $p < 0.01$, ** $p < 0.05$, * $p < 0.1$.

and somewhat inconsistent with Vogl (2007) and Galiani and Schargrodsky (2004). While property rights are not associated with children's BMI scores, both Vogl (2007) and Galiani and Schargrodsky (2004) found that children's BMI scores improved in households that had property title. However, the findings were characterized as suggestive for Vogl (2007), while Galiani and Schargrodsky (2004) found that these health improvements were only short-term. Galiani and Schargrodsky (2004) offer useful insights for all three studies and the field, suggesting that other nutrition-related government programs may already be at work, such that addition of property rights does not affect food security. Indeed in 2009, the government of Kenya began to implement the Home-Grown School Feeding (HGSF) Program, which has reached over half a million schoolchildren. Supported by the World Food Program, meals under HGSF have been provided to school-age children at primary schools in Kibera (World Food Programme 2016).

Table 5.7 further reveals that Canaan residents have better psychological health than Langata residents, meaning that real property rights improve psychological health. The anxiety disorder scale scores are lower on average by 2.56 to 2.86 points for Canaan participants. Each of these differences is significant at the 1 percent level. Findings confirm existing suspicions in the literature that real property rights are associated with better psychological health. In a different study, Gandelman (2010) provided the interpretation that real property rights may lead to lower stress levels and hence a lower frequency of chronic diseases. What remains to be tested is the mechanism. The mechanism is most likely that real property rights are associated with stronger tenure security, which is associated with lower levels of anxiety and stress arising from fear of eviction. In turn, this improves psychological health and ultimately reduces frequency of chronic diseases such as hypertension. Further work in property rights and health needs to test the abovementioned mechanisms, perhaps through path analysis. Further work also needs to interrogate the mechanism by which mortgage-based real property titling impacts income and health in low-income households in sub-Saharan Africa.

Table 5.7 shows that poor people with property rights have fewer children than those without. Fewer children lived in Canaan households, demonstrating that property rights are associated with a lower fertility rate. Table 5.7 shows that there were 18 to 21 percent fewer children in Canaan than Langata. This could be the effect of being in a transitory period, or the fact that fewer poor people than middle-class people found their way into the houses.

5.2.4. Social Capital

The Soweto East Pilot Project led to a reduction in social capital, but this cannot be attributed to property rights. As tables 5.8 and 5.9 demonstrate, there were no significant differences in various social capital measures between untitled households and freeholders, or between those with usufruct tenure

Table 5.8. Average Treatment Effect on the Treated (ATT) for Social Capital Indicators Using Nearest Neighbor, Radius, Kernel, and Stratification Propensity Score Matching

Zone B (Untitled) vs. Canaan (Freehold)

	Matching Method			
Outcome Variable	Nearest Neighbor	Radius	Kernel	Stratification
Social Capital				
Membership in Associations	−0.20	−0.10	−0.14	−0.13
	(0.10)	(0.08)	(0.07)	(0.08)
Bonding Social Capital	0.24	0.80	0.42	0.64
	(1.41)	(1.18)	(1.22)	(1.05)
Bridging Social Capital	−0.99	−1.10	−0.98	−0.58
	(1.36)	(1.07)	(1.08)	(0.97)

Note: Standard errors in parentheses; *** $p < 0.01$, ** $p < 0.05$, * $p < 0.1$.

Table 5.9. Average Treatment Effect on the Treated (ATT) for Social Capital Indicators Using Nearest Neighbor, Radius, Kernel, and Stratification Propensity Score Matching

Langata (Usufruct) vs. Canaan (Freehold)

	Matching Method			
Outcome Variable	Nearest Neighbor	Radius	Kernel	Stratification
Social Capital				
Membership in Associations	−0.16	0.18	0.19	0.08
	(0.28)	(0.20)	(0.91)	(0.07)
Bonding Social Capital	0.76	−0.14	−0.20	−0.33
	(1.37)	(0.98)	(1.00)	(1.15)
Bridging Social Capital	0.68	0.52	0.50	0.35
	(1.07)	(0.84)	(1.03)	(0.71)

Note: Standard errors in parentheses; *** $p < 0.01$, ** $p < 0.05$, * $p < 0.1$.

and freeholders. No evidence was found to support the claim that real property rights reduce social capital.

Instead, the relocation of residents may explain the negative impact on social capital among beneficiaries. During in-depth, one-on-one interviews, several interviewees pointed out ways that their move from Zone A reduced their connections and influenced their ability to do business away from their temporary housing. The subsequent move to Canaan exacerbated the decline in social capital. It was a process of starting over, getting connected, and then starting over again. As Zawadi puts it:

> First were the relations. Among us, it was kind of like you know everybody. So, moving from [Zone A] to [Langata], you find that because you just became close and then you move [to Canaan]. . . . You have to start over again because you are placed with people you don't know. Kibera was quite a good place. Just getting to live together people who are not that close to them, it took time. The relationships changed. It is both a good thing and a bad thing. For the good thing, . . . [y]ou can see some blocks, they have shops, they can rent it out to people who have businesses or a business idea. It is good for them to start something new here, to catch the market for people because all of us are new to this place.

By contrast, Chitundu did not lament the separation from neighbors because she felt that there was no help from neighbors during health emergencies. However, she did lament the disruption of informal business that came with moving from Langata and Canaan:

> It's not guaranteed that they will go with the same neighbor together. The government's plan could bring strangers alongside them. There is no guarantee that the same neighborhood would go together and live together. For instance, in Kibera when I get sick, among people that I don't know, I can never call any neighbor to bring me to the hospital. Here, I am used to the people around me; we know each other. I could easily call a friend to take me to the hospital. There, I might just even die. . . . Even if they're removed, the guys that are doing small businesses, they are going to be affected. Because you move that person doing a small business to another area, you disrupt his business. There is no way he can start the same business he has in other places. So, it means you have the stress of not saving the money the government wants us to save. Disruption mostly is about income. The biggest issue is income generation.

5.2.5. Self-Esteem, Satisfaction with the House, Neighborhood, and Life, and Sense of Belonging

Table 5.10 demonstrates that freeholders experienced remarkable improvements to their self-esteem and satisfaction with their houses, neighborhood, and life in general, and reported a deeper sense of belonging. On a scale from 0 to 10, freeholders reported an average of 1/2 to 2/3 of a point higher on the self-esteem scale than untitled households. They also reported 1 point higher on their satisfaction with their house, about 1 1/3 points higher in satisfaction with the neighborhood, 1/2 to 2/3 points higher in satisfaction with life in general, and nearly 1 1/2 points higher in their sense of belonging.

Finally, table 5.11 reveals that beneficiaries on the Kibera East pilot project have higher self-esteem, are more satisfied with their house and neighborhood, are less likely to move, and are more satisfied with life in general compared to those in Langata. This means that property rights are linked to higher self-esteem. People with ownership of property were proud of attaining higher status as homeowners and of having achieved an important milestone. As Odhiambo puts it, "I am proud of myself because I have something

Table 5.10. Average Treatment Effect on the Treated (ATT) for Self-Esteem, Satisfaction with House and Neighborhood, and Sense of Belonging Using Nearest Neighbor, Radius, Kernel, and Stratification Propensity Score Matching

Zone B (Untitled) vs. Canaan (Freehold)

	Matching Method			
Outcome Variable	Nearest Neighbor	Radius	Kernel	Stratification
Self-Esteem	0.55***	0.71***	0.68***	0.61***
	(0.21)	(0.18)	(0.16)	(0.19)
Satisfaction with House	3.04***	2.58***	2.50***	2.54***
	(0.52)	(0.25)	(0.47)	(0.43)
Satisfaction with Neighborhood	2.43***	2.31***	2.28***	2.32***
	(0.52)	(0.26)	(0.29)	(0.36)
Satisfaction with Life in General	1.13***	0.87***	0.73***	0.69***
	(0.29)	(0.24)	(0.25)	(0.28)
Likelihood of Moving	−2.84***	−2.69***	−2.71***	−2.77***
	(0.45)	(0.33)	(0.36)	(0.43)

Note: Standard errors in parentheses; *** $p < 0.01$, ** $p < 0.05$, * $p < 0.1$.

Table 5.11. Average Treatment Effect on the Treated (ATT) for Self-Esteem, Satisfaction with House and Neighborhood, and Sense of Belonging Using Nearest Neighbor, Radius, Kernel, and Stratification Propensity Score Matching

Langata (Usufruct) vs. Canaan (Freehold)

	Matching Method			
Outcome Variable	Nearest Neighbor	Radius	Kernel	Stratification
Self-Esteem	0.66***	0.59***	0.60 ***	0.54***
	(0.22)	(0.15)	(0.17)	(0.14)
Satisfaction with House	1.09***	1.13***	1.14***	1.09***
	(0.29)	(0.20)	(0.19)	(0.18)
Satisfaction with Neighborhood	1.29***	1.43***	1.43***	1.33***
	(0.31)	(0.20)	(0.20)	(0.20)
Satisfaction with Life in General	0.54***	0.58***	0.63***	0.62***
	(0.23)	(0.18)	(0.19)	(0.19)
Likelihood of Moving	−1.24***	−1.45***	−1.43	−1.32***
	(0.36)	(0.28)	(0.23)	(0.28)

Note: Standard errors in parentheses; *** $p < 0.01$, ** $p < 0.05$, * $p < 0.1$.

that I can call my own. I did something to get this. I will not leave my children without a house. When I go to my children, they will be able to have the house, it will be comforting." Odhiambo shows that the house builds self-esteem and allows him to pass it on to his children. Not only does he pass on the dwelling, he begins a legacy of homeownership. Some interviewees spoke of talking to their children about moving to another slum to finish up paying for the house, while others encouraged the children to work hard so they could finish paying for the house; ultimately, it is theirs.

Property rights are associated with satisfaction with house and neighborhood. People with more bundles of property rights were less likely to move, implying that they have a stronger sense of belonging. They were also more satisfied with life in general compared to those with a smaller bundle of rights.

5.3. CONCLUSION

Ownership rights are associated with stronger tenure security, higher income and household wealth, better psychological health, lower fertility, higher self-esteem and satisfaction with the house and neighborhood, and a stronger sense of belonging. Ownership rights are also associated with social production and intergenerational transfer of homeownership culture through the family. Owners work hard to pass down to their children both their houses and their beliefs about the value of a house. Freehold ownership rights are not associated with the theoretically consistent mechanisms for capital accumulation, such as access to credit, higher labor-market participation, and income-generating activities, which suggests that there are unobserved mechanisms through which income and durable goods are accumulated. Qualitative interviews suggest that rent-seeking behavior and corruption are at play.

The present chapter concludes that ownership rights are bundles of rights to idle capital, as demonstrated by a lack of evidence for their economic utility. However, clear benefits such as tenure security may reduce worry about eviction, thereby improving psychological health, self-esteem, sense of belonging, and home and neighborhood satisfaction. When we extend our research beyond a focus on economic utility, we see such benefits. Further, we see that untitled households score higher than freeholders in income-generating activities, if we extend beyond a focus on ownership tenure.

Although the case revealed that beneficiaries had higher income than those in Langata, there was no evidence for the theorized mechanisms through which these differences can arise. This implies that an unobserved factor was responsible for the income differences. The most likely factor is the selection of higher-income households through both the process of eviction among poorer households, and the apparent corruption and fraud involving the SEC, employees of the Ministry of Land and Housing, and structure owners' efforts to benefit from KENSUP. While the project aimed to provide housing for the poor, the poorest did not benefit. Even more concerning, the project did not pay attention to how orphans, widows, and older people could be included as beneficiaries when they could not afford to raise the amount required for selection.

Considering that there was no evidence for the theorized mechanisms, ownership of mortgage housing for the income-poor as a capital resource is structured idle capital. Beneficiaries are not using their property rights to access credit, because the state is holding title deeds, supporting Albertus's (2020) property rights gap theory. Nor are beneficiaries using their ownership rights to increase labor-market participation. Indeed, their income-generating activities are not significantly different from those who only have occupancy rights. Perhaps beneficiaries will utilize their ownership rights to obtain credit when they possess the deed, when property values increase to levels competitive with middle-class housing, or when employment opportunities are more widely available. But so long as these constraints are in place, real property in the hands of the poor represents idle capital, and real property rights delivered to beneficiaries on the Soweto East Village Pilot project and KENSUP will remain idle capital.

CHAPTER 6

The Homeowner Ideology and Freehold through Subsidized Housing in Cape Town

Let us revisit Mpho, the person from Khayelitsha, who received a government housing subsidy with freehold tenure from the post-apartheid government. After living in a shack in Site C of Khayelitsha for three decades, Mpho is now a happy and respectable "madam" who owns and runs her house. While she cannot borrow against her house, she is much healthier physically. Not only does she feel that she has respectability, decency, and dignity—especially after decades of dehumanizing experiences under apartheid—her self-esteem has improved, she is proud of her house and neighborhood, and she feels satisfaction with her life. But there are also unexpected developments—her teenage daughter got pregnant in the new house. Mpho's story is typical among housing subsidy beneficiaries in Khayelitsha. Her story and those of others like her challenge the economic focus on the benefits of real property rights, by elevating non-economic dimensions of human welfare as well as counterintuitive consequences.

This chapter demonstrates that persistent ideological claims about the economic utility of freehold property rights obscure social reality. Freehold property rights delivered through housing subsidy programs represent a bundle of rights to idle capital among the poor in Khayelitsha. Even so, informality and weaker forms of tenure have utility. Furthermore, the sole focus on freehold economic utility obscures evidence of positive effects on health and other indicators of human welfare, such as self-esteem. Counterintuitive effects such as teenage pregnancy are also part of this social reality. The first part of the present chapter discusses the quantitative methods employed in this case. The second part offers evidence on the futility and utility of ownership tenure.

6.1. MEASURING THE EFFECTS OF FREEHOLD TENURE IN KHAYELITSHA, CAPE TOWN

The case of Khayelitsha presented an ideal research opportunity to investigate the effects of real property rights on beneficiaries relative to squatters with temporary protection against eviction. The close adjacency of housing beneficiaries and nonbeneficiaries offers an the opportunity for a treatment and comparison group. Those who remained in shacks in Site C, Site B, Town One, and Town Two were in the comparison group, while those who had moved to serviced sites in Site B, Makhaza, and Kuyasa, and later into state-built houses, were the treatment group. Further, subsidy allocation was completed in phases, meaning that Khayelitsha beneficiaries and nonbeneficiaries coexisted, making comparison possible. Nonbeneficiaries who remain on the waiting list on both serviced and unserviced sites offer a useful comparison. Despite the problems in subsidy allocation described in chapter 4, the case of Khayelitsha provides an opportunity to investigate the effects of freehold relative to administrative recognition of occupancy.

6.1.1. Data

Data from the ongoing Cape Area Panel Study (CAPS) were analyzed to examine effects of real property. CAPS follows the lives of a large representative sample of young adults living in metropolitan Cape Town as they undergo multiple transitions from adolescence to adulthood. CAPS also administers household-level questionnaires, including a survey for household heads. The first wave commenced in 2002. There have been four subsequent waves, with the latest wave at the writing of this book being wave 5, carried out in 2009. CAPS covers a range of topics, including schooling, entry into the labor market, housing, neighborhood, sexual and reproductive health, and family relations. The panel asks questions about whether the household head or anyone in the household received a government housing subsidy to acquire land or build the house. The panel consisted of approximately 4,750 randomly selected individuals between ages 14 and 22 in 2002 and between ages 22 and 35 in 2009. Households were sampled using probability proportional to size, and stratified according to population group. First, 440 clusters roughly corresponding to the 1996 census enumerator areas were selected. Then households were selected from each cluster. From each household, up to three young adults were selected. Since CAPS covers all of Cape Town, a subsample consisting of only respondents from Site C, Khayelitsha, in 2002 was selected.

Analysis was restricted to respondents who reported no housing subsidy in wave 1 (2002) of CAPS, but reported one in wave 3 (2005). The total sample size in 2002 was 330. By 2005, 111 had obtained subsidies (treatment) and 219 had not (control). The effects were examined four years later in 2009 using wave 5 data. Only those who reported that they had a housing subsidy and lived in their houses in both 2005 and 2009 were considered part of the treatment group. Similarly, only those who reported living in a shack in both 2005 and 2009 with no housing subsidy were part of the control group. The same individuals were tracked, since CAPS follows individuals even when they move. Table 6.1 describes the variables used in the analysis.

Table 6.1. Variable Descriptions

Variable	Response Categories	Description
Labor Participation	Group average	"How many hours do you work on your current job per day?"
Per Capita Income	Group average	Log of household income per capita from imputed per capita income variable
Household Durables	Average scale	"Does anyone in your household own . . . ?" (e.g., radio, television, microwave, refrigerator, car, etc.)
Physical Health	Ordinal scale	"How good is your health?" 0 = poor, 1 = fair, 2 = good, 3 = very good, 4 = excellent
Teenage Pregnancy	Dummy	"Have you ever been pregnant?" 1 = pregnant, 0 = otherwise, restricted to females below age 18
School Dropouts	Dummy	Average number of respondents who had not completed matriculation and were above 18 years. 1 = dropout, 0 = otherwise
Neighborhood Stability	Dummy	"Did your household move in the past five years?" (Wave 1) / Have you moved since the last interview? (Waves 4 and 5) 1 = Moved in last 4/5 years, 0 = otherwise
Membership in Associations	Composite scale	"Are you a member of . . . ?" (e.g., youth group, political party, church . . .)

6.1.2. Analytical Strategy

In the estimation strategy, difference-in-differences (DID) was used to estimate the effect of a housing subsidy for the outcome variables. The models are of the form

$$Y_{it} = \beta_0 + \beta_1(\text{treatment period})_{it} + \beta_2(\text{RDP homeowner})_1 + \beta_3(\text{treatment} \times \text{RDP homeowner})_{it} + \beta_{ki}X_{ki} + e_i$$

where Y_{it} is any of the outcome variables for observation i at time t, *treatment period* is a dummy variable with the value of 1 for the post-treatment period and 0 for the pretreatment period, *RDP homeowner* is a dummy taking the value 1 if the individual is in the treatment group (owns a Reconstruction and Development Programme home) and 0 if they are in the control group, and the coefficient of the interaction between *treatment period* and *RDP homeowner*, β_3, is the OLS DID estimator or the logistic regression odds ratio. The vector X_{ki} specifies the pretreatment covariates or controls.

Difference-in-differences coefficients are estimated for labor market participation, per capita income, assets, physical health, and membership in associations using OLS regressions. The DID is estimated using odds ratios for teenage pregnancies, stability, and the proportion of dropouts using logistic regressions.

6.2. (F)UTILITY OF FREEHOLD IN KHAYELITSHA

6.2.1. Credit

Subsidy beneficiaries are found to rarely use their property titles for credit purposes in Khayelitsha. Where they are used, they are alone insufficient to obtain credit and are used alongside other requirements, such as evidence of regular income. Evidence from qualitative interviews is overwhelmingly convincing that the poor do not use their subsidized houses as collateral to get a loan more than do nonbeneficiaries who live in shacks. This is despite some expressing the need for money to complete or extend their houses. There were three main reasons. First, they were not aware they could use their house to get a loan. Second, those who were aware feared defaulting on credit repayments and losing their home. Third, whether aware or not, employed household heads felt that they did not need a loan. However, Zoleka was a unique case of a state subsidy beneficiary who managed to obtain loans with her friends. Her story is juxtaposed with that of Sibongile, a nonbeneficiary living in slum conditions in an undeveloped part of Khayelitsha. Zoleka and her friends obtained several loans from the Kuyasa Fund to extend their houses, though the property title was not the only requirement. She was also required to provide pay slips. In previous loans, Zoleka used her own pay slips. Since retirement, she used pay slips from her daughter, who was in a police reserve in the South African Police Service. She noted that Kuyasa did not use evidence from her pension:

> Kuyasa cannot lend you money if you don't have a house. . . . I borrowed money . . . and they need your house title deed. But now Kuyasa don't lend people who gets pension grant. . . . Kuyasa do not want people who live in a shack, but people with brick houses. [W]e used to get it without title deeds. I only realize that when I went to get a loan for my daughter. . . . I had to bring my title deed. . . . All of us in this neighborhood are getting loans from Kuyasa, and we pay well. . . . I was going to put ceiling and geyser [hot water heater] . . . but I haven't bought the geyser yet because of my poor health. I think I'm tired from working. . . . I was working, when I started borrowing from Kuyasa, I was working. . . . Kuyasa is the one that built for me. I extended this side of my house with the money from Kuyasa. . . . All of us here . . . the only thing now is that Kuyasa do not accept pensioners; you need to have a child who is working to go and stand for you—that's why the geyser failed. Because you cannot rely on the youth, as they work now and stop tomorrow. The only child I relied on was the one who is a police reservist.

The Kuyasa Fund is a South African nonprofit microfinance institution that provides microcredit for housing to the marginalized, those in informal employment, women, and pensioners (Mills 2007, 458). The fund was set up to address the failure of formal microfinance to reach low-income clients, particularly those who were beneficiaries of housing subsidies (Kuyasa Fund 2022). Banks see low-income clients as a credit risk. According to their website, by 2021, the Kuyasa Fund had provided loans worth R25 million (US$1.76 million), worth up to R10,000 (US$700) each to people earning less than R3,500 (US$245) per month. They served over 5,000 clients. The fund leverages household savings as collateral, but not the house. The Kuyasa Fund expected that clients would use the loans for renewable energy products such as solar water heaters, stoves, and lamps, along with general renovations such as tiling, tubing, electrification, plastering, painting, fencing, flooring, and structural extensions. The criteria for awarding loans were that clients needed to have a South African ID, a pay slip, or proof of income if informally employed or remittance dependent, and a title deed, proof of savings, and a bank account.

By comparison, Sibongile is not a housing beneficiary and could not use his shack to get a loan. However, he was able use his relatively stable job to access a loan to start a small business and fix his shack. Sibongile arrived in the (unserviced) QQ section of Site B in 1996 from the Eastern Cape. He first lived with his mother, who had come earlier, in 1992. He moved because he wanted to become independent. Since he was getting married, he decided to buy a better shack than the one he had built for himself. There is a thriving market for shacks in Khayelitsha, where buyers can view and pick a shack like any home furniture. Using all his money on the shack, Sibongile acquired a small business loan of R3,000 from the First National Bank (FNB). He used part of the loan for burglar bars and other house needs. Sibongile describes his need for a loan after upgrading his shack:

> I got it [a loan] from FNB after I bought this house. I bought it because . . . I wanted to buy a fridge, but I didn't have the money, I spent all my money on buying this house. . . . I bought it for R3,800 [US$260], but other things were not here . . . things like these fridges and all that, burglar gates were not there. I borrowed a loan of R3,000 [US$210] at FNB. . . . I pay it every month; my monthly instalment is R417 [US$30].

Together, these stories demonstrate that for the few who access loans, the property title is either unnecessary or insufficient to obtain a loan. In general, there is no difference in access to loans between the poor who live in shacks with temporary protection against eviction and those who live in subsidized housing with freehold rights. A steady-paying job or other flow of income was the most important criterion. As with those who lived in shacks, even when some expressed interest, they did not meet the criteria of South African banks, and only met two of the criteria for the Kuyasa Fund, which required a South African ID, a stable job, and a title deed.

In the broader scheme, the evidence from the research in Khayelitsha confirms that titling may not be associated with access to credit. Other studies (mainly qualitative) in South Africa that researched a similar question found similar results (see Boudreaux 2006; Kingwill et al. 2006; Lemanski

Table 6.2. Effects of a Housing Subsidy on Labor Participation, Household per Capita Income, Household Durables, Physical Health, and Membership in Voluntary Associations: Difference-In-Differences Estimation (Multivariate OLS Regression)

	(1) Hours Worked per Day		(2) Per Capita Household Income (log)		(3) Number of Household Durables Owned		(4) Health Self-Report		(5) Membership in Voluntary Associations	
	Pre-treatment	Post-treatment	Pre-treatment	Post-treatment	Pre-treatment	Post-treatment	Pre-treatment	Post-treatment	Pre-treatment	Post-treatment
RDP Homeowners	3.24	0.62	6.0	6.6	0.21	0.35	2.99	3.04	0.09	−0.02
	(1.85)	(1.86)	(0.41)	(0.41)	(0.08)	(0.08)	(0.52)	(0.52)	(0.10)	(0.10)
Shack Dwellers	3.16	0.06	6.2	6.64	0.16	0.32	3.35	2.89	0.12	0.04
	(1.84)	(1.83)	(0.40)	(0.40)	(0.08)	(0.08)	(0.51)	(0.51)	(0.09)	(0.09)
Difference	0.08	0.68	0.22*	0.05	0.06**	0.03	0.35**	0.14	−0.03	−0.06**
	(0.49)	(0.50)	(0.11)	(0.12)	(0.02)	(0.02)	(0.14)	(0.14)	(0.02)	(0.03)
Difference-in-Differences		0.60		0.16		−0.02		0.50**		−0.03
		(0.70)		(0.16)		(0.03)		(0.20)		(0.04)
Adjusted R^2		0.21		0.24		0.28		0.04		0.12
Observations	464		417		437		436		440	

Note: * $p < 0.10$, ** $p < 0.05$; *** $p < 0.01$. Standard errors are in parentheses. Only demographic and significant variables are controlled for in each model. Regression of hours controls for sex, marital status, children, education, household size, and physical health. Regression of per capita income controls for age, sex, marital status, children, education, hours of labor, and household size. Regression of household durables controls for age, sex, marital status, children, education, employment status, and household size. Regression of physical health controls for age, sex, marital status, education, hours of labor, household size, water, and toilet. Regression of membership in associations controls for age, household size, education, civic duties, and political awareness. Number of observations is a combined total of the baseline and endline observations.

Table 6.3. Effects of the Housing Subsidy on Teenage Pregnancy, Proportion of School Dropouts, and Neighborhood Stability: Difference-in-Differences Estimation (Multivariate Logistic Regression)

	(1) Proportion of Teenage Pregnancies	(2) Proportion of School Dropouts	(3) Stability
Treatment Period	25.79***	0.53	4.01***
	(30.53)	(0.23)	(2.05)
RDP Homeowner	49.25***	1.51	2.05
	(65.85)	(0.94)	(1.16)
Treatment Period * RDP Homeowner	0.02***	0.77	1.42
	(0.03)	(0.55)	(1.75)
Pseudo R^2	0.19	0.08	0.18
Observations	116	273	409

Note: * $p < 0.10$, ** $p < 0.05$, *** $p < 0.01$. Standard errors in parentheses. Only demographic and theoretically important variables are controlled for. Regression of teenage pregnancies controls include age, marital status, education, and per capita income. Regression of school dropouts controls include age, sex, marital status, children, household size, per capita income, and mother's education. Controls for stability include age, sex, marital status, children, household size, education, per capita income, hours of labor, and memberships. Number of observations is a combined total of the baseline and endline observations.

2011; Tomlinson 2007, 53–65). These works found that low-income homeowners were reluctant to use RDP houses as collateral for credit and that banks cannot lend to the poor because the poor cannot sustain repayments. Further, Kingwill et al. (2006, 53–65) drew on several case studies to conclude that real property rights do not increase lending to the poor.

6.2.2. Labor Market Participation

The study's evidence does not support the view that freehold titling increases labor-market participation among the poor by freeing up tied labor. Rather, housing subsidy beneficiaries in Khayelitsha experienced no change in the number of hours they worked prior to and after housing subsidies. The statistical analysis presented in table 6.2 shows that the marginal effect implied by the estimated coefficient on the interaction term between RDP homeowner and treatment period is −0.84 hours. This coefficient corresponds to a reduction in number of hours of labor resulting from freehold title. However, the estimate is not statistically significant. By interpretation, there is no evidence that a government housing subsidy with the full bundle of real property rights increases labor-market participation.

Likewise, qualitative evidence is consistent with the statistical analysis. Beneficiaries who were employed often had part-time menial jobs. Others eked out livelihoods in business. Some sold illicit alcohol from their homes, while a few worked full time. There was no difference between freeholders and those living in shacks. Those who worked were employed as taxi (local commercial minibus/minivan) drivers, domestic workers, and casual workers in heavy industries or in the services sector, especially in supermarkets and restaurants. The unemployed were mainly youth who had completed high school or dropped out. The families of those who had completed high school could not afford to send them for tertiary education. Unemployed youth spent time chatting in groups while sitting in the sun along the streets. Those who were elderly were either living as pensioners or surviving on old-age grants. Mothers were surviving on child-support grants.

Based on the many in-depth one-on-one interviews, Bakhulu's and Zanele's stories are quite representative of experiences with employment after obtaining freehold ownership. A 62-year-old mother and grandmother, Bakhulu came to a serviced site, Site B, in around 1994. Before that, she lived in a shack covered with railway tents in Site C. She only remembers that she got the housing subsidy after 2000. Bakhulu describes her work life and mode of survival:

> It's only me who was working until I was 62 years old, but now I am not working. I only started to get my pension from two years ago when I turned sixty years old. People are not working especially in this area. If you look going down the street, people are not working; and if you move to the other streets, you will find people sitting in the sun. There are no jobs. If they are going to look for a job, they just leave their CVs [curriculum vitaes] and are promised to be called, but they will wait until the end of the year. These promises are from all over[,] we have been to submit our CVs in parliament, but it's almost three years now we have been waiting for the responses.

Bakhulu reports high unemployment and scarce employment opportunities. When one loses a job, one is lucky to qualify for a grant. She qualified for the older person's grant two years before she stopped working. Depending on one's circumstances, the South African government put a maximum ceiling of R1,600 (US$95) per month for the older person's grant, which Bakhulu calls an old-age pension because that was what it was formerly called. One qualifies for it at age 60, with income less than R44,880 ($3,200) per annum and ownership of assets worth less than R752, 400 ($53,000) if not married and less than R1,504, 800 ($106,000) for a married couple.

Many depend on social services while they are unemployed against their will; they wish to work. For example, Zanele lost her job and now survives on a child-support grant. Her eldest son lost his job and decided to leave Cape Town in frustration. As she notes:

> It's difficult since I lost my job, so now I'm surviving with the money for social services because my children are getting child grants. It's only Vuyolwethu who was working, but after he lost his job, he decided to go back to Eastern Cape to his uncle.

Both Zanele and her eldest son found it difficult to support themselves after losing their jobs. Their jobs were short term, unstable, and an unsteady source of income. A lack of stability can be a source of frustration. Zanele was fortunate to have children under 18 when she lost her job, as she later lived on child support grants from the government.

6.2.3. Income-Generating Activities

Freehold rights in Khayelitsha are an unnecessary and insufficient condition for the poor to engage in income-generating activities. Although some beneficiaries participate in income-generating activities, many do not due to challenges of accessing capital. Zoleka, Sefiso, and Nkhosi used to operate *shebeens*—illegal taverns that sell illicit alcohol. Zoleka switched to selling vegetables and meat, which she was doing at the time of the interview. Sefiso gave up on her business because the *shebeen* took away the dignity of her house, and she felt that it was not right for her as a devout Christian. Nkhosi, who had come to Site C in 1994 and now lives with her children in Kuyasa, used to run a *spaza* grocery store and *shebeen* while living in the shack. Once she moved into the RDP house, she did not have enough space to run the business. Another former business owner, Mamela obtained her house in 2001 and lived with her husband and children in Site B. She ran business selling potato chips from their new home, until they took a trip to the Eastern Cape. She did not resume the business on return.

Since there is no evidence that subsidy beneficiaries started doing business after they obtained their housing, real property rights matter less than financial capital for small-business activities. Those who did business in the new houses also ran them in their old shacks; those who did not run businesses in the new houses also did not run them in their shacks. None attributed starting business activities to moving into new housing or to having their title deeds. Zoleka even suggests that her business did better when she lived in the shacks of Site C than in Site B where her house was built. As she notes:

> I conducted many businesses. I was selling alcohol, and the business was going very smooth before the law became very strict about licences . . . it was going very well, but when this thing of licenses came, I stopped, as having a license you need to have a lot of money; but I was also selling vegetables and everything. I stopped selling alcohol completely; I'm now selling vegetables and meat . . . it's not going well because now a lot of people are selling in this area; but at first, I was the only one selling here. I was selling the same things [in the shacks] I'm selling now. I started there and my people followed me, and it was going very well before coming here. My business was going very well before I came here; that's why I say life in the shacks was much better than here. . . . People who do business were not as many by then, and now almost everybody is doing business. For instance, I think most of us in this street are selling [the same] thing, and that is not business. Now I am starting to sell clothes. I'm going to see how it goes . . . I just started.

It was a similar story in the shacks. For instance, Thabo moved to the SST section of Site C in 1993 and still lives there with his wife and three children. He is on the waiting list for a government housing subsidy. He runs a *shebeen* and does tailoring from his shack. Thabo reflects on his work history:

> Yes, I am running a business of selling alcohol. . . . I have got five years now. . . . I was working in Bellville in 1993, and I have not found any job since that time. . . . [Business] is doing well, but I need the money to make it stronger. . . . I have tried at First National Bank, but I failed because they want me to have security, so that they can give me the money. Unfortunately, I do not have even a cent in my account. I have one [other business] doing some sewing in the shack when I am not busy. . . . The problem that I am facing is that people don't pay when you have done something for them.

In general, it did not matter whether interviewees lived in brick houses or shacks for them to start a business when they had the capital. As seen in interviews with Zoleka and Thabo, those living in shacks and those living in subsidized houses run similar businesses. Interviewees had tried several businesses while living in shacks and RDP houses. Ownership rights were not the problem for establishing a business in these neighborhoods. A source of starting capital was the problem, as exemplified by Thabo's failure to get a loan at the First National Bank.

6.2.4. Investments in Housing

Housing improvements were associated with narratives of success among beneficiaries. Success was measured in terms of conspicuous consumption, particularly the extent to which beneficiaries extended or improved their homes. Houses with extensions or significant improvements were deemed "high status." An unintended consequence of the subsidy was that the "high status" of some individuals affected relationships by generating gossip and jealousy. Following long periods living in relative parity with neighbors, the slightest visible differences caused animosity, envy, jealousy, and gossip. The theme of jealousy, gossip, and envy is revisited in section 6.2.12.

The extension and use of a house and renting out a room to tenants as a source of income is a widely recognized way of generating income, which was legally available to subsidy beneficiaries. However, none of them rented out any of their rooms or houses—not even backyard shacks, which were instead occupied by older children or extended family, or in some cases strangers who needed a place to stay for a while. When asked whether they thought of getting tenants, interviewees answered that there were not enough rooms, that they were avoiding fights with tenants, that tenants can bring such things as witchcraft into their homes, and that they intended to let out rooms in the future.

6.2.5. Household Income

There was no evidence of increases in household income among subsidy beneficiaries. In table 6.2, the difference-in-differences estimate shows an increase of 10 percent in household per capita income attributed to the housing subsidy. However, this was not statistically significant, showing there was no real difference in household income between subsidy beneficiaries and households living in shacks. The evidence from the statistical analysis complements the qualitative findings presented thus far.

6.2.6. Wealth in the Form of Durable Goods

Data showed that a housing subsidy had no effect on the number of household durable goods. Table 6.2 shows that the estimated treatment effect is

−0.25, implying a reduction in the number of household items, but this effect is not statistically significant. For sure, there were households that bought more durable goods following their move into the new houses, but the rate was not discernibly different from that of those who lived in shacks.

Counter to the idea that increased investments were the process through which households accumulate durable goods, subsidy beneficiaries accumulated household goods because of the protection provided by the dwelling. Although some subsidy beneficiaries bought household durables when they were still living in shacks, many avoided doing so due to risks of fire, theft, wind, and rain. Second, interviewees felt that living in a brick house comes with the norm of furnishing one's house. One is compelled to furnish a brick house, whereas one need not furnish a shack due to its temporary nature and the risks associated with a shack. By contrast, beneficiaries felt social pressure to buy a lounge suite, curtains, television sets, and other electronic goods. Mpepeto expressed it this way:

> A brick house [is expensive] because you are supposed to decorate it by buying furniture and other things. The shack is not that expensive because there is nothing much needed. For example, now, look at this floor. It needs tiles and if you look at the shack, there is no need for tiles. If you put a carpet, it's fine.

In noting, "you are supposed to decorate," Mpepeto expressed a conviction that it is a social norm that one must furnish a brick house. This emphasis on furnishing resonates with what Meintjes (2000) found in her comparison of Soweto and Lusaka.

In sum, beneficiaries of the housing subsidy were able to increase the number of household durables in their houses, but not significantly more than those in shacks. Better protection and social norms compelled beneficiaries to purchase these goods. Our finding corroborates that of Mentjies (2000), who found that residents in Soweto Township in Johannesburg felt compelled to furnish their houses.

6.2.7. Physical Health

Housing subsidies improved the general physical health of beneficiaries, but this seems more to do with the improved housing conditions than with real property rights. In table 6.2, the marginal effect of a housing subsidy on self-reported physical health is positive and statistically significant. The difference-in-differences estimator ($\beta = 0.47$) represents the estimated improvement in health attributed to being a beneficiary of a government housing subsidy. This coefficient means that a government housing subsidy increases physical health by 0.5 on a scale of 0 to 4, with 0 being poor and 4 being excellent. In other words, there is a 10 percent increase in self-reported health following titling. The difference-in-differences estimators for physical health remained significant when demographic and other explanatory factors were controlled for.

Intuitively, we should expect that moving shack-dwellers to houses under the housing subsidy would improve self-reported health. The mechanism is that the improved housing with standard walls, floors, and roofs, and access to piped water and flushed toilets, translates to better health. Shacks in Khayelitsha and other townships are susceptible to fire, flooding, and dust, which are common sources of respiratory and waterborne diseases.

6.2.8. Psychological Well-Being

There was no indication that the housing subsidy affected psychological well-being in Khayelitsha. Psychological well-being was moderately high among subsidy beneficiaries, with reports on average that they experienced psychological stresses "some of the time" to "a little of the time." However, the evidence is not conclusive, because the existing data fail to satisfy essential assumptions. The analysis nevertheless may indicate a positive direction in the relationship, especially in Nairobi, where the result suggested that subsidy beneficiaries did have improved psychological well-being.

6.2.9. Education

Housing subsidies improve human capital by enabling better learning environments for children. Having title and a home reorients households away from solely meeting housing needs and toward investing more in human capital (Moser and Felton 2007). In Khayelitsha, households reported extraordinarily positive changes that came from living in a higher-quality housing environment.

First, children needed less preparation time in the morning. A change in housing quality and environment made preparing for school easier. In the shacks, mothers would go early to draw water for the children. Those living on serviced sites shared with three other families, which sometimes meant waiting. Living in a house with their own bathroom allowed for both faster preparation and cleaner and healthier children. As Mpho shared:

> A person can wash and be clean, but you are different when you are clean but living in a shack [laughter]. There are lots of things here, a child would put his cereal in a microwave, and everything is easy. You take his clothes and put them in a washing machine—how do you like that? They would have improved a lot. I wish I had a child who was studying living in a shack and who is here with me now, so I can compare his life. I sometimes look at my grandchildren and laugh, thinking the way they would be if they were living in a shack. They are beautiful and healthy now.

Second, they experienced increases in school attendance due to reduced safety concerns. Noluthando felt that her child was able to go to school more often because he felt safer in the neighborhood of brick houses than in the shacks. Shacks were in close proximity, and there were a lot of unsafe areas. Noluthando felt that a lack of safety contributed to her son's poor school performance.

Third, electricity allowed more time for homework and study. Interviewees also felt the brick houses were quieter, which created a better studying environment. As Mahala notes,

> It's hard in the shack because the time you are studying its cold and sometimes it's raining, and the drops of water fall into the books; and if it's cold, you can't concentrate. But in a house, it's not cold, and there is no water coming through; you are safe.

Shack dwellers used candles to provide light for study; thus, evening study time was limited to how long it took a candle to burn out. As Lindiwe reflects,

> It [school performance] has improved a lot because when we lived in a shack, there was not even electricity. If they want to study at night, we would light a candle; and if they want to study the whole night, I would shout at them saying we should save that candle for the next day. . . . Now my children can study for the whole night because we have electricity.

Fourth, students experienced improved performance in school because of improved sleeping conditions. In Noluthando's view, her children did better in school and slept because of the safety provided by their home. Her point of view is supported by science on the benefits of sleep. Not only were shacks unsafe, the noise from wind and rain impeded high-quality sleep.

Freehold ownership is not responsible for better educational outcomes. Nevertheless, it has been found elsewhere that titling leads to better school performance among children (Galiani and Schargrodsky 2004). Galiani and Schargrodsky (2004) attribute this to a reduction in the number of school days missed. Further research is needed to determine the role played by real property rights in education.

6.2.10. Membership in Formal Associations

Homeowner ideologists claim that freeholders participate in voluntary associations because of the stake they have in their homes and community. However, no effect of a housing subsidy on participation in voluntary associations was found in Khayelitsha. Table 6.2 shows that the estimated difference-in-differences coefficient is −0.30, representing a reduction in memberships, but this is not statistically significant. This means there is no difference between housing subsidy beneficiaries and nonbeneficiary shack-dwellers. Various reasons for this finding emerged among shack dwellers. Many interviewees said they lacked access to community organizations, except political organizations like the South African National Civics Organization (SANCO). SANCO seemed to be responsible for organizing street committees. It also organized informal arrangements such as savings groups where some neighbors put together money to cope with deprivation. SANCO also organized burial societies where residents contributed money for use by the bereaved.

In contrast to owner ideologist claims, beneficiaries do not seem to have enough of an economic or other stake in their neighborhood to act on it, for two possible reasons. First, they were constantly struggling to meet their basic needs, which drained much of their energy. Second, they did not participate in the process that brought about their housing and location. During the process of beneficiary selection, beneficiaries were not involved in the negotiations. They were represented by committees. Beneficiaries registered on the waiting list; when their house was ready, they were given a short induction and handed their keys. Even more, they did not expend much beyond the R2,479 (US$330) to obtain the houses (Tomlinson 2007). By contrast, Oldfield (2000, 2004) found in her study of the "door-kickers" of Delft, Cape Town, that the group of invaders of government-subsidized houses developed strong bonds after they occupied, fought for, and won their housing in the courts. Participation in the process of delivery is therefore an important condition for beneficiaries to have a stake in their houses and neighborhood.

6.2.11. Civic Participation

As table 6.4 shows, there is no relationship of association between freehold tenure and participation in civic duties. The coefficient ($\beta = -0.02$) is not significant in all models including in the final model, when only significant variables were included in the equation.

At a basic level, civic participation among subsidy beneficiaries was reflected in informal social control around community safety, if at all. In-depth interviews reveal that residents of subsidized housing used both informal and formal mechanisms of social control. When in shacks, they could only rely on informal mechanisms sanctioned by street committees—a system used to counter crime in African townships during apartheid. Street committees have persisted in many African townships, informal settlements, and new neighborhoods. Street committees were elected from households in

Table 6.4. OLS Regression of Civic Participation against Housing Subsidy

Independent Variables	Model 1	Model 2	Model 3	Model 4
Housing Subsidy	−0.03	−0.03	−0.01	−0.02
	(0.02)	(0.02)	(0.03)	(0.02)
Age		−0.02*	−0.02	
		(0.01)	(0.01)	
Married		0.081	0.08	0.09*
		(0.05)	(0.05)	(0.05)
Child		0.05*	0.05*	
		(0.03)	(0.03)	
Male		−0.02	−0.03	−0.04*
		(0.03)	(0.03)	(0.02)
Working		0.03	0.04	
		(0.02)	(0.03)	
Income			−0.01	
			(0.01)	
Education			−0.01	
			(0.01)	
Political Awareness			0.08***	0.07***
			(0.02)	(0.02)
Constant	0.28***	0.41***	0.35**	0.16***
	(0.02)	(0.09)	(0.15)	(0.04)
Adjusted R^2	0.00	0.04	0.08	0.07
Observations	220	214	191	202

Note: Standard errors in parentheses; * $p < 0.10$, ** $p < 0.05$, *** $p < 0.01$.

the area. Up to a hundred households could be covered by the street committee. The elected committee head was usually an elderly member called the street chairman. The committee dealt with day-to-day neighborhood affairs, such as complaints and disputes among neighbors, and issued appropriate sanctions for crimes. The street committee could sanction corporeal punishment and expel a household following multiple offenses. As Mpepeto recalls, "the police were going around the area every day, but they did not find these places that are selling drugs. After we found out as community members, we called a meeting. We took the decision that it's our kids, so let us beat them on the bums."

In addition to street committees, RDP neighborhoods worked with the police under the rubric of community policing. Often, the police were invited to street committee meetings and worked with residents in conducting neighborhood patrols. Within informal neighborhoods, the police did not work with street committees. This perhaps explains why residents felt safer in RDP neighborhoods.

The street committee system functioned effectively in dealing with crime in both RDP neighborhoods and shack neighborhoods, though some residents felt it had grown increasingly ineffective. Few people attended meetings, unless they involved crimes committed within the vicinity of their area. In addition, given the poor socioeconomic conditions, street committees are unable to address many of the problems, such as unemployment.

6.2.12. Community Cohesion

As table 6.5 shows, no association is found between a housing subsidy and community cohesion. In the bivariate model, being a homeowner is not associated with higher scores on the community cohesion scale ($\beta = 0.00$). The model fit is poor, with R^2 being less than 2 percent. The evidence therefore does not point to a stronger community resulting from freehold tenure.

Owner ideologists claim that freeholders have better neighborly relations because they expect to live longer together as neighbors and have a greater stake in their communities. To provide a bit more context, residents who became neighbors in these new neighborhoods were spread across sections when they lived in shacks; they were not neighbors. When they assigned houses, authorities mixed people from different backgrounds. Many met for the first time as neighbors. This process of housing allocation maimed established social networks and brought strangers together as neighbors. However, since most beneficiaries had previously migrated to Cape Town from

Table 6.5. Housing Subsidy and Community Cohesion: OLS Outcomes

Independent Variables	Model 1	Model 2	Model 3	Model 4
RDP Homeownership	0.01	−0.01	0.00	0.00
	(0.04)	(0.04)	(0.04)	(0.04)
Age		−0.00	−0.01	
		(0.02)	(0.02)	
Married		0.01	0.00	
		(0.08)	(0.08)	
Male		0.08*	0.08*	0.08**
		(0.04)	(0.04)	(0.04)
Child		−0.00	0.01	
		(0.04)	(0.04)	
Working		0.03	0.03	
		(0.04)	(0.04)	
Income		0.01	−0.00	
		(0.03)	(0.03)	
Education		0.01	0.00	
		(0.01)	(0.01)	
Move			0.06	0.06
			(0.05)	(0.04)
Constant	0.37***	0.29	0.34	0.32***
	(0.02)	(0.26)	(0.27)	(0.03)
Adjusted R^2	0.00	0.02	−0.02	0.02
Observations	207	187	188	201

Note: Standard errors in parentheses; * $p < 0.10$, ** $p < 0.05$, *** $p < 0.01$.

the Eastern Cape via village and ethnic social networks, randomly assigned neighbors felt disconnected. The difficulty of starting again imposed stresses on establishment of new relationships. Interviewees guarded themselves against intimate friendships to avoid jealousy and gossip, which were widespread in these neighborhoods. Many interviewees preferred to relate within kinship networks rather than with the strangers who had come to be neighbors. They felt that family members were less likely to share information or gossip with a third party. Particularly when they obtained financial support from kin, they reported more flexibility and concessionary repayment terms.

As scholars researching similar neighborhoods in South Africa have pointed out, intimate knowledge among neighbors is an important ideal of good neighborliness; however, close relations are undermined by gossip, secrecy, and jealousy (Ross 2021, 162–63). Jealousy, gossip, secrecy, and envy breed conflict and physical violence among members of interdependent households, as Ramphele (2002) recounted. Indeed Ross (2021, 162–63), Bray et al. (2010, 108), and Ashforth (1998) also discussed how jealousy undermines relationships in South African neighborhoods. Ashforth (1998, 507) noted that the new post-apartheid opportunities in Soweto generated inequalities among Africans who in previous generations had been compelled to live in conditions of relative socioeconomic parity. Emerging disparities in the post-apartheid township expanded the prospects for jealousy, envy, and gossip, though the privacy of home offered some assured level of protection.

6.2.13. Status Attainment, Decency, and Respectability

Having a house under freehold tenure is a symbol of status and respectability. Respectability, decency, and dignity are recurring themes in the urban ethnographic literature on new housing in South Africa (Ross 2005a, 2005b, 2021) and elsewhere. It manifests in different ways. A person who owns a house expects respectability in the mundane realities of everyday life. For Mpho, respectability may involve everyday pleasantries such as eating breakfast at her table in the comfort of her home. Although emanating from ownership of a house, respectability extends beyond the mere residential abode. At the everyday level of informal neighborly mixing elsewhere in Cape Town, respectability can mean greeting in the streets, visiting homes, intermarriage, and sharing common spaces.

6.2.14. Sense of Belonging

Resident experiences of belonging, place identity, and neighborhood are important attributes of neighborly relations. Such dimensions should be examined because neighborhoods are symbols of personal and social identity, and loci of sentiment, meaning, and home. In qualitative interviews, freeholders and shack-dwellers alike felt that their neighborhoods were not their homes, for varied reasons. Almost all interviewees traveled back to the Eastern Cape yearly. Indeed, within the households of our interviewees, some elderly members had returned to the Eastern Cape, leaving their adult children the houses. Some pensioners spoke of plans to be buried at "home" in Eastern Cape, and others expressed that they were in Cape Town for work, with intentions to go back later.

A freeholder named Zuma noted that Cape Town is only good for work, while the Eastern Cape is good for social relationships. Zuma moved to Cape Town from the Eastern Cape in 2000 to join his mother and look for work.

Mr. Stevens, also a homeowner, agreed with Zuma, noting that he was satisfied living in Makhaza when working, but not after he lost his job. Another freeholder, Simphakazi, noted that she was forced to live in Cape Town for health reasons and would be in the Eastern Cape if it not for that. She went to the Eastern Cape every year to compensate for her absence. Mpepeto said he was planning to move because there was nothing beautiful in his neighborhood, only jealousy.

The few others who were satisfied with their neighborhood reported pride in their RDP houses; they were happy housing beneficiaries. As Mahala put it, "I saw myself as a special person because there are people who have been applying for houses for a long time but even now, they are still living in the shacks."

When beneficiaries moved, they did not sell or abandon them, but left them to their children, who constructed their social identities in the city and neighborhood. Passing the property on to children reflects intergenerational transfer of both the home and the culture around homeownership.

The sentiments of shack-dwellers were similar albeit with stronger emotion. Shack-dwellers felt that they did not intend to stay when they moved to Cape Town. They planned to raise enough money to build their house in Eastern Cape and then return someday.

In sum, the sense of belonging, identity, and home for many interviewees in both RDP and shack neighborhoods was still in Eastern Cape. Interviewees did not have much stake in their houses and neighborhoods, as they viewed them as temporary spaces. Lemanski (2011, 62) reported that only 18 percent of houses were sold by their original beneficiaries in Westlake village. The Western Cape Occupancy Study (Vorster and Tolken 2008, 13) estimated that about 28 percent of people living in subsidized housing were not the original beneficiaries.

6.3. CONCLUSIONS

Freeholders in Khayelitsha rarely utilize property rights as a capital resource. Even if they did, they expected that it would produce no economic benefit. The observed impact on subsidy beneficiaries can be attributed to the change in housing quality and the housing environment, rather than to the difference between real property rights and squatting with temporary protection.

Nevertheless, real property rights do empower the urban poor with ownership of a dwelling, which increases their status. In short, whether or not one has freehold title makes no difference in subsequent experiences in this context—except in terms of social status. Property rights to land and housing in the hands of the poor in Khayelitsha produce idle capital, but the poor face structural constraints that disincentivize use of their capital. Even so, they enjoy the respectability and higher status that accompany ownership rights. Even though they prefer their rural homes and hope to return there, they pass on to their children their houses and a culture of homeownership.

CHAPTER 7

The Homeowner Ideology and Privatization of Council Housing in Lusaka

A beneficiary of the privatization of public rental housing in Matero, Mary sought a loan to buy a second home for investment purposes. Mary felt that income from the investment property would assure that she would not lose her primary house. Although she was not able to obtain a loan, and her businesses have failed, she is still happy she owns a home.

Using the case of privatization of low-cost low-income housing in Matero, Lusaka, this chapter examines claims that real property rights improve property values, credit access, employment, household income, and participation in income-generating activities among the poor. Matero housing is contrasted with self-built housing in George—a neighborhood that was part of the World Bank–funded Lusaka slum upgrading program. The present chapter compares outcomes between households with leasehold ownership rights in Matero and occupancy or usufruct rights in George. The chapter shows that Matero residents living under leasehold rights are associated with significantly higher property values and less participation in income-generating activities. Yet these property values are still not high enough to allow access to credit. No significant differences in tenure security were found. In fact, those with stronger rights reported greater fears of property loss in the face of property taxes and bills. The Matero case further demonstrates that freehold rights are bundles of rights to idle capital, and a focus on freehold ownership obscures evidence of the utility of usufruct rights.

7.1. MEASURING THE EFFECTS OF LEASEHOLD TENURE IN MATERO, LUSAKA

Variation in tenure rights between Matero and George presented a research opportunity to understand the effects of ownership rights compared to usufruct rights. Indeed, exploring the evolution of housing provision in Matero and George may advance understanding of the consequences of providing real property rights through titling relative to the administrative recognition of occupancy. In assessing claims about ownership in Lusaka, a mixed-methods approach was employed. Methods include using quantitative data from a household survey, regression analysis, and propensity score matching techniques, as well as qualitative data from in-depth semi-structured interviews.

7.1.1. Household Survey

Comprised of seven data collectors and a principal investigator, the research team conducted a survey and qualitative interviews as part of the study, as no existing datasets were readily available in both neighborhoods. The survey was conducted from July to August of 2011–15 years after the privatization of houses in Matero. A structured questionnaire was used for data collection. Data collectors received training over the course of a week, and a pilot study was implemented. During the pilot study, each data collector conducted one interview as part of training. The final questionnaire was reviewed and revised using the results of the pilot study. The survey interviewed heads of households or their competent adult proxies. In Matero, the ideal respondent was the household head who was a direct beneficiary of the privatization of housing, and who held a title deed or deed of sale.

7.1.2. Sampling

For Matero alone, the targeted sample was 350 out of 5,097 existing households (Government of the Republic of Zambia 1996a). In George, another 350 holders of occupancy licenses were targeted, out of approximately 20,000 households. Czaja et al.'s (2014, 126–33) formula for calculating sample size was employed to arrive at the number of households to interview. Google Earth maps of the neighborhoods were used to create a sampling frame. From the sampling frame, households to interview were selected using the method of interval sampling with a random start. In the George compound, the initial plan was to draw a matched sample using a database from the Zambian census of population as a sampling frame. While it was available at the Central Statistical Office, the database was not publicly available, and our study was not given permission to access this database. Thus, the study proceeded with selection of an unmatched sample of 350 households from George, with the intention of including analysis that would mathematically match respondents using propensity score matching techniques.

The total realized sample size came to 623 households (89 percent response rate). In Matero, 312 interviews were completed, and 311 were completed in George. However, the council offered 50 survey participants opportunities to purchase houses after the original owners had failed to complete payment. Those respondents were excluded from the analysis. In George, 75 participants obtained their occupancy titles and entered housing after 1997. They were also excluded, because they arrived after treatment had occurred. The final dataset comprised 498 individuals, with 262 participants from Matero and 236 from George. The sample remained representative, but with less precision (wider confidence intervals) than the original calculated sample size. With this sample size, significance for computations assuming normality is at less than 0.07. Variable descriptions are presented in table 7.1.

Table 7.1 is largely self-explanatory, but it is important to highlight the property value variable. Typically, studies use housing prices for untitled and titled households, and use the difference as a measure of this effect. This effect is also considered a tenure security premium (Durand-Lasserve and Selod 2009, 118). Respondents were asked to provide their property value based on the most recent government valuation. A separate question asked those who had not yet valued their houses to estimate based on neighborhood comparisons. This question was assumed to arrive at an estimate reflecting the government value, as houses were uniform with similar plot sizes. Valuations had taken place between 1997 and 2011 as part of the purchase. Property values based on government valuation were provided by 149 (57%) respondents from Matero. Government valuations were used, rather than the going market rate, because they are the most recent official and objective estimates of property value in Matero. Thus, limiting self-reported values was a way to limit the influence of social desirability bias (overreporting value) and recall bias (inaccuracy of memory). Nevertheless, property prices rose considerably in Lusaka since 1997. This suggests that the difference between Matero and George among the 43 percent who used market rate may be more significant. Government valuations are not available for George because the land belongs to the government and cannot be sold. Participants from George were asked

Table 7.1. Variable Descriptions

Variable	Description
Independent and Control Variables	
Leasehold Title	Tenure type, 1 = leasehold title, 0 = occupancy license
Age	Age of household head
Gender	Gender of household head. 1 = male, 0 = female
Education	Number of years of education completed by head of household
Employed Members of Household	Are there other members of this household who have full-time paid jobs? 1 = yes, 0 = no
Occupational Skill Level	International Standard Classification of Occupations (ILO, 2012) skill level 1 (simple, routine, physical and manual jobs) = 0; skill level 2 (operating machinery and electronic equipment) = 1; skill level 3 (complex technical and practical tasks) = 2; and skill level 4 (complex problem-solving, decision-making, and creativity based on established theoretical and empirical knowledge) = 3
Father's Education	Number of years of education of father of head of household
Household Size	Number of household members residing in the dwelling
Rooms	Number of rooms in the dwelling
Duration	Number of years respondent has lived in the house
Dependent Variables	
Square Root of Property Value	Two questions. 1. What is the market value of the dwelling (in Zambian Kwacha) according to the last valuation? 2. Please provide an estimate if your house has not been valuated.
Credit Access	Have you used this house in any way (e.g., as collateral) to obtain loans or credit? 1 = yes, 0 = no
Employment Status	Employment status of head of household, 1 = employed, 0 = not employed
Income-Generating Activities	Has the house been used for any income-generating activities? 1 = yes, 0 = no
Logged Per Capita Income	What is the total monthly income for this household?

to provide a value for their house using the going rate of houses on the active informal housing market in the neighborhood (several handwritten posts of "House for Sale" were posted in George). Participants were aware of these prices, as many had neighbors or knew of people who sold their houses.

7.1.3. Analytical Strategy

Ordinary least squares and logistic regression analyses were employed to estimate the effects of leasehold tenure rights on property value, credit access, employment, income-generating activities, and household income. The equation to make the regression estimates was as follows:

$$Y_i = \alpha + \gamma \text{Leasehold rights}_i + \beta X_i + \varepsilon_i$$

Y_i is any of the above-mentioned outcome measures for observation *i*. γ is the coefficient that indicates the size of effect of the "leasehold rights" measure. In the equation, "leasehold rights" is a dummy variable that equals 1 for individuals with leasehold rights and 0 for those with occupancy rights. X is any of the covariates controlled for, mainly but not limited to background characteristics, including age, gender, number of years of education, father's number of years of education, mother's number of years of education, and marital status. Finally, ε_i is the error term that represents the amount of variation in the outcome variables that is unexplained by the regression model.

PROPENSITY SCORE ANALYSIS

Like our work in Kibera, this study was observational, which presents the similar problem of failing to eliminate selection bias. Participants from Matero differed from participants in George for reasons other than their tenure status, which could determine differences in outcomes. This called for employment of propensity score matching, described in chapter 5. Thus, the following is only an explanation of how the methods were applied to the Matero case.

ESTIMATING THE PROPENSITY SCORES

An initial propensity score model was estimated using 107 variables. A probit regression model was employed to estimate the propensity scores. The treatment status was holding of leasehold rights (treatment) vs. holding of occupancy rights (control). The treatment status variable was regressed on baseline characteristics. The baseline characteristics variables are plausible predictors of property value, credit access, and employment, participation in income-generating activities, and household income in households with stronger tenure rights. These variables were included in the propensity score model because of the need to ensure balance on variables that are predictive of these outcomes. Additionally, demographic and other attitudinal variables were included in the model to ensure that observed characteristics were included as necessary.

MATCHING ON PROPENSITY SCORES

Treated and untreated participants were matched based on similar propensity scores. More participants (262) received leasehold title than occupancy title—that is, there were more treated than untreated participants. Inferences are therefore made only in the region of common support—the space where the distributions of the propensity scores of the two groups overlap. The objective was to match a treated participant to each participant who did not receive leasehold rights. As in the Nairobi case, participants were matched on the propensity score using nearest neighbor, radius with calipers of width equal to 0.1, kernel, and stratification matching.

STRATIFICATION AND BALANCE ON PROPENSITY SCORES

Balancing the data ensures that there are no confounding effects across distributions of propensity scores (Guo and Fraser 2015). Quintiles of the estimated propensity scores were computed. The region of common support ranged from 0.08 to 1. Participants in the overall study sample were stratified into five approximately equal-size groups using the quintiles of the estimated propensity score. The distribution of scores across groups is as shown in figure 7.1, and the results of the tests of equality of means in propensity scores within each quintile block—shown in table 7.2—are not significant, showing that the means are equal.

ESTIMATING TREATMENT EFFECTS

As noted earlier, the book examines the effect of a stronger bundle of rights on property value, credit access, employment, participation in income-generating activities, and household per capita income, by comparing leasehold rights in Matero and occupancy licenses in George. The average treatment effect for the treated (ATT), that is, the average response to treatment for individuals who were assigned treatment—leasehold rights—was estimated for matched samples derived using nearest neighbor, radius, kernel,

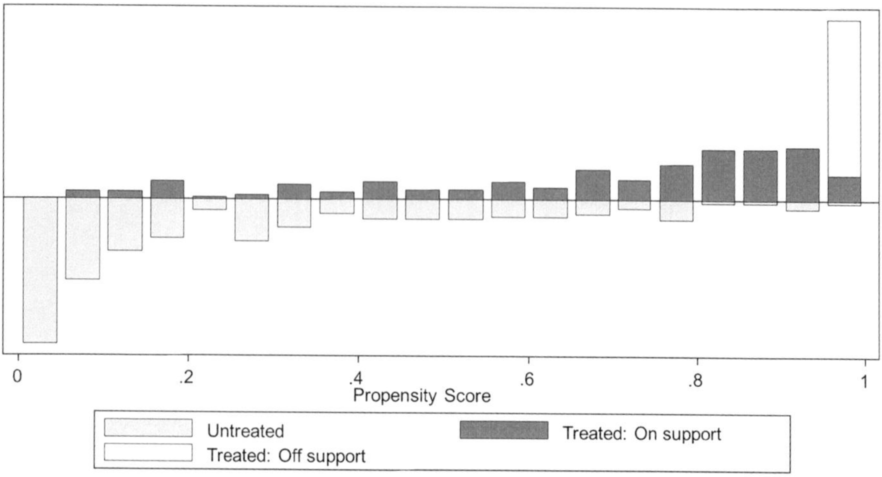

Fig. 7.1. Balance of Propensity Scores across Treated (Leasehold Tenure Rights) and Untreated (Occupancy Tenure Rights) Groups

Table 7.2. *t*-tests of Equality of the Means of Propensity Scores between Treated and Untreated Groups in Each Block

Block of Propensity Score and Minimum	Untreated (n = 129)	Treated (n = 227)	t
Block 1–0.08	0.14	0.14	−0.57
Block 2–0.2	0.29	0.31	−1.37
Block 3–0.4	0.50	0.50	−0.24
Block 4–0.6	0.70	0.71	−0.94
Block 5–0.8	0.90	0.94	−1.27

and stratification-matching techniques. The models do not control for unobservable or unknown factors that may be driving observed variation in the outcomes. The assumption of the propensity score models in using observed characteristics is that there are no unobserved factors correlated with the outcome.

7.1.4. Qualitative Data: In-depth Semi-Structured Interviews

In a similar approach to the Kibera case in chapter 5 and the Khayelitsha case in chapter 6, in-depth semi-structured interviews complement the findings of the quantitative analysis. Such interviews were conducted with 35 households—25 in Matero and 10 in George. Interviewees were selected from the survey sample pool. A purposive sampling technique based on geographical clustering was used to select interviewees. Google Earth images of the terrain guided the identification and selection of clusters and households. Matero and George were the two large clusters. Matero was then divided into subclusters made up of households. The objective was for the Matero sample to be as geographically representative as possible. The boundaries of the clusters were defined by road networks. Households were then selected to represent concentrations of households within the cluster. One to three households were sampled from each cluster, depending on cluster size and density. George interviews were conducted for control purposes. Geographical spread and long-term residency were the main factors in purposively selecting George households.

An interview schedule was developed to guide data collection. The interview schedule was loosely structured to allow interviewees to be as expressive as possible. The topics on the guide included questions about individuals and the dwelling, economic benefits, social benefits, and benefits under human capital. The idea behind structuring the questions this way was to avoid biasing the interviewee. This ensured that interviewees provided what *they* thought was the benefit rather than being asked whether a specific preconceived factor, such as credit access for example, was a benefit. However, interviewees were probed to give more details. For example, we asked, "What businesses do you conduct from this house?" and "Have you ever got a loan for business or for other purposes?"

To facilitate analysis, each interview was recorded, with the permission of the interviewee. Audio recordings of the interviews were stored on a computer with password encryption. Each interview was transcribed and analyzed. Eleven interviews were conducted in English, seven in Bemba, and seventeen in Chinyanja. The interviews conducted in Bemba and Chinyanja were translated into English. A thematic analysis method was employed following transcription of all the interviews.

7.2. (F)UTILITY OF LEASEHOLD IN MATERO

The estimated treatment effects of leasehold tenure on property value, credit access, employment status, participation in income-generating activities, and household income using propensity score matching reveal that leasehold rights are associated with higher property values and less participation in income-generating activities; they have no effect on the rest of the examined outcomes. Computations using propensity score matching methods revealed that property values in Matero are K64 million (US$12,300), and K36 million (US$6,900) in George—a 44 percent difference. When household heads are matched, property values are higher in Matero by about K3 million ($650) to K8 million ($905) on average, and there are about 22 percent fewer households engaged in income-generating activities than in George.

As table 7.3 shows, matching using nearest neighbor techniques yields an ATT of 1,962.31 in property values. This means that participants from Matero report an average of K3.85 million (US$740) more in property values than those in George. The radius-matching technique yields an ATT of 2,169.67, which translates to K4.7 million (US$905). The kernel matching method yields an effect similar to that of the nearest neighbor matching technique. Using stratification matching, we see an ATT of 1,836.59, which translates to K3.37 million (US$650). Each of these is statistically significant at the 1 percent level. Although the estimated treatment effects on property values from propensity score matching are lower than those from regression analysis, they nevertheless support the hypothesis that households with stronger rights have houses with higher property values. The difference is 44 percent. Privatization of public rental housing and titling opened participant houses in Matero to the private market and raised property values.

Tenure rights have been found to substantially increase property values. Findings from Matero and George suggest a 44 percent increase. The percentage difference could be significantly higher today, given that the study has used property valuations for the 2009–2011 period. Moreover, land and housing prices have rapidly appreciated in recent years in Zambia, and in Lusaka in particular. Scholarly studies that capture property values in African cities are scarce, which makes it a challenge to place the findings in a broader context.

In addition to leasehold rights, the differences in property values between George and Matero can be explained by their different histories and status within the city. Matero was purposely built by the colonial government in the 1950s to house government employees and private-sector employees (Schlyter 2004, 1). Matero maintained its status as a formal area, while George began as an informal area earmarked for demolition and was later formalized.

Table 7.3 shows that leasehold rights are significantly associated with less participation in income-generating activities. Stronger property rights have

Table 7.3. Average Treatment Effect on the Treated (ATT) Using Nearest Neighbor, Radius, Kernel, and Stratification Matching

	Matching Method			
Outcome Variable	Nearest Neighbor	Radius	Kernel	Stratification
Property Value	1,962.31***	2,169.67***	1,961.51***	1,836.59***
	(944.63)	(575.27)	(861.01)	(901.99)
Credit Access	0.02	0.01	0.02	0.02
	(0.01)	(0.02)	(0.01)	(0.01)
Employment Status	0.03	0.08	0.08	0.08
	(0.15)	(0.10)	(0.15)	(0.15)
Income-Generating Activities	−0.23***	−0.15**	−0.24***	−0.27***
	(0.06)	(0.09)	(0.04)	(0.04)
Log of Household Income	0.20	0.15	0.15	0.17
	(0.15)	(0.20)	(0.16)	(0.17)

Note: Standard errors in parentheses; *** $p < 0.01$, ** $p < 0.05$, * $p < 0.1$; models control for all demographic and behavioral characteristics listed in table 7.1.

an ATT of −0.23 using nearest neighbor, −0.15 using radius, −0.24 using kernel, and −0.27 using stratification matching techniques. These are statistically significant at the 1 percent level, indicating that households with stronger tenure rights engage in significantly fewer income-generating activities by 15 to 27 percent.

Qualitative evidence also shows no difference between Matero and George interviewees. Indeed, income-generating activities were of different types but mostly had to do with renting out, turning an entire house or part of the house into a shop, selling groceries on a stand in the yard, or using the premises to prepare products that would be taken to the market to be sold. For example, Banda was aged 18 when his mother died, the year before I interviewed him. As the eldest child and without a father, he was forced to become the breadwinner for six siblings and an aunt. He turned part of the house into a *shebeen*.

In George, even though they enjoyed only usufruct rights, renting out an extra room was the main business. However, the income realized from rent was generally lower than from rentals in Matero. Rentals in George generated about K100,000 ($50) per month less for a room than in Matero. One interviewee used to sell scrap metal from her premises in the past. Others sell groceries and vegetables.

The quantitative analysis also showed that stronger property rights were not associated with significantly more durable goods, and qualitative interviews corroborate this finding. Interviewees in Matero expressed that owning a house provides an incentive to accumulate large, high-quality durable items. When interviewees lived in the smaller council houses, they bought household durables, but their purchases were not as large and not of very high quality. The lack of room and threat of eviction discouraged purchases of large durable assets.

In George, on the other hand, even though the statistical analysis showed no difference, the theme did not emerge as a benefit in any of the interviews. Perhaps it can be attributed to a lack of space for residents to extend their houses, except in the George extension area. Because the houses remain small, there is not much room to put large and expensive assets. The further restriction comes from the fact that the household sizes are large; hence, accumulation of assets does not serve already crowded houses. In her comparison of Lusaka and Cape Town, Meintjes (2000) found similar results.

The findings underscore the fact that tenure security matters more for a household's participation in income-generating activities than stronger tenure rights per se. The literature has shown that weak tenure rights can be sufficient to provide tenure security and support an increase in informal income-generating activities. Research from other parts of Africa supports the view that households in informal settlements engage in income-generating activities in the informal sector, even though regulations do not permit such activities (Prassana 2007). Prassana (2007), who studied the effects of tenure security on income-generating activities in informal settlements in Dar es Salaam, concluded that upgrading land tenure rights alone cannot address the needs of the urban poor; it must be accompanied by providing basic infrastructure facilities that support livelihood activities. Also, in the barrios of Quito, Ecuador, Riano (2001, 3) found that the main use of land in informal settlements is not only as sites to build shelter, but also as centers of economic production such as brick-making, agriculture, and housing production.

7.2.1. "Are These Our Houses? They Just Lied to Us": Tenure Security

Although privatized houses were associated with higher property values in Matero, beneficiaries found themselves at risk of losing their property. Getting a title deed meant higher property values and tenure security in the short run, but it did not mean long-term tenure security. Beneficiaries feared losing their houses due to failure to pay the newly introduced land rates. Immediately following privatization, residents did not have to pay rates. Perhaps the council was waiting for the valuation of property and registration of title to be completed. Respondents were frustrated that the council did not introduce land rates, because it nullified some benefits of homeownership. Instead of paying council rent, they now had to worry about paying land rates. The penalty for lack of payment of land rates was eviction via court bailiffs. The council would sell the beneficiary's property to recover both arrears and costs incurred in the process of recovery. Chongo encapsulates the lament of beneficiaries:

> [The City Council] reminded us of the way it was a long time ago . . . with these land rates, the council comes with court bailiffs to come and remove property from our house. It is not a good system. Because when you give someone something, you cannot come back again in another way saying no you will be doing this. Am I going to be proud that this is my house, while another is waiting for me to take money for a license to live in the house? No! It should have remained there, "we have given you the houses." . . . Already many are saying "Are these our houses? They just lied to us." That's what people are saying now because they have been taken aback. They are being reminded of a long time ago of paying rent for the houses.

For some respondents, this evoked memories of past evictions in Matero and the accompanying fear felt by residents. With the unpredictable flow of income that many of the households are undergoing, this fear was resurrected and comes with a feeling of insecurity.

Similarly, interviewees in George noted that they enjoy a similar benefit with their houses. Only in 2011 did they feel insecure, when they were told they could not renew their occupancy licenses if their ground rent arrears were not settled. For a long time, interviewees felt the houses were theirs and that no one could take them away from them or their descendants. In the 1980s, some boycotted the service fee. The boycott was to protest that the council was not providing services, even when residents paid their service fees. However, interviewees became worried about the evictions from private land that they were hearing about in several informal settlements. They were also worried about the elections at the end of 2011. They wondered whether the new government would allow them to stay. Mabo and her daughters and grandchildren expressed eviction worries. Mabo's daughter notes, "they send us papers saying they want the money for land." She paraphrases their sentiment as, "If you don't pay, we will come and remove you from our land." Mabo's granddaughter elaborates on the challenges of back payment and notes the council's understanding:

> [T]hey say that, if the arrears are too high, then they tell you that if you don't pay until a certain maximum value, they send the bailiffs. So, they will come and evict you from the house. So, if they evict you, then you have to find where to go. So that is what happens. They remove all the property from the house and leave it outside just like that, and they lock the house. . . . At this time, it is not too common because the council understands. . . . It's not too common that they come and evict.

Even though they possess an occupancy title, they fear they may be evicted for violating the terms. If they lost the protection from their occupancy license, residents provide another basis for which they should not be evicted: Christianity. Essentially, they argue that the land belongs to God. Since we are all God's children, we deserve it. Interviewees express faith that the council will provide alternative ways of sorting out the problem. Even after administrative recognition of occupancy, the possibility of eviction lingers.

Real property rights may reduce tenure security in the case where the poorest households may not have the means to pay the costs associated with formalization. In Senegal, some households guard against such types of insecurity by beginning the process of formalization in order to be tenure secure, but then suspending it indefinitely to avoid the costs (Payne, Durand-Lasserve, and Rakodi 2009, 407). Titling and the ensuing increase in property value can lead to reduced tenure security, as market-driven displacements are common following titling (Durand-Lasserve and Selod 2009, 107). Indeed, following the transfer of housing, Matero experienced rapid gentrification, with higher-income families buying up properties and extending them for their families (Schlyter 2002, 2004, 12). Petty landlords bought up properties to turn them into extended rental units, and sitting "tenants moved out and sold or let their houses to prosperous families" (Schlyter 2004, 12).

7.2.2. Access to Credit

Despite appreciation in property values, 98 percent of respondents had not used their house as collateral to access credit. They wanted to get loans, but they found that none of the banks would accept their homes as collateral. Others feared they would lose the house if they failed to repay. Informal loans were a popular alternative, but some interviewees were defrauded in the process. Interviewees in George were aware that their occupancy licenses were not acceptable in banks for getting loans.

The property title was neither a necessary nor a sufficient condition for getting a loan from banks in Lusaka; on the other hand, employment was a necessary condition.

7.2.3. "Most People Are Not Working": Employment Status

I found no evidence supporting a relationship between labor market participation and differences in bundles of rights. Unemployment was high in both neighborhoods, such that respondents depended on the informal sector, meager retirement benefits, and remittances from adult children for their livelihoods. The International Labor Organization (2018) reports that 91 percent of the working-age population works in Zambia's informal sector, which includes agriculture. Hence, it is no surprise that most people in both poor neighborhoods work in the informal sector. The few who were fortunate enough to be formally employed held clerical and menial jobs (general workers) either in the government or erstwhile state-owned enterprises that were privatized during the 1990s.

A few secured jobs that were technical in nature. Phiri positions himself as an outlier, noting that most people "were general workers, mostly civil service." He notes, "I stood out in the crowd. I used to work for the University of Zambia then, School of Medicine, yeah, I was in the lab." Phiri represents a unique and fortunate case, having worked for a reputable institution that honored his pension, while many others were not as fortunate. Many interviewees who retired have exhausted their pension benefits. Those who were retrenched during the economic reforms of the '90s have exhausted their severance packages, which were inadequate.

The adult children of the heads of household are mainly involved in informal activities, such as piecework, while others have formal full-time jobs, mainly in companies established by foreign investors from China, Korea, and the Middle East. Foreign investors are known to pay very low wages for long hours of manual labor. Chomba offers insight into the kind of work available to those in formal employment:

> The investors who come now are the Chinese who just open a shop and then gives you a K200,000 [$10] at the month-end. Now, where will the K200,000 take you? Because you will just buy a bag of mealie meal and a container of

> cooking oil, and that money will be finished. So that's the problem. Though, now at least the investors are opening some companies.

The employment conditions in George are similar to those in Matero. With limited formal employment opportunities, respondents depend on scarce blue-collar jobs from foreign investors, and informal business and piecework. Again, it is worth revisiting Gilbert's (2004) question of whether the provision of title is realistic given the high unemployment, widespread poverty, and high income inequality. Leasehold ownership is unlikely to lead to increased employment if the economy in general cannot support a larger labor force.

7.2.4. "We Extended and Put Someone for Rent, and It Brings in Some Money": Housing Improvements and Investments

Housing improvement after titling was one of the most cited benefits in Matero. Interviewees had won the right to build extensions and additional units on their land. They also pointed out their option to sell, if they wanted to make money. However, extensions were primarily made to accommodate large families, rather than to gain income from tenants. Original homes came with a bedroom, sitting room, kitchen, and bathroom with an outdoor toilet. Household sizes were approximately eight people, which meant four people per room. The houses were overcrowded. Figures 7.2 and 7.3 show one original house and two extended houses.

In his interview, Chongo describes family comfort as his reason for extending the house, noting, "We were in a two-roomed house with the number of children over ten. How can they sleep? So, I extended for children to sleep well." The primary objective for extensions for Chongo and others was to create room for their families. Although it did not increase income, it did generate higher property values as shown in the statistical analysis.

Data show that once Matero beneficiaries obtained their houses, they invested in them. George residents did the same when they had space, even though they did not have the legal right to do so. George residents were permitted to use only the land on which their house was built. However, many residents extended their houses and built new structures without consent of the council. Bwalya was working on extending his house during our interview. His plan was to add a rental house. The unit would support additional tenants, as he had already extended for renters. When I asked about requesting approval from the council, Bwalya notes:

Fig. 7.2. Original House in Matero

Fig. 7.3. Extended House in Matero

> Normally we don't, normally people here don't get approval from the council . . . [residents] do the planning on their own; they will do everything on their own, so it means there is no need for someone to approach the council and seek their approval before anything can be done.

Council enforcement is weak, and Bwalya reports open disregard for council regulation among his neighbors. Almost no interviewees from George had had any direct communication with the council since obtaining their occupancy titles some 30 years ago. At the time of data collection, the 30-year occupancy licenses were up for renewal. Many residents were surprised to learn that they had unpaid bills in ground rent. For some, the ground rent had accumulated to unsustainable levels, contributing to growing eviction fears.

Figure 7.4 shows a newly extended house along Commonwealth Road in George. It shows how people with usufruct rights have been able to invest in their property. Commonwealth Road extends west from Matero, forming the northern boundary with George. Thus, despite the regulations, there is no difference in housing improvement between Matero and George interviewees, as they all extended their houses.

7.2.5. "It Has Given Me Pride that I Own Property": Status Attainment and Satisfaction with Life

Interviewees in Matero, but not in George, reported pride in ownership. Interviewees also felt that they had property over which they could exercise control. Much like Mpho's experience as a respected "madam," owning a house conferred status and social esteem. For example, Chongo was not able to use his house for any income-generating activity. Despite extending his house with financial assistance from his children, all rooms were occupied by his 14 children. Instead, he points to his ownership as a source of pride:

> It has given me the pride that I own a property. That is how it has helped me. I have property, even when I look at it this is money. If I want, I can sell and go somewhere.

By noting "if I want, I can sell," Chongo is expressing his agency to exercise control and power over a valuable possession. Such power yields personal pride, dignity, esteem, and satisfaction. Poverty is characterized by lack of ownership and control, and owning an asset over which one has control can be dignifying.

Fig. 7.4. Extended Houses in George with Regular Houses in the Background

7.2.6. "As You Know, We Are Africans": Neighborly Attachment and Social Capital

No evidence indicated that leasehold rights led to diminished neighborly attachment. Qualitatively, neighborly relations in both Matero and George are considered healthy by interviewees. When asked how relationships with their neighbors were, all interviewees responded that they were positive, using various adjectives and phrases, such as "we live well," "we get along well," and relations are "cordial." According to interviewees in Matero, there were three main sources for this situation. The first source of cordial relationships was referred to as the "African setup." Interviewees referred to being African as the embodiment of expectations and knowledge about each other in an urban situation, with relationships modelled on those that exist in rural areas. Problems are not considered purely personal; rather, neighbors help and support one another in solving them. This was well explained by Mambwe, who referred to being African as a source of cordial relationships. As he notes, the "relationship with the neighbors is very good, as you know we are Africans. We all live one, yeah, like in the community; we live more like in a village."

Among interviewees, it was a given that Africanism embodies values, beliefs, and interpersonal bonds that transcend familial boundaries. Hyden (2013) refers to this theme as the economy of affection (72–93).

Second, there were no fences between houses on most streets. This allowed neighbors to interact more frequently and walk to each other's houses at any time of day. As Sibeso explained, the lack of fences facilitated mutual assistance. Sibeso contrasts this situation with that in Lusaka's most affluent neighborhood, where most expatriates and government elites live behind very high walls or fences.

Several interviewees also cited Christianity as an important source of cordial relations. Interviewees often assumed that all neighbors were devout Christians, and therefore expected them to adhere to Christian values in neighborly relations. Principles for neighborly relations were often cited in the interviews, such as those noted by Kalyata:

> We live well because for us people, respect is about yourself. . . . So, at all times, the Lord Jesus said you should humble yourselves, don't be proud, no? Even if you have strength or you have gone to school or have not gone to school, be humble. If you humble yourself, you will have peace. No, we live very well with neighbors. The neighbors love us.

In the Zambian context, Christianity was institutionalized on December 29, 1991, when Zambia was formally declared a Christian nation by President Chiluba. This declaration was included in the preamble of Zambia's 1996 constitution. Thus, Christianity serves as a source of principles for both government and social relations in the nation.

Some interviewees were unsympathetic to the mainstream values, particularly values thought to embody Africanism. Despite acknowledging that relationships are cordial, Chando, who lived in a semi-detached house, felt his privacy was being violated by the very values of Africanism other interviewees regarded as a source of accord. As Chando reports:

> The biggest problem I have found with our friends our neighbors here, they don't want to mind what is happening in their own houses. They want to know what is going on in their neighbors' houses. That's one. Then two, what I have found as a problem, like these houses that are not independent, like this one, coz these are semi-detached, they give us problems instead of hygiene. . . . Here you might be clean, but those on the other side are unclean.

> For example, even if you treat cockroaches, you could treat here, but they will run to the other side. Then after some time, they come back like that.

Meanwhile, the departure of some neighbors and the large influx of new owners and renters has upset the neighborly dynamics. The large influx of new owners and renters came about when some neighbors sold their houses to new people and others either rented out part or all their property and/or built new houses on their premises where they took in renters. Indeed, many renters stayed only for a few months and moved. This affected relations negatively, as they did not get to know each other.

New entrants are also serious about enforcing sanctions against trespassing. In the past, this has been socially unnecessary due to the assumed Africanism among prior owners. However, new owners have built high walls and fences, and renters do not take kindly to strangers passing through uninvited. Many interviewees referred to renters as *abalendo* (visitors or guests), implying that they were not fully accepted as Matero citizens, but rather as guests or temporary residents.

Studies elsewhere in Africa, such as Meinzen-Dick and Mwangi (2009), have noted the effects of property rights on social relationships. Though their study was conducted in rural Kenya, it found that formalization of property rights created exclusive forms of ownership, injuring preexisting webs of overlapping interests. This appears to be the case in parts of Matero.

On the other hand, interviewees in George felt that nothing had changed in neighborly relations over time, even though many original heads of household are dying and bequeathing the houses to their children. Interviewees explained how well they lived together and even described each other as family. The relationships with the younger generations were described as strong.

However, conflicts involving land boundaries were more common and harder to resolve than in Matero. Some residents sold part or all their plots without clear delineation and consent from the council. Though residents could not go to the council, they resolved to go to the local court.

7.2.7. "We Take Them to the Elders": Civic Participation

More civic participation was reported in Matero than George, with evidence of formal and informal action against crime. Informal action included collective responses by neighbors against criminal actors in their communities. Formal action involved participation in neighborhood watch and street committees. Interviewees in Matero were unanimous in their agreement that when a crime is in progress and a neighbor calls for help, the other neighbors collectively rush to their aid. Some interviewees pointed out, however, that only the original neighbors help, while renters and recent buyers stay locked inside their houses.

In addition to answering calls for help, Matero maintained a social control system organized by section chairmen, and a functional, albeit irregular, neighborhood watch. Responsible for resolving conflicts between neighbors and mobilizing residents for community issues, the Matero street chairman was similar to the street committee chairmen in South Africa. The chairman organized neighborhood watch and engaged police officers from Matero Police Post to accompany residents on patrol.

Although this social control arrangement seemed to be working for many interviewees, others felt that neighborhood criminals had infiltrated the neighborhood watch and suspected that some crimes were committed during patrols. Though they believed it strongly, no interviewees had seen this happen.

George implemented similar informal reactions to crime, but it lacked a formal system of chairmen and section committees. Interviewees pointed to a system of chairmen before the introduction of multiparty democracy in Zambia in 1991. Such arrangements were required by the United National Independence Party (UNIP) at the time. In terms of civic participation, Matero residents are more organized than those in George.

7.2.8. "They Will Just Think that You Want to Use Up Their Money for Personal Gain": Membership in Voluntary Associations

Based on survey data, the hypothesis that leasehold titling is associated with more memberships in voluntary associations was not supported. Qualitative interviews revealed that although Matero had a functioning social-control system through chairmen and a neighborhood watch, interviewees did not belong to any other voluntary community organizations. While interviewees reported no awareness of associations operating in their neighborhood, the most cited reason for lack of civic engagement was that they did not trust each other. Interviewees reported skepticism and distrust when a neighbor proposed a community initiative, project, or plan.

Interviewees in George confirmed that associations existed under the UNIP government, but they no longer exist. By interviewee accounts, the organizations and initiatives were functional, and residents lamented the loss.

In general, leasehold rights do not provide enough of a stake in the neighborhood to instigate participation in voluntary associations. In many respects, residents are so busy attempting to meet basic needs that there is not enough time left for civic activities.

7.3. THE FAMILY HOUSE AND SOCIAL PRODUCTION AND INTERGENERATIONAL TRANSFER OF TENURE

The family house emerged as an important theme in the Matero case. A family house is one in which some members are caretakers, appointed by extended family to live in the house following the passing of the owner. Caretakers were typically siblings of the head of the household. In this situation, the house was bequeathed to all the children of the primary beneficiary, but only one person could be officially added to the title. The collective nature of families forced the deed office to include a string of names on the title. While some interviewees in George regarded their homes as family houses, there was no legal provision for several members to be included on the occupancy license, and the license was not legally transferrable.

The family house is emblematic of the disconnect between the collective societal orientation in Zambia and the individualistic orientation of neoliberal ideology. While extended family may view the home as a collectively owned asset, property rights institutions developed based on private ownership only provide for individuals. Here we see the social production and intergenerational transfer of homeownership tenure through the family. The circumstance also illuminates the compromise necessitated by neoliberal ideology in the social production of ownership tenure. Neoliberalism demands only one name on a deed, but under a collective orientation, a collection of individuals could sign the deed.

7.4. CONCLUSION

The homeowner ideology in Lusaka's Matero township has not lived up to its claims. Leasehold rights delivered through privatization and slum upgrading are a bundle of rights to idle capital there, too. Evidence from Matero and George corroborates much of what we know in terms of a positive association between property rights and property value. However, the appreciation in value is too small for leaseholders to access formal credit. Moreover, the fact that fewer people who have ownership rights participate in income-generating activities relative to those with usufruct rights highlights the importance of context. The evidence casts further doubt on the ability of ownership rights to lead to higher labor market participation, household income, investments, and household wealth as measured through durable goods. In short, beneficiaries of leasehold rights through privatization of public housing receive a bundle of rights to idle capital, because they are discouraged from utilizing their land and housing to engage with the market and advance their livelihood.

In the context of a poorly performing macroeconomic environment characterized by high unemployment, low incomes, and high prevalence of poverty, stronger rights have little impact on individual household economies. Further research is required to ascertain optimal economic conditions for stronger rights to have a positive effect on employment and income, through increases either in home businesses or tenure security.

However, despite the personal and structural constraints to economic utility gains, ownership rights do provide holders with certain social benefits, such as higher status and life satisfaction, as compared to those with usufruct rights. Yet this does not suggest that there are no gains from usufruct rights. Indeed, income-generating activities were higher in George, and housing investments took place, despite regulations prohibiting them.

In sum, contention and compromise regarding the idea of the family house reveal the social production of ownership tenure, through the family's practices of production and intergenerational transfer, as inflected by the individualistic values of neoliberalism.

CHAPTER 8

The Antitheses of the Homeowner Ideology through Usufruct Rights to Social Housing in Luanda

Recall the story of Rosana in Luanda in chapter 1. Rosana was evacuated by the government from Boa Vista and relocated to temporary housing in Zango, 40 kilometers (25 miles) away. Five long years later, she was provided with a house under usufruct rights. Through her *guia de entrega* (a housing occupancy receipt), Rosana agreed to use the house for habitation only. However, with the help of her family, Rosana built a wall and fence, converted the dwelling to a two-story house, and painted the exterior an unapproved color (only green, yellow, orange, purple, and white are allowed). Yet Rosana's story is not unique. Even though they have gone against the terms of their occupancy, Rosana and her neighbors in Zango express little to no fear of eviction by the government. Their health is much better since moving, and they have more income and durable goods than the people who moved to Paraiso. Many opened businesses and rented out rooms, despite rules against doing so. Rosana is satisfied with her house and her neighborhood, and she has a strong sense of neighborhood and no intention to move. Her story challenges the assumptions of homeowner ideology. Rosana's story teaches us that even without ownership rights, the poor can maximize economic utility. What matters is that they feel, think, and assess that they have security of tenure.

Chapters 5, 6, and 7 provided evidence to support the argument that freehold is structured idle capital among the urban poor, and that a focus on the economic utility of real property rights obscures the social reality that such rights affect non-economic dimensions of welfare. This chapter adds to those assertions to suggest that although property rights empower the possessor with ownership and security of tenure, the homeowner ideology obscures the benefits of usufruct property rights. The present chapter demonstrates that in cases of untitled tenure and state recognition and administration of usufruct rights, the urban poor engage in trading, investment, and informal business on the land.

8.1. MEASURING EFFECTS OF USUFRUCT RIGHTS IN ZANGO, LUANDA

Our study team used a quantitative approach in Zango and Paraiso. Working with the research contractor that administers the Afrobarometer in Angola, I conducted a household survey from December 3 to 21, 2019—thirteen years after the first transfer of housing to families in Zango in 2006. The targeted sample size was 650. The study population was made up of 3,000 Zango household heads who are housing beneficiaries, and about 120,000 dwellers who live in the musseque of Paraiso (Tvedten et al. 2018). There were no requirements for representation in terms of gender, ethnicity, or health. Only adult heads of household or adult proxies were interviewed.

The target sample size was 10 percent of the number of households in Zango. The government built 3,000 homes. Our target sample size was 300 in Zango, and an unmatched sample of 350 households was targeted in Paraiso. Systematic sampling with a random start was chosen; this is a probability-based sampling method that ensures that every person in the study population has an equal and random chance of being selected. Google Earth images of the two areas were used to select the random start because there was no publicly available and reliable housing registry of either Zango 1 or Paraiso that could be used as a sampling frame. A random start was assigned by a field supervisor. Data collectors requested to interview every second household from the random start in each location. Paraiso was divided into eight sectors in line with Waldorf (2014). The sectoral division allowed for geographical representation during data collection. In both neighborhoods, data collectors were instructed to request to speak to the household head or a proxy 18 years old or older. The realized total sample size was 634 households (a 97.5 percent response rate). However, during data cleaning, it was found that some of the respondents had indicated that their households had moved into Zango later than 2006. These were probably recent buyers and not original owners or dependent proxies, who supplied information about their own arrival date rather than that of the household head. These were removed from the dataset.

In the final unmatched dataset, there were 297 observations from Zango and 298 from Paraiso.

Twenty-two data collectors were trained in survey administration and ethical considerations. During the training, a pilot study was conducted, wherein each enumerator conducted one interview, and the questionnaire was reviewed according to the comments made. Data collectors proceeded to their random starts under the guidance of a field supervisor and began to administer questionnaires. Data collectors carried password-protected smartphones, and the questionnaire was programmed into the secure online platform SurveyToGo. Data collectors did not have access to the data once they had conducted and uploaded an interview. Data was stored in a secure and encrypted cloud account. The principal investigator downloaded the datafile in excel.csv format. After data collection, a research assistant assisted with data cleaning and preliminary analysis. The research assistant possessed a current CITI Human Subjects Research Certification.

8.1.1. Analytical Strategy

As in the cases from Nairobi and Lusaka, propensity score analysis was employed to eliminate selection bias and achieve comparability of the groups. Although some households self-selected and moved from Boa Vista to Paraiso, there were already people who had settled there. They did not settle in one location but mixed into Paraiso. There were no records to help trace and isolate these households. Thus, the sample was limited to those who had settled there from 2001. Participants who moved to Zango 1 may differ, for reasons unknown. The fact that they obliged and did not resist, while those who went to Paraiso resisted going to Zango, suggests that they could be a reason for the difference. The general reason for self-selection into Paraiso was that evictees wanted to stay close to economic opportunities, but there might be other, unknown reasons why specific individuals self-selected in the way they did. These reasons might determine differences in outcomes. The propensity score balances scores between the two groups on observed characteristics, thereby eliminating selection bias and making the two groups comparable on baseline characteristics. This means that conditioned on their propensity scores, participants from both groups will have a similar distribution of measured or observed baseline covariates. Procedures were similar to the Kibera and Matero case studies, but specific adjustments were made. Below is the description of the specific application of propensity score matching for this case study.

ESTIMATING THE PROPENSITY SCORES

I estimated an initial propensity score matching model, using the matching variables described in table 8.1.

To estimate the propensity score, a probit regression model was employed to predict treatment status—that is, usufruct rights in Zango vs. untitled or no tenure rights in Paraiso. The probit model regressed tenure status on baseline characteristics. Income and demographic characteristics were plausible predictors of outcome variables in households with stronger tenure rights. These were included in the propensity score model because of the need to ensure balance on variables that are predictive of these outcomes.

MATCHING ON PROPENSITY SCORES

Treated and untreated participants were matched based on similar propensity scores. The ideal is to have fewer treatment observations and more untreated

Table 8.1. Variable Descriptions for Matching Variables

Matching Variables		
Age	Group average	[Q_17] Age of the head of the household
Sex	1 = male, 2 = female	[Q_16] Sex of head of household
Education	Group average	[Q_19] Highest level of education of the head of household
Marital Status		[Q_18/Q_18_S] Marital status of the head of household
Employment Status	0 = Unemployed, but not actively seeking work 1 = Unemployed 2 = Unemployed and job searching in the last 4 weeks 3 = Employed	[Q_22/Q_22_S] Employment status of the head of household
Employment Type	0 = informal 1 = formal	Q_23 If the head of household is employed, is the employment formal or informal?
Employed Household Members	0 = no 1 = yes	[Q_24] Besides the head of the family, are there any other family members who work?
Number of Rooms	Group average	[Q_29] Total number of rooms
Dwelling Area	Group average	[Q_30] Total construction area of your housing in m^2

observations, to have a larger pool from which treatment group matches can be selected. After matching, the realized matched sample size was 162 households for Zango 1, which is the treatment group, and 214 for Paraiso. Multiple matching methods, such as nearest neighbor, radius, kernel, and stratification methods, were employed. Inferences were made only in the region of common support—the space where the distributions of the propensity scores of the two groups overlap. The objective was to match a treated participant to each untitled participant.

STRATIFICATION AND BALANCE ON PROPENSITY SCORES

Balancing the data ensures that there are no confounding effects across distributions of propensity scores (Guo and Fraser 2015). Balance is achieved by computing quintiles of the estimated propensity scores such that each quintile has no differences. When propensity scores are constant within each quintile, the distribution of matching variables is approximately the same between treatment and control groups (Rubin 2006, 449). The region of common support ranged from propensity scores 0.15 to 0.92. Participants in the overall study sample were stratified into five approximately equal-size groups of the estimated propensity score. The distribution of scores across groups is as shown in figure 8.1, and the results of the tests of equality of means in propensity scores within each quintile block, as shown in table 8.2, are not significant, showing that the means are equal. Figure 8.1 and table 8.2 show that the extent of overlap is satisfactory, and balance is achieved across the two samples within each quintile.

ESTIMATING TREATMENT EFFECTS

Estimates were made of the average treatment effect for the treated (ATT)—that is, the average response to treatment for individuals who were assigned usufruct rights. Nearest neighbor, radius, kernel, and stratification matching techniques were applied to derive and estimate ATT. The models do not control for unobservable or unknown factors that may be driving observed variation in the outcomes. The assumption of the propensity score models in using observed characteristics is that there are no unobserved factors correlated with the outcome. For variable descriptions of outcome variables, please see appendix C. See appendix D for descriptive statistics.

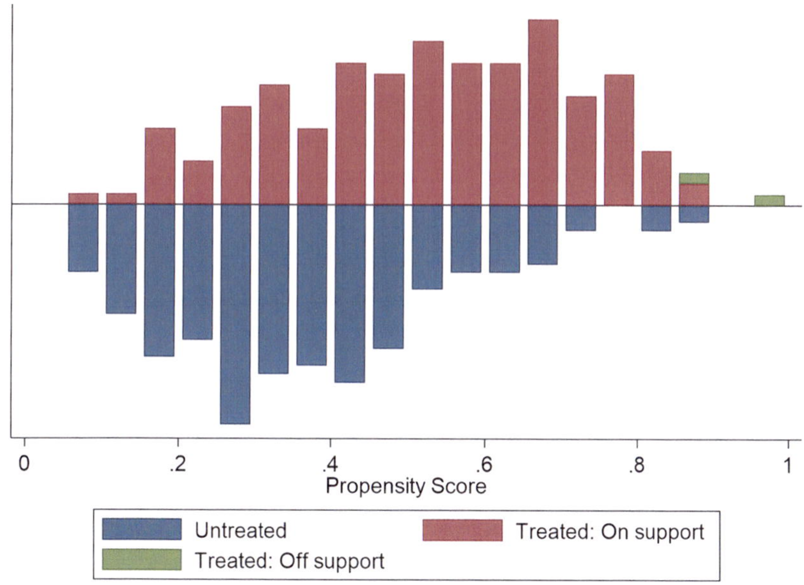

Fig. 8.1. Balance of Propensity Scores across Treated (Usufruct Rights) and Untreated (Untitled) Groups

Table 8.2. *t*-tests of Equality of the Means of Propensity Scores between Treated and Untreated Groups in Each Block

Block of Propensity Score Inferior Bound	Untreated (Paraiso) ($n = 214$)	Treated (Zango 1) ($n = 162$)	t
Block 1–0.09	0.15	0.16	−0.51
Block 2–0.2	0.30	0.31	−1.06
Block 3–0.4	0.48	0.50	−1.79
Block 4–0.6	0.65	0.69	−2.29
Block 5–0.8	0.86	0.85	−0.32

8.2. UTILITY OF USUFRUCT RIGHTS IN ZANGO

8.2.1. Tenure Security

Zango residents had more tenure security than Paraiso residents, as the government allocated houses, moved families to Zango, and provided a document to signify occupancy.

8.2.2. Housing Investments and Consolidation

After matching, an independent samples t-test was used to examine whether Zango 1 households from the matched sample engaged in investments despite the guidelines to the contrary in the *guia de entrega*. Croese (2013) observed that households in Zango did make house modifications, but did not quantify the extent and significance of these modifications. Several studies have shown that households with usufruct rights tend to make investments contrary to regulation, where enforcement of regulations is weak (Muyeba 2018; Payne, Durand-Lasserve, and Rakodi 2009). The analysis reveals that the average dwelling size in Zango 1 is significantly greater than the initial size of houses delivered by the government. The average size of the dwelling is 115 m^2, while the initial size was 52 m^2, which represents a statistically significant difference of an average of 63 m^2, with t (161) = 5.49, p = 0.00. This means that since housing delivery, households in Zango 1 have more than doubled the sizes of their dwellings on average. Evidence of household investments was further corroborated by Google Earth satellite images and author photographs.

Satellite images are used here to visually identify investments taking place over time. Since the dwellings were built in a single contiguous area, satellite

Table 8.3. Average Treatment Effect on the Treated (ATT) for Perceived Tenure Security Variables Using Nearest Neighbor, Radius, Kernel, and Stratification Matching

	Matching Method			
Outcome Variable	Nearest Neighbor	Radius	Kernel	Stratification
Fear of Eviction	−1.82***	−1.03***	−1.05***	−0.98***
	(0.60)	(0.43)	(0.45)	(0.34)
Possibility of Eviction	−2.22***	−1.42***	−1.49***	−1.27***
	(0.56)	(0.41)	(0.43)	(0.47)

Note: Standard errors in parentheses; *** $p < 0.01$, ** $p < 0.05$, * $p < 0.1$.

Fig. 8.2. Northwest Section of Zango in 2008

Fig. 8.3. Northwest Section of Zango in March 2020

images can identify structural changes that took place over years. The images were obtained using Google Earth Pro. The first image was taken in 2008, shortly after the houses were built and delivered to 3,000 residents. The second image was taken in March of 2020. The two maps are compared to depict any investments that had occurred.

Satellite imagery confirms investments in housing. Figure 8.2 shows the northwest part of Zango 1 in 2008, while figure 8.3 shows the same location in 2020. Many dwellings have an additional structure or extension, which confirms the statistical analysis. Over time, residents made many house modifications, even though they were prohibited by the government. Some homeowners remodeled the government-built houses into mansionettes such as one might see in an American suburb. Other modifications were driven by a desire for increased security, such as walls, burglar bars, and barbed wire. Zango residents took concrete steps (no pun intended) to invest in their houses based on their security. The development is so significant that it can be difficult to distinguish boundaries between houses on the map. Even with usufruct rights, residents of Zango felt secure enough to make costly investments in homes that technically belonged to the government.

The critical question is whether observed levels of investments in Zango 1 were more significant than those made by Paraiso residents. Table 8.4 shows the results of the propensity score analysis on differences in dwelling area and number of rooms between the two neighborhoods. There was no significant difference in housing investments and number of rooms between households in Zango 1 and Paraiso. The difference in dwelling area ranges from 0 to 12 m^2, but this is not statistically significant. The difference in the absolute

Table 8.4. Average Treatment Effect on the Treated (ATT) for Dwelling Area and Number of Rooms Using Nearest Neighbor, Radius, Kernel, and Stratification Matching

	Matching Method			
Outcome Variable	Nearest Neighbor	Radius	Kernel	Stratification
Housing Investments				
Dwelling Area	3.44	31.89	32.06	30.57
	(28.64)	(18.47)	(19.73)	(18.53)
Number of Rooms	0.75***	0.61***	0.63***	0.53***
	(0.19)	(0.16)	(0.18)	(0.14)

Note: Standard errors in parentheses; *** $p < 0.01$, ** $p < 0.05$, * $p < 0.1$.

number of rooms is 0. This means that higher perceived tenure security and possession of the *guia de entrega* does not mean higher housing investments. Untitled households in Paraiso invested as much as Zango residents in their housing, despite having no formal document.

8.2.3. Labor Market Participation

Table 8.5 reveals no significant differences in type of employment or employment status of the head of household and other household members. This means that labor market participation is not a mechanism through which property rights affect income in Zango. The labor market participation mechanism probably does not work, for two primary reasons. First, as the analysis shows, perception of tenure security is very high in both Zango and Paraiso, which means that changes in title and housing status have no impact. Where tenure security is high, households do not need to leave an adult at home during the day to protect the dwelling from eviction. Second, it is very likely that formal employment opportunities are so few that changes in property rights do not lead to labor market participation. Almost half of all household heads in the Zango sample are either unemployed and not seeking employment, unemployed and seeking employment, or report only that they are unemployed. Thus, the evidence suggests that property rights increase tenure security, which leads to increase in home business activities.

Table 8.5. Average Treatment Effect on the Treated (ATT) for Labor Market Participation and Home Business Activities Using Nearest Neighbor, Radius, Kernel, and Stratification Matching

	Matching Method			
Outcome Variable	Nearest Neighbor	Radius	Kernel	Stratification
Employment Status	0.07	0.07	0.06	0.02
	(0.13)	(0.13)	(0.13)	(0.12)
Employed Members of	−0.07	0.01	0.00	0.04
Households	(0.09)	(0.06)	(0.06)	(0.06)
Employment Type	0.15	0.04	0.02	0.03
	(0.12)	(0.09)	(0.10)	(0.09)
Home Business	0.03	0.11**	0.10*	0.12*
Activities	(0.07)	(0.05)	(0.06)	(0.06)

Note: Standard errors in parentheses; *** $p < 0.01$, ** $p < 0.05$, * $p < 0.1$.

8.2.4. Income-Generating Activities

Table 8.5 also shows evidence that property rights are associated with higher participation in home-business activities in Zango. Radius matching shows that ATT = 0.11, $t(334) = 1.97$, $p < 0.05$. Kernel matching demonstrates that ATT = 0.10, $t(348) = 1.76$, $p < 0.10$. Stratification matching reveals that ATT = 0.12, $t(348) = 1.94$, $p < 0.10$. This means that Zango has 10 to 12 percent more households engaged in home business activities than Paraiso. This evidence is based on radius, kernel, and stratification matching. Analysis using nearest-neighbor matching shows no significant differences.

8.2.5. Household Income

Table 8.6 presents strong evidence that Zango households have higher household income than Paraiso households. All four matching methods reveal a higher ATT, ranging from Kz9,106 to Kz11,735 (US$21 to $28). The analysis shows an ATT = Kz9,106, $t(314) = 2.73$, $p < 0.01$ using nearest neighbor; ATT = Kz9,225, $t(314) = 3.42$, $p < 0.01$ using radius matching; ATT = Kz9,489, $t(314) = 3.41$, $p < 0.01$ using kernel matching; and ATT = Kz11,735, $t(348) = 3.93$, $p < 0.01$ using stratification matching (US$21.54, $21.83, $22.46, and $27.77). This means that the *guia de entrega* for households that benefitted from social housing in Zango is associated with a higher range of income than for those who lived in Paraiso. The analysis using log of household income is consistent, showing that Zango households have more income than Paraiso households. To use alternative indicators of income, the analysis using dura-

Table 8.6. Average Treatment Effect on the Treated (ATT) for Household Income, Log of Household Income, and Households Durables Using Nearest Neighbor, Radius, Kernel, and Stratification Matching

	Matching Method			
Outcome Variable	Nearest Neighbor	Radius	Kernel	Stratification
Households Income	9106.03***	9225.36***	9489.04***	11734.89***
	(3335.22)	(2694.32)	(2783.03)	(3772.82)
Log of Household Income	1.23***	1.05***	1.13***	1.39***
	(0.44)	(0.30)	(0.31)	(0.37)
Durable Household Goods	2.45***	2.10***	2.14***	2.00***
	(0.72)	(0.58)	(0.61)	(0.61)

Note: Standard errors in parentheses; *** $p < 0.01$, ** $p < 0.05$, * $p < 0.1$.

ble household goods shows that Zango households have two more durable goods than Paraiso households.

8.2.6. Usufruct Rights and Health

There was no significant difference in scores on health indicators between Zango and Paraiso residents. In terms of physical health, this might be attributed to the fact that Paraiso residents build their houses using brick and mortar. Gastrow (2017a) has shown that houses built of brick and mortar reflect efforts to legitimize settlements in Luanda. A lack of difference in psychological health can be explained by high levels of tenure security. Despite Zango residents having higher scores, perception of tenure security is generally high in both Zango 1 and Paraiso. As shown in appendix D, Paraiso's score on fear of eviction is an average of 4 out of a possible 10. Zango is 2.77. Perception of the possibility of eviction is also a low 4 out of 10 for Paraiso households, while that of Zango 1 is 2.31.

The high perception of tenure security can be explained by multiple factors. For Zango 1 residents, it probably emanates from the *guia de entrega*, the low likelihood of a second eviction, and the social housing assumptions of a Marxist tradition. The *guia de entrega* is assurance of government backing, even though its guidelines are violated. The modification guidelines are also

Table 8.7. Average Treatment Effect on the Treated (ATT) for Health Indicators Using Nearest Neighbor, Radius, Kernel, and Stratification Propensity Score Matching

	Matching Method			
Outcome Variable	Nearest Neighbor	Radius	Kernel	Stratification
Self-Reported Physical Health	0.63	0.51	0.50	0.49
	(0.41)	(0.32)	(0.33)	(0.30)
Adult BMI	1.02	0.32	0.53	0.66
	(0.53)	(0.57)	(0.43)	(0.42)
Child BMI	2.05	−0.95	−0.90	−0.04
	(2.60)	(1.21)	(1.38)	(1.61)
Fertility	−0.06	−0.16	−0.07	−0.05
	(0.23)	(0.15)	(0.15)	(0.14)
Anxiety Disorder Scale	−0.51	−0.58	−0.55	−0.86
	(0.74)	(0.50)	(0.52)	(0.58)

Note: Standard errors in parentheses; *** $p < 0.01$, ** $p < 0.05$, * $p < 0.1$.

open enough that residents made them without fear of eviction. Poor monitoring and guideline enforcement also contribute to a sense that residents can make changes without sanction. In addition, there is no delimitation of tenure duration. Perpetual usufruct rights may be interpreted as permanent possession and use. Also, the government eviction of households from Boa Vista and subsequent resettlement in Zango 1 may suggest to residents that a second mass eviction was unlikely.

Culturally, Marxist values and traditions persist and provide a broader context for higher security of tenure. For many Paraiso households, even without official communication or title, the government promise to build housing provided a level of tenure security. As noted, brick-and-mortar building materials in Luanda further legitimized the settlement (Gastrow 2017b). Most houses in Paraiso, as shown in figure 4.18, are built of brick and mortar. Even more, establishment of a police post and water tanks through JICA contributed positively. Further, when evictions have taken place, it was often in response to dangerous conditions or urban development (Croese 2013). Instances from this latter category are concentrated in Luanda's city center.

There was no difference in any of the indicators of social capital. However, this is not surprising—residents in both neighborhoods have been together for at least two decades. Once they moved from Boa Vista, Zango residents lived in informal housing structures while waiting for their housing. However, social capital can develop in the next generation after titling, as shown in Moser and Felton (2007). Perhaps a definitive answer can only be found after the children of residents in Zango become adults.

Table 8.8. Average Treatment Effect on the Treated (ATT) for Social Capital Indicators Using Nearest Neighbor, Radius, Kernel, and Stratification Propensity Score Matching

	Matching Method			
Outcome Variable	Nearest Neighbor	Radius	Kernel	Stratification
Membership in Associations	0.43	0.46	0.26	0.24
	(0.28)	(0.73)	(0.17)	(0.22)
Bonding Social Capital	−1.05	−0.15	−0.03	−0.65
	(1.06)	(0.69)	(0.62)	(0.94)
Bridging Social Capital	−0.02	−0.21	0.05	−0.38
	(1.16)	(0.64)	(0.73)	(1.08)

Note: Standard errors in parentheses; *** $p < 0.01$, ** $p < 0.05$, * $p < 0.1$.

Table 8.9. Average Treatment Effect on the Treated (ATT) for Self-Esteem, Satisfaction with House and Neighborhood, and Sense of Belonging Using Nearest Neighbor, Radius, Kernel, and Stratification Propensity Score Matching

	Matching Method			
Outcome Variable	Nearest Neighbor	Radius	Kernel	Stratification
Self-Esteem	−0.02	0.01	−0.01	−0.23
	(0.31)	(0.20)	(0.21)	(0.19)
Satisfaction with House	−0.35	−0.14	−0.15	−0.25
	(0.47)	(0.36)	(0.36)	(0.37)
Satisfaction with Neighborhood	0.01	0.54	0.50	0.51
	(0.40)	(0.28)	(0.37)	(0.39)
Satisfaction with Life in General	0.41	0.33	−0.04	−0.11
	(0.42)	(0.28)	(0.31)	(0.29)
Sense of Belonging	1.52***	1.71***	1.72***	1.45***
	(0.57)	(0.41)	(0.43)	(0.35)

Note: Standard errors in parentheses; *** $p < 0.01$, ** $p < 0.05$, * $p < 0.1$.

Zango residents have a higher sense of belonging than Paraiso residents. All four matching methods reveal an ATT higher for Zango, ranging from a difference of 1.45 to 1.72. The analysis shows an ATT = 1.52, $t(352) = 2.69$, $p < 0.01$ using nearest neighbor; ATT = 1.71 $t(352) = 4.15$, $p < 0.01$ using radius matching; ATT = 1.72, $t(352) = 4.00$, $p < 0.01$ using kernel matching; and ATT = 1.45, $t(374) = 4.11$, $p < 0.01$ using stratification matching. It is likely that having the government deliver housing with a document backing occupancy provides Zango residents with a higher sense of belonging than residents of Paraiso. Residents of Paraiso have little assurance from the government that they belong in the land that they occupy and possess.

It appears that living in Zango does not evoke the same level of self-esteem as we saw in Kenya, South Africa, and Zambia. Residents of Zango do not own their land and housing, which remain the property of the government. Residents are not more satisfied with their dwelling and neighborhood than Paraiso residents.

8.3. CONCLUSION

A focus on the economic effects of ownership rights obscures the broader view of social reality, including the non-economic benefits of usufruct property rights. The present chapter demonstrated that usufruct rights are associated with stronger tenure security, higher household income, more household durable goods, and a better sense of belonging compared to those who are untitled in Paraiso. It also showed that the absence of freehold ownership title does not imply absence of tenure security. Thus, freehold tenure is a source of tenure security, but usufruct rights and being untitled can also be associated with high tenure security. Indeed, the homeowner ideology's focus on the utility of ownership obscures evidence for benefits of usufruct property rights.

CHAPTER 9

Conclusion

Persistence of the Homeowner Ideology in Africa

Over the course of six decades following political emancipation from colonialism, the urban housing crisis has unfolded and grown to unsustainable levels in Africa. The continent is home to over 1.2 billion people, with 400 million living in inadequate dwellings and 234 million living in slums. Housing poverty is rife, with 51 million households lacking adequate housing. The future poses even greater challenges. Projections of the 2030 urban tipping point and population growth to 2.5 billion by 2050 suggest unprecedented population stress on African cities. Making things worse, African governments are still recovering from unsustainable international debt incurred while trying to meet housing and other socioeconomic needs during what Malawian-Swedish economist Thandika Mkandawire called Africa's Great Depression from 1973 to 2002, and the more recent borrowing from China and international financial institutions from 2002 to 2020.

During the same period, neoliberal market fundamentalism gradually became a pervasive idea. With defaults on loans spreading across the developing world, market fundamentalist economists such as Milton Friedman, Harry Johnson, Bela Balassa, Anne Krueger, and others diagnosed the involvement of the state in the economy as a major cause of the 1973 to 2002 crisis (Todaro and Smith 2020). These economists prescribed the market as a solution through adjustment and stabilization programs, and institutionalized Washington Consensus policies in the form of SAPs. The market fundamentalists held influential positions at the World Bank and IMF, and in African government. To them, the solution to poverty was the market, and ownership is central to the functioning of markets.

Market fundamentalists and libertarian philosophers made ideological claims about the utility of ownership forms of property rights in addressing poverty, and such claims became pervasive following the fall of the Soviet Union and the triumph of neoliberalism.

In this book, the libertarian philosophical system of beliefs, values, assumptions, and claims about permanent ownership of real property are referred to as the homeowner ideology. The homeowner ideology is based on several unsubstantiated claims, positioning ownership as the norm, the most desirable and cheapest tenure, a status symbol, a pathway to community engagement and satisfaction, and the natural preference of rational people (Acolin 2020; Acolin, An, and Wachter 2022). It is also argued that lack of well-defined property rights—especially ownership rights—contributes to the failure of nations (Acemoglu and Robinson 2012). More operationalizable claims include that real property rights increase tenure security, allow access to credit markets, increase property values, increase investments and housing consolidation, allow for accumulation of household wealth, allow freeholders to engage in income-generating activities, lead to higher labor market participation and income, and in general reduce poverty. Non-economic claims suggesting that freehold is related to better physical and psychological health and better citizenship have been marginalized by the focus on economic effects.

Markets have failed the urban poor in Africa so profoundly that some governments decided to address these market failures and provide housing to their poor, despite meaningful disincentives to do so. The government of Kenya implemented KENSUP and built 824 apartments in 21 high-rise blocks. The country still faces a housing backlog of two million homes with a rapid urban population growth rate of 4.5 percent per year. The South African government built houses for the poor who were marginalized during apartheid, knowing well that markets had failed them. In Cape Town, 300,000 houses were built, and the project continues. In Lusaka, the poor could not afford to buy houses at market rate, which led the government to transfer colonial-era homes to them at no cost. Similarly, even though it has the option of opting for market-rate housing, the government of Angola decided to provide social housing, transferring houses under usufruct rights for free.

Using these cities as case studies, I argue that ideological claims about the economic utility of real property rights are both ambiguous and assumed to be accurate, and they powerfully obscure social realities and persist through the social production of homeownership tenure. Contrary to market fundamentalist claims, real property rights among the urban poor in African cities are actually bundles of rights to structured idle capital on the formal market. The evidence for economic utility is weak. In addition, the focus on the economic outcomes of ownership has obscured evidence that real property rights are associated with improvement in non-economic dimensions of human welfare. Indeed, the freehold and leasehold case studies in this book demonstrate that the utility of freehold extends beyond economic utility. Similarly, a focus on the utility of ownership obscures evidence of the benefits of weaker forms of property rights, such as usufruct rights. Finally, social production processes driven by the neoliberal homeowner ideology account for the persistence of using real property rights as a tool to eradicate poverty. In the following sections, I offer a summary of evidence for each part of the argument.

9.1. (F)UTILITY OF REAL PROPERTY RIGHTS

It is clear from the evidence that freehold ownership produces structured idle capital. Cases from Nairobi, Cape Town, and Lusaka revealed that ownership rights actually do little for the poor as an economic resource on the formal market. Indeed, neoliberal market-dominated economies functionally disincentivize investment in low-cost or low-value property, such as where slum conditions once existed. Ownership rights fail to fulfil their promise of prosperity and freedom for the poor, and they fail to fulfil promises of increased access to credit, sufficient increases in property values, labor market participation, investment, household wealth and income, and overall reduction in income poverty. In some cases, they even fail to assure tenure security. Ownership rights do not overcome the potential perils of low returns for banks and property developers, given conditions of low savings rates, poor credit, insufficient insurance markets, and widespread informal employment and unemployment among the poor in former slums.

Ownership rights do not lead to better access to credit. Freehold and leasehold titleholders fear losing their property if they fail to repay the loan. The market is reluctant to lend to these high-risk clients. In addition, a few beneficiaries of housing subsidies and shack-dwellers alike who have a stable source of income have managed to secure small loans in Khayelitsha—fewer than 5 percent. In these cases, property titles were often unnecessary, and where necessary, they were not alone sufficient to qualify for the loan. Beyond Africa, access to credit from private-sector lenders is unaltered by titling, and credit rationing is still a key feature of the microlending environment in urban Peru (Field and Torero 2006). In another example, informal finance was available from the onset of the formation of an illegal settlement in Bogota, and there is little formal financing forthcoming after legalization (Gilbert 2000). In Buenos Aires, low-income freeholders are not different from untitled households in accessing credit cards, bank accounts, and non-mortgage formal credit from banks, government, and labor unions or cooperatives (Galiani and Schargrodsky 2010). However, rates of access to informal credit are higher among freehold households than untitled ones. Only in Indonesia does freehold increase formal credit access, with the help of the state (Dower and Potamites 2005).

Ownership rights do not increase labor market participation. However, the issue is not that residents fail to reallocate time away from activities aimed at securing services such as service delivery protests toward employment. Rather, in economies with high unemployment and decreasing market demand for unskilled labor, it may be unrealistic to expect ownership rights to lead to improved employment status or an increase in number of hours worked. Similarly, given high levels of unemployment, poverty, and inequality in the broader economy, it may be unrealistic to expect freehold and leasehold titles to affect labor market participation and income. In the broader literature on property rights and labor market participation, Gilbert (2004) asked whether providing housing subsidies in South Africa, Chile, and Brazil is worth it; the question may be especially apt given the high unemployment, widespread poverty, and vast income inequality we see in 2022.

Evidence on the effects of ownership rights on labor market participation was not found in any of the case studies. The evidence is similarly scarce in other developing countries, and findings are ambiguous. In the COPOFRI program that issued property titles to 1.2 million urban households in Peru, the net effect of property titling was an increase in hours of labor and a reallocation of work hours from inside the home to the outside labor market (Field 2003b, 2007). Households with no legal claim to their property spent an average of 13 hours per week guarding their houses from eviction, and they were 40 percent more likely to work at home. Between 1997 and 2000, households that converted to freehold increased household labor supply by 16 hours over untitled households. These households were also half as likely as untitled households to work at home. Similarly, a natural experiment in Brazil demonstrated that freehold tenure increased labor market supply and household income (Moura and Bueno 2009). By contrast, freehold titling had no effect on labor market outcomes 20 years after titling in Buenos Aires (Galiani and Schargrodsky 2010).

Income-generating activities are not exclusive to freehold and leasehold homeowners. Rental investments are not a priority, and houses are too small to accommodate renters. Context seems important here, as titling has led to investments in some neighborhoods but not others. In Khayelitsha, it may not have worked because in the prevailing economic conditions, the poor are too poor to purchase from each other. In a society with one of the highest rates of inequality in the world, the poverty is profound, with purchasing power so weak that it cannot sustain businesses. Counterintuitively, Matero residents participated significantly less in income-generating activities, which challenges the claim that owners are associated with significantly higher participation in such activities.

Ownership rights increase property values among the poor, but the home values are lower than what is required to participate in the formal market. Elsewhere, conversion to freehold raised property values by up to 23.5 percent on the formal market in Guayaquil (Lanjouw and Levy 2002), by 73 percent in Jakarta (Dowall and Leaf, 1991), and by an astounding 100 percent in Brazil (Alston, Libecap, and Schneider 1996). Increases recorded in Lima, Jakarta, and Manila amount to 25 percent (Cantuarias and Delgado 2004; Dowall 1998; Friedman et al. 1988). Self-assessed property value gains from freehold in Costa Rica amount to 40 percent of the original value (Méndez 2006). Nevertheless, these increases do not necessarily mean the values are sufficient to be used as collateral in obtaining loans.

Ownership rights do not result in increased household income. Since there is no evidence of an increase in labor-market participation, and income-generating activities are similar to those of individuals living in shacks, a finding of no increase makes sense. Other scholars have made similar discoveries in other developing countries. Furthermore, in cities outside of Africa, income increases were preceded by an increase in labor market participation (Field and Torero 2006; Piza and de Moura 2016). There are no differences between titled and untitled households in terms of household head income, total household income, total household income per capita, total household income per adult, and employment status of the household head. There are also no significant differences in the pension status of the household heads, in female employment, and in child labor. To add to this ambiguity, in Quito and Guayaquil, there is no significant difference in aggregate weekly household labor hours between freeholders and untitled households, and freehold households are 42 percent more likely to have at least one adult member working primarily inside the house (Rose 2006). However, freehold households are 6 percentage points less likely to use child labor to contribute to household income (Rose 2006).

Although owner economic ideologists claim that freehold titling results in increases in wealth, no evidence of this was found. Freeholders and leaseholders seem to feel no obligation to fill up their houses as Meintjes (2000) expected. It may also be that they could not afford many assets. Leasehold tenure is associated with investments in housing, but these are not wealth-generating in Lusaka. Elsewhere, in Lima, freehold formalization has a large positive effect, a 68 percent increase in housing renovations within four years of titling (Field 2005, 286). This effect does not operate exclusively through greater access to credit, and investments were limited to small renovations (Field 2005, 286–87). In a poor suburban area of Buenos Aires that received freehold, the proportion of houses with high-quality walls rose by 40 percent, and high-quality roofs rose by 47 percent; houses with a constructed surface rose by 12 percent, and houses with sidewalks rose by 16 percent; the titled neighborhoods had an overall improvement score of 37 out of 100 (Galiani and Schargrodsky 2010). This is not a wealth-creating effect from households that became wealthier after titling, but rather an incentive to invest because of titling (Galiani and Schargrodsky 2010).

It turns out that belief in free-market ideology happens after, not before, the poor become freeholders and leaseholders. The change from untitled individuals to freehold and leasehold ownership drives individuals to trust the market and decide to invest. Change in beliefs regarding ownership occurs after freehold or leasehold titling (Di Tella, Galiant, and Schargrodsky 2007). A widely cited natural experiment by Di Tella, Galiant, and Schargrodsky (2007) investigated whether titling influenced four beliefs that appear fundamental to the workings of a capitalist society: individualism, materialism, the role of merit, and trust. Two decades before their study, in 1981, about 1,800 families occupied a large tract of land in San Francisco Solano, Buenos Aires. In 1984, the state expropriated the land, but offered the squatters an opportunity to surrender their plot in exchange for compensation and a subsequent transfer of ownership to them. Some squatters surrendered and were given formal titles in 1989. Others challenged the expropriation in court, demanding better compensation. The group of squatters that obtained real property rights became the treatment group, while the ones who challenged the state became the control group. They found a significant difference in the beliefs of the squatters with real property rights relative to those with no property title. The beliefs espoused by squatters with freehold were pro-market, while those without title were less pro-market.

9.2. OBSCURITY OF THE NON-ECONOMIC EFFECTS OF FREEHOLD

Our four cases also provided evidence that the focus on the economic utility of ownership rights is so pervasive that it obscures the social reality that property rights are associated with improvement in non-economic dimensions of human welfare. Freehold tenure is associated with better psychological health in Nairobi, and with higher self-esteem in Nairobi, Cape Town, and Lusaka. Freehold increased owners' sense of belonging and satisfaction with their houses, neighborhoods, and life in general in all three cities. It also improved physical health in Nairobi and Kenya. Counterintuitively, freehold tenure is associated with higher rates of teenage pregnancy among the urban poor in Cape Town.

Formal housing has electricity, which permits longer study time, contributing to better education outcomes. With investments in stronger wall materials that can more effectively block noise, children in households of real property have quieter study environments. Children of freeholders also experience fewer school absences because of the safety provided by formal streets, unlike the hidden paths found in informal slum conditions.

Freeholders are modestly healthier, but this only happens if they invest in a better living environment or are given adequate housing by the state. Moving from slum conditions into houses improved self-reported physical health by 10 percent in Khayelitsha. The mechanism seems to be that improvement in the housing environment from increased access to piped water and sanitation translates into better health. Shacks in Khayelitsha and other townships are susceptible to fire, flooding, and dust, which are sources of respiratory and waterborne diseases. Once these conditions improve, health status improves. This is consistent with the finding in the city of Nairobi, where property rights delivered with housing also improved the health of beneficiaries.

Elsewhere, in Montevideo, having property title is not associated with lower rates of housing-related diseases (Gandelman 2010). To the contrary, the effect of freehold on individuals is to lower rates of non-housing-related diseases; in fact, overall health status is significantly better because of lower levels of stress among homeowners. Children from freehold titled households enjoy better weight-for-height scores than those from untitled households in Buenos Aires, but similar weight-for-age scores (Galiani and Schargrodsky 2004). There were fewer occurrences of wasting although stunting remained unaffected. There is suggestive evidence that children in freehold households in Lima experienced an increase in weight but not in height (Vogl 2007). In addition, freehold titling seems to raise the risk of children being obese, which may mean that weight gain might not indicate improved nutritional status.

Evidence suggests that ownership rights are associated with psychological health in Kibera, but in Khayelitsha there is no indication that freeholders have better psychological well-being than shack dwellers. Respondents reported moderately high levels of psychological well-being, meaning they experienced psychological stresses some or a little of the time. Because of the methodological shortcomings, the evidence is not conclusive. The analysis nevertheless indicates the direction of the relationship. The state of knowledge on African cities is such that more empirical study and theory building are needed to understand the relationship between titling and psychological well-being.

In all three freehold case studies, there is no effect on social capital. The evidence does not support the claim that freehold titling positively affects citizen behavior in terms of memberships in voluntary associations, civic participation, neighborhood attachment, and political awareness. Freeholders do not demonstrate behavior consistent with people who have an economic or other stake in the neighborhood, mainly because they did not participate in the process that brought them their houses. What we know from the very few studies that examine the effects of freehold on neighborhood outcomes and on aspects of social capital in developing countries is that there is no effect in Latin America (Pecha and Ruprah 2010). Pecha and Ruprah (2010) investigated whether homeownership affects membership in community and religious organizations, trust in local entities, good citizenship, civic and political activism, voting behavior, satisfaction with neighborhood, and political ideological inclination. The study sampled 17 Latin American countries using the Latin Barometer opinion survey and found no effect of homeownership.

In Nairobi, fewer children were born to freehold families, indicating that women are more empowered. Overall, there is a dearth of research on the effects of freehold on empowerment of vulnerable individuals in urban areas in the developing world, much less in African cities. Evidence from Lima and Buenos Aires seems to indicate a reduction in fertility. Freehold titling reduced annual birth rates by 21 percent among beneficiaries in Lima because of an increase in female bargaining power (Field 2003a). In Buenos Aires, fewer children are born to the household head after titling compared to untitled households, an average of one less person than in untitled households (Galiani and Schargrodsky 2010). Further, untitled households seem to have more extended relatives living with them than those with freehold.

There is no evidence of a reduction in school dropout rates due to freehold rights in the three case studies. However, the claim that freehold rights reduce school dropouts is supported by evidence from Buenos Aires. Children in freehold, titled households experience less grade repetition than those from untitled households (Galiani and Schargrodsky 2004).

Finally, freeholders experience higher status attainment and a sense of decency and respectability. Untitled households do not claim increases in any of these characteristics.

9.3. OBSCURITY OF THE UTILITY OF USUFRUCT RIGHTS

The homeowner ideology's emphasis on utility obscures the social reality that usufruct rights or untitled tenure do not imply absence of tenure security and utility. In Paraiso, households improve and invest in their dwellings in the absence of title, just like those in Zango, who ignore government regulations. This is also the finding elsewhere (Angel et al. 2006; Calderón 2004). Where there is considerable de facto tenure security, dwellers do not wait for title to invest in their homes (Angel et al. 2006, 14; Calderón 2004, 298). Also, income can be a constraint for some households with a title. Angel et al. (2006) argue that the lack of improvements in Mexico reflects lack of income more than lack of title. Payne et al. (2009) pointed out the extent to which title can achieve the objective of increasing housing investments, concluding that although title is a means of achieving housing improvement and investment, it is by no means the only one. In Bogotá, sales of houses are more common when people lack legal title (Gilbert 2000). Informal property rights can substitute effectively for formal property rights in Guayaquil, Ecuador (Lanjouw and Levy 2002). In fact, a property-rights gap exists in the developing world where governments begin the process of delivering property rights, but to maintain political control do not complete the process (Albertus 2020). In Lusaka and Cape Town, simple binaries of owner and nonowner fail to capture the lived experiences of their interviewees. This is because rights to houses are not embedded in legal title, but are shaped by shifting economic, social, and cultural realities (Butcher and Oldfield 2009).

Lack of formal freehold or leasehold title does not limit the occurrence of transactions and investments. In Angola, 96 percent of transactions take place without documented ownership (Cain 2013). In Argentina and Indonesia, there is no significant difference in housing improvements between those with formal legal title, perception of tenure security, and informal/de facto tenure (Reerink and van Gelder 2010; van Gelder 2007). A sense of perceived tenure security results in dwellers investing in their habitat through psychological pathways including both thinking and feeling, which influence how dwellers make decisions about the probability of eviction and which determine fear of eviction. In this regard, titling should lead to a lower perceived probability of eviction and to less fear of eviction, which in turn should lead to investment in housing (van Gelder 2007).

Ownership title is a source of tenure security, but not the only one. Even though it is equated with tenure security, households can have tenure security without title (Durand-Lasserve et al. 2007, 22). In metropolitan Manila, it is possible to have tenure security based on de facto tenure rights (Porio and Crisol 2004). Those without formal title on informal land settlements perceive law and order, basic services, and job opportunities to be more important elements of their security and make investments on that basis.

Moreover, ownership title in some contexts reduces tenure security (Payne, Durand-Lasserve, and Rakodi 2009). Freehold titling programs are often used in informal settlements in countries or cities that already have some degree of de facto tenure security. In India and Afghanistan, tenure security was reduced after titling, because titles do not protect one from eviction. There are also market-driven displacements of titled households in Cambodia, Rwanda, Egypt, and India through gentrification. Tenure security can be achieved through several means other than titling, and titling may sometimes lead to increased tenure insecurity.

There is a need to go beyond the economic claims about real property rights in development. Market fundamentalist neoclassical economics has focused the debate about real property rights on economic outcomes. It has neither considered nor tested a wider range of effects, including many potential human and social capital effects. The consequence has been the obscuring of knowledge on non-economic dimensions of human welfare. This limits understanding of the full extent of effects of titling in different contexts.

I do not suggest that freehold and leasehold ownership be denied to the poor; rather, below the low-income threshold, there is a need to break from an ideologically informed view that ownership of real property among the poor is an economic capital asset. A paradigm shift is needed, from ideologically based claims in policymaking to developing an awareness of social production of tenure processes that inform the persistence of homeowner preferences. An understanding of the social production of homeownership tenure—not only through neoliberal ideology and policies informed by neoclassical economics, but through intergenerational transfer of knowledge about homeownership, through the institution of the family, and through the state as an institution that re/produces a preference for homeownership through policy support. Such a shift should recognize the role of neoliberal ideology, the family, and the state in social production processes, and it should develop an appreciation of social reality through empirical evidence.

9.4. SOCIAL PRODUCTION OF HOMEOWNERSHIP TENURE

This section discusses the fourth part of the supporting argument and suggests that the case for homeownership based on presumed economic benefits among the urban poor in African cities is ideological, and its persistence is driven by the social production of tenure preferences. For decades, scholars have challenged mainstream thinking about the economic paramountcy of ownership of real property among the poor, yet claims about ownership persist because of the pervasiveness of the homeowner ideology.

Advanced by Poggio (2006) and further developed by (Ronald 2007), the social production of tenure theory has the most explanatory value. The theory suggests that any emphasis on a particular tenure must be explained by the process of social production. Social production can result from a combination of sources, including the intergenerational production and transmission of culture, liberal market channels, and state support for homeownership. Ronald (2007) notes that the process of social production involves economic, cultural, and ideological elements. Thus, homeownership persists due to liberal market channels guided by market fundamentalist neoliberal ideological claims about homeownership. Such claims also interact with demand for housing and homeownership (Potts 2020), based on the cultural values of families, as well as deliberate efforts by the state to meet housing needs through specific forms of tenure.

The main social production element perpetuating ownership as a tenure of preference in scholarship and international development practice in Africa is the market fundamentalist neoliberal ideology. As discussed in chapters 2 and 3, it has turned homeowner ideology into a pervasive ideology in African cities through manipulation using development finance conditionalities imposed by international development organizations through SAPs.

The cultural element of the social production of homeownership is the sanctification of the status of the homeowner and cultural orientation toward homeownership, which has been enhanced by market fundamentalist neoliberal ideology. Although most people are renters, there is more support for homeownership than for renting. The renter is stigmatized, and the landlord is treated as royalty in a neoliberal dispensation. The liberal ideology holds sacred individual freedom, private property rights, and individual responsibility; therefore, homeownership is the preferred form of tenure (Ronald 2007, 7), even where collective values are entrenched. Cultural values preferring homeownership were unquestionably present during colonialism, even though they were only enjoyed by colonizers. Following independence and even under one-party socialist-oriented regimes in Africa, values of homeownership persisted, and constitutions allowed for ownership tenure. Then, the cultural orientation was collective, having been informed by African customs and endorsed by socialist ideals. Nevertheless, with state provision of housing, many did not actively pursue homeownership. Liberalization and privatization policies, along with removal of housing subsidies, stimulated ideological values of individual ownership in Africa.

One might argue that the calls for homeownership are not ideological, but rather follow the economic expansion thesis, which suggests that home ownership emerges as the dominant tenure preference as economies grow. It is true that African economies showed rapid expansion, with average growth rates of 3 percent from 1999 to 2015 (African Development Bank 2016, 4). However, it is also true that the growth of this period was accompanied by significant growth in within-country inequality, and poverty levels remained unresponsive to growth (African Development Bank 2016; Chancel et al. 2022; World Bank Group 2016). Moreover, despite such rapid economic expansion, homeownership rates remain low, as shown in table 1.1. The emphasis on owner occupation is not a function of expansion of economic growth under globalization in Africa.

An alternative to the economic expansion thesis is the cultural disposition thesis, which suggests that some societies are culturally disposed toward particular housing tenure. For example, societies that highly value individualism are more likely to veer toward homeownership, while collectivist societies are oriented more toward social housing. Ideally, in collectivist states, the belief is that housing should not be a commodity and that its costs should be distributed to guarantee good housing conditions for all households. Although this theory holds explanatory power in Western industrialized societies, it fails to explain the push for ownership forms of tenure in Africa. African societies are oriented toward collectivism, which can perhaps explain low levels of ownership.

Still others might agree with Kemeny's (1981) political dominance or "home ownership ideology" theory, which suggests that the persistence of the push for homeownership can be explained by the classical Gramscian theories of hegemony and dominance by the political elite (Kemeny 1981, 2015). This thesis suggests that dominance by hegemonic elites whose ideology favors a particular tenure type occurs through the mechanism of state control and political power. Thus, the push for homeownership tenure occurs when bourgeois elites—who hold a libertarian ideology and favor homeownership—become hegemonic and gain political control of the coercive state apparatus. Thus, there is a certain level of manipulation of society by elites to expand home ownership. Ronald (2004) offers a useful distinction between Kemeny's "homeownership ideology," as a more Marxist structural theory about the relationship between homeownership and society, and "homeowner ideology or ideologies," which focus on ideological claims about owner-occupied housing.

Kemeny's theory has some explanatory value in that it introduces the role of ideology in ownership tenure and identifies an elite pushing the homeownership agenda. The theory, however, presupposes the existence of a well-defined class structure, political parties, and elites with well-defined ideologies. Clearly defined class societies are less common in Africa (Chabal and Daloz 1999), as are political parties with clearly defined ideologies. Political parties tend to have very similar agendas. What is more, in the context of a poor society with collectivist ideals, it does not make sense for political actors to dangle economic benefits in an attempt to manipulate the poor into homeownership. Even more, given the considerable clout of former colonial powers, donor countries, international financial institutions, and emerging powers, few African countries meet the criteria of a society with a hegemonic, dominant ideological group.

Another theory pertains to restructuring the welfare state through a one-off transfer of an economic asset to the poor. In industrialized societies, it is argued that homeownership expanded because of the restructuring of the welfare state from direct state provision to a one-time transfer of assets—particularly housing—to poorer households (Ronald 2008). The restructuring is explained as a convenient policy for addressing fiscal difficulties encountered by the shrinking state. Indeed, the South African case examined in this book involved transferring a one-off housing subsidy to the poor who were marginalized under apartheid. One might also suggest that the privatization of public rental housing at a 100 percent discount in the Matero case lends credence to this thesis, in that it, too, involved the one-off transfer of an economic asset to the poor. As credible as this view may seem, emphasis on ownership tenure does not reflect the restructuring of the welfare state in Africa; it is an anachronistic argument. Welfare-state building has occurred more recently in Africa, expanding through noncontributory welfare programs such as social cash transfers (Seekings 2017). In fact, welfare-state building is occurring while the state is shrinking in Africa. The South African case was driven more as a response to apartheid injustices than as part of a welfare state policy. Moreover, in Zambia, privatization of council housing was part of a broader neoliberal process by the government, although it has been argued that it was politically motivated by others. The president announced the transfer of housing, not the Ministry of Local Government and Housing. The president also personally went to hand out houses. The transfer occurred in April, some months before the presidential election in November 1996 (Free Library 1997). Thus, a prominent interpretation is that it was more of a patronage act than a welfare state policy act. Also, it may be considered a convenient policy in response to fiscal difficulties encountered by the African state following SAPs, in that it relieved the state of expenditures on maintenance of the large public housing stock. However, city governments have protested the loss a major source of revenue where public housing was privatized (Schlyter 1998, 2002, 2004).

9.5. CONCLUSION

Claims about real property rights are ideological, and they persist ideologically. While important in some contexts, real property rights are not a means of eliminating slum conditions and poverty among the urban poor in the examined cities. Clearly, ownership rights have failed to eradicate poverty among the urban poor—as demonstrated by the large, persistent, and growing scale of slum conditions in sub-Saharan Africa.

Several governments have transferred ownership rights to slum-dwellers, yet slum conditions and poverty persist. Rather than providing a pathway to economic opportunity, the approach represents a literal transfer of responsibility from the state to the urban poor, who lack the financial resources to build adequate housing, let alone withstand the power of distress sales and gentrification. In many cases, they cannot withstand any new forms of vulnerability to their tenure.

The solution to the lack of low-cost, low-income housing will always be more low-cost, low-income housing. With the exception of Kenya, the countries under study here provide a state-led supply of new dwellings. Each country used its own resources for the projects, because World Bank funding demands private sector–led housing provision.

The book makes an empirical contribution to the few existing quantitative studies and the rich qualitative literature that challenges claims about real property rights in African cities. It offers an original contribution of quantitative knowledge on real property rights among low-income housing beneficiaries in Cape Town, Luanda, Lusaka, and Nairobi.

Theoretically, the book explores the limits of the homeowner ideology, and introduces the idea of structured idle capital to expand our understanding of real property rights among the urban poor in Africa. Further, it extends beyond the focus on the economic utility of real property rights to consider various potential human and social capital effects. In future studies of real property rights, scholars should consider analyzing mechanisms through which the homeowner ideology maintains the persistence of claims about real property rights in both theory and international development practice. The role of the homeowner ideology in the persistence of unequal access to real property rights for women in Africa also requires attention.

Ideological claims about the economic effects of real property rights are taken for granted as true, yet they obscure the social and economic reality. It is important to recognize and acknowledge the existence of the homeowner ideology and especially the social production of homeownership tenure preferences. There is a real need to recognize the flawed nature of the taken-for-granted theoretical paradigm guiding solutions to the housing crisis. While real property rights have utility in non-economic aspects of human welfare, they are futile as an economic resource for the urban poor. Considering the recognized flaws in neoliberal market fundamentalism following the 2008 Great Recession, and in light of Sustainable Development Goal 11 and the future urban tipping point, scholars and international financial institutions should conduct research with more institutional reflexivity about the ownership ideology and the social production processes involved in preferences for homeownership as an intervention.

APPENDIX A

Understanding Property Rights and Tenure Security

The most dominant understanding of property rights is utilitarian-based, rooted in the right to decide how a resource is used, alongside the complementary right to exclude another from using it (Alchian 1965; Demsetz 1966). Utilitarian sources of property rights can be seen in the seminal definition offered by Demsetz (1966):

> Property rights are an instrument of society and derive their significance from the fact that they help a man form those expectations which he can reasonably hold in his dealings with others. Those expectations find expression in the laws, customs, and mores of a society. An owner of property rights possesses the consent of fellow men to allow him to act in particular ways. An owner expects the community to prevent others from interfering with his actions, provided that these actions are not prohibited in the specifications of his rights. (347)

In the same vein, Barzel (1997) provides that individual property rights represent the powers to consume an asset, obtain income from it by exchanging it through the mutual ceding of rights, and by alienating it. Thus, one's rights over property allow it to be used as an asset. Thus, property rights not only constitute legal title signifying ownership and provision of security from others' attempts to dispossess, they accord the owner the power to maximize utility.

Property rights are sometimes defined as a bundle—a definition useful for delineating the differences between ownership and usufruct rights in this book. Bundles of rights are the list of rights that individuals and communities possess, including ownership, occupancy, use, development, inheritance, and transfer rights (Durand-Lasserve and Selod 2009). Bundles of rights show how one comes to have legal access to real property, spell out the rules that govern access and utility, and define the social relationships among people based on their access or lack of it. A specific bundle of rights enables individuals and communities to exercise power over real property (Durand-Lasserve and Selod, 2009; Payne 2001, 2004). A full bundle of property rights includes the right to:

- Use the property
- Exclude unauthorized people from using the property
- Control how the property is used
- Derive income from the property
- Protect against illegal expropriation of the property
- Transmit property rights to successors
- Alienate all rights to the property (e.g., through sale), or apportion the property (e.g., subdivide it)
- Alienate a portion of the rights (e.g., lease) and retain them when partially alienated rights lapse (e.g., lease expiry)
- Enjoy property rights into perpetuity, as desired
- Use the asset such that it is not harmful to other members of society
- Surrender the property when withdrawn through lawful action (e.g., insolvency, tax default). (Food and Agriculture Organization, 2002)

Some users may access the entire "bundle" with full use and transfer rights. Other users may be limited (i.e., on such conditions as nature of use, length of use, etc.). Different contexts elicit variations in the nature and content of these rights, in level of confidence that they will be honored, and in level of recognition by public authorities and communities; these factors are contextual and have a direct impact on how land will be used (Durand-Lasserve and Royston 2002).

Tenure rights do not exist as a de jure/de facto dichotomy, as previously thought; rather, they reflect a rights continuum from informal to full ownership (Payne 2001, 2004; van Gelder 2007, 2009). De facto tenure occurs when occupants of usually state-owned land obtain a guarantee of tenure either by living on the land for a duration or by buying guarantees from politicians (Davis 2006). Payne (2001, 2004) identifies a 10-point continuum based on his case studies of more than ten developing countries: (1) pavement dweller,

(2) squatter tenant, (3) squatter owner—in an unregularized settlement, (4) tenant in an unauthorized subdivision, (5) squatter owner—in a regularized settlement, (6) owner—in an unauthorized subdivision, (7) legal owner—with unauthorized construction, (8) tenant with a contract, (9) leaseholder, and (10) freeholder.

Through bundles of rights and the tenure continuum, the proprietor's tenure security or insecurity may be ascertained. In developing countries, people who live in slum conditions in informal settlements are characterized by tenure insecurity. According to the United Nations Centre for Human Settlements (UNCHS), "a person or household can be said to have secure tenure when they are protected from involuntary removal from their land or residence, except in exceptional circumstances, and then only by means of a known and agreed legal procedure, which must itself be objective, equally applicable, contestable and independent" (UN-Habitat, 2003). In simple terms, tenure insecurity refers to the risk of forced eviction (Durand-Lasserve and Selod 2009; Reerink and van Gelder 2010; van Gelder 2007, 2009)—or the lack of protection under national and international law against "the permanent or temporary removal against their will of individuals, families and/or communities from the home and/or the land they occupy" (Durand-Lasserve and Selod 2009). Tenure insecurity is often but not always caused by tenure informality (Durand-Lasserve and Selod 2009).

APPENDIX B

Summary of Claims about the Effects of Freehold and Lessons from the Developing World

Claim	Lessons from the Developing World
Scholarly Knowledge on the Economic Utility of Freehold	
Housing investment	Positive effect, but not a wealth-creating effect
Property value	Increase, but too low to allow access to credit on the formal market
Access to credit	No effect in Africa
Labor market participation	Not examined
Female labor market participation	Not examined
Child labor	Not examined
Home-based business investments	Weak evidence of increase in Langa, Cape Town. No real wealth created from businesses.
Household per capita income	Generally, no effect
Wealth (consumer durables)	Not examined
Belief in capitalism/political ideological inclination	Not examined in Africa
Scholarly Knowledge on Non-Economic Effects of Freehold	
Tenure security	Positive and in some cases negative, but freehold households are more likely to feel secure
Perceived tenure security	Positive effect
School dropouts	Unexamined
Children's education	Unexamined
Teenage pregnancy	Increased in Cape Town
Physical health	Improvement in Nairobi
Psychological health	Unexamined
Chronic diseases	Unexamined

Status attainment	Positive effect on economic status in Mufulira, Zambia, using qualitative evidence
Fertility	Unexamined
Satisfaction with life	Unexamined
Membership in voluntary associations	Unexamined
Volunteerism	Unexamined
Neighborly attachment	Unexamined
Civic participation	Unexamined
Political awareness	Unexamined
Neighborhood satisfaction	Unexamined
Sense of belonging	Unexamined

APPENDIX C

Variable Descriptions for Chapter 8

Variable	Response Categories	Description
Dependent Variables		
Tenure Security		
Fear of Eviction	Scale of 0–10	[Q_34] Looking back at the time you lived in this house or neighborhood, to what extent would you be worried about an eviction or eviction action? (Interviewer: Use a scale from 0 to 10.)
Possibility of Eviction	Scale of 0–10	[Q_35] To what extent would you agree with the statement that "The possibility of being evicted or displaced from this neighborhood is always present"? (Interviewer: Use a scale from 0 to 10.)
Economic Utility		
Credit	Binary	[Q_52] Have you ever used this house as collateral to get loans or credit? (Interviewer: If the answer is no, go to question E.1.)
Employment Status	1. Employed 2. Unemployed 3. Unemployed and job searching in the last 4 weeks 4. Unemployed, but not actively seeking work Changed to binary—1 = employed, 2 = unemployed	[Q_22/Q_22_S] Employment status of the head of household

Income-Generating Activities	Binary	[Q_91] Has the house been used for some income-generating activity? 1 = yes, 2 = no
Household Income	Group average	[Q_25] What is the total monthly income for this family? (Interviewer: If the respondent cannot remember, use the following table of income categories.)
		[Q_26/Q_26_S] What is the total monthly income for this family?
Household Assets/ Wealth	Group average	[Q_61–89] Does anyone in your home own the asset listed below in working/ running conditions?
Physical and Psychological Health		
Self-/Reported Physical Health	Ordinal	[Q_97] On a scale of 0 to 10, how do you describe your health?
Adult BMI	Group average	[Q_95] How tall are you in meters?
		[Q_96] What is your weight in kgs?
Child BMI	Group average	[Q_98] How many children under the age of 18 live in this house? If 0, jump to Q97
		[Q_99] How tall is the first child?
		[Q_100] What is the weight in kgs of your first child?
Fertility	Group average	[Q_39] Of the children who live in this house, how many were born here (in this same house)?

Anxiety Disorder	Scale, group average	[Q_113] On a scale of 0 to 10, how much distress/sadness have you felt in the last two weeks, including today? [Q_114] In the last two weeks, how many times have you felt anxious, nervous, or on edge? 0. Not at all; 1. several days; 2. more days than not; 3. almost every day [Q_115] Over the past two weeks, how many times have you not been able to stop worrying or control your worry? 0. Not at all; 1. several days; 2. more days than not; 3. almost every day [Q_116] In the last two weeks, how many times have you felt down, depressed, or hopeless? 0. Not at all; 1. several days; 2. more days than not; 3. almost every day [Q_117] Over the past two weeks, how many times have you felt little interest or pleasure in doing things? 0. Not at all; 1. several days; 2. more days than not; 3. almost every day [Q_118] Did you suffer a personal loss or misfortune last year? (For example: a loss of employment, disability, divorce, separation, jail time, or the death of someone close to you.)
Social Capital		
Membership in Associations	Scale, group average	[Q_125] You are a member of . . .

Bonding Social Capital	Scale, group average	[Q_147] In this neighborhood there are several people I trust to help solve my problems. (1 = strongly agree, 2 = agree, 3 = neither agrees nor disagrees, 4 = disagree, or 5 = strongly disagrees) [Q_148] In this neighborhood there is someone I can turn to for advice on how to make very important decisions. [Q_149] In this neighborhood there's someone I feel comfortable talking to about intimate personal problems. [Q_150] In this neighborhood, when I'm lonely, there are a lot of people I can talk to. [Q_151] In this neighborhood if I need an emergency loan from Kz20,000, I know someone I can turn to. [Q_152] In this neighborhood, the people I interact with would put their reputation at risk for me. [Q_153] In this neighborhood, the people I interact with would be good work references for me. [Q_154] In this neighborhood, the people I interact with would share their last secret with me. [Q_155] In this neighborhood I know a lot of people to get them to do important things. [Q_156] In this neighborhood, the people I interact with would help me fight an injustice.

Bridging Social Capital	Scale, group average	[Q_158] Interacting with people makes me take an interest in things that happen outside the home or neighborhood. [Q_159] Interacting with people here makes me want to try new things. [Q_160] Interacting with people makes me take an interest in what people different from me are thinking. [Q_161] Talking to people makes me curious about other places in the world. [Q_162] Interacting with people makes me feel like I'm part of a larger community. [Q_163] Interacting with people makes me feel connected to a bigger picture. [Q_164] Interacting with people reminds me that everyone in the world is connected. [Q_165] I am willing to spend time to support the activities of the community at large. [Q_166] Interacting with people gives me new people to talk to. [Q_167] In this neighborhood I interact with new people all the time.
Self-Esteem, Sense of Belonging, and Satisfaction with the Dwelling, the Neighborhood, and Life in General		
Self-Esteem	Ordinal	[Q_186] On a scale of 0 to 10, how much do you feel that you are worthy of respect from others?
Satisfaction with the Dwelling	Ordinal	[Q_183] On a scale of 0 to 10, how satisfied are you with your home?
Satisfaction with the Neighborhood	Ordinal	[Q_184] On a scale of 0 to 10, how satisfied are you with your neighborhood?
Satisfaction with Life in General	Ordinal	[Q_188] On a scale of 0 to 10, how satisfied are you with life in general?

Likelihood of Moving	Ordinal	[Q_185] On a scale of 0 to 10, what's the likelihood of you leaving this neighborhood?

APPENDIX D

Comparison of Paraiso and Zango 1 Households on Key Variables

	Paraiso (n = 214)	Zango 1 (n = 162)	t-statistic
Fear of Eviction	4.17	2.77	3.98***
	(0.24)	(0.25)	
Possibility of Eviction	4.00	2.31	5.04***
	(0.23)	(0.24)	
Dwelling Area	81.53	115.30	2.40**
	(8.56)	(11.53)	
Age	40.14	43.38	−2.47**
	(0.86)	(0.99)	
Sex			
0. Female	35.05	34.57	X = 0.01
1. Male	64.95	65.43	
Education	3.56	5.02	−6.39***
Marital Status			
0. Never married	26.79	26.42	X = 3.98
1. Divorced	1.44	1.26	
2. Separated	11.00	10.06	
3. Lives with partner	43.06	38.36	
4. Married	10.05	16.98	
5. Other	7.66	6.92	
Employment Status			
0. Unemployed and Not Actively Looking	2.43	1.27	X = 3.43
1. Unemployed	45.63	38.85	
2. Unemployed and Searching for Employment	5.83	4.46	
3. Employed	46.12	55.41	

Employment Type			
0. Informal	52.34	30.86	$X = 26.35^{***}$
1. Formal	20.09	43.21	
2. Unemployed	27.57	25.93	
Employed Household Members			
0. No	66.82	51.23	$X = 9.34^{***}$
1. Yes	33.18	48.77	
Number of Rooms	2.59	3.19	−4.56***
Household Income	20,630.96	32530.89	−5.15***

Note: Standard errors in parentheses; *** $p < 0.01$, ** $p < 0.05$, * $p < 0.1$.

REFERENCES

Abrams, C. 1966. *Squatter Settlements: The Problem and the Opportunity*. Washington, DC: Office of International Affairs, Dept. of Housing and Urban Development.

Acemoglu, Daron, and James A. Robinson. 2012. *Why Nations Fail: The Origins of Power, Prosperity, and Poverty*. New York: Crown Business.

Acolin, Arthur. 2020. "Housing Wealth and Consumption Over the 2001–2013 Period: The Role of the Collateral Channel." *Journal of Housing Research* 29, no. 1: 68–88. https://doi.org/10.1080/10527001.2020.1826664

Acolin, Arthur, Xudong An, and Susan M. Wachter. 2022. "Lending Competition, Regulation, and Nontraditional Mortgages." *Real Estate Economics* 50, no. 2: 340–65. https://doi.org/10.1111/1540-6229.12366

Adams, M. 2003. *Land Tenure Policy and Practice in Zambia: Issues Relating to the Development of the Agricultural Sector, Draft Document for DfID*. Oxford: Mokoro.

African Development Bank. 2016. *African Development Report 2015 Growth, Poverty and Inequality Nexus: Overcoming Barriers to Sustainable Development*. Abidjan: African Development Report. https://www.afdb.org/en/documents/document/african-development-report-2015-chapter-1-africas-recent-growth-has-been-widespread-and-persistent-89688

Albertus, Michael. 2020. *Property without Rights: Origins and Consequences of the Property Rights Gap*. Cambridge: Cambridge University Press.

Alchian, Armen A. 1965. "The Basis of Some Recent Advances in the Theory of Management of the Firm." *Journal of Industrial Economics* 14, no. 1: 30–41. https://doi.org/10.2307/2097649

Alchian, Armen A., and Harold Demsetz. 1973. "The Property Right Paradigm." *Journal of Economic History* 33, no. 1: 16–27. https://doi.org/10.1017/S0022050700076403

Aldrich, Brian C., and Ravender S. Sandhu. 1995. *Housing the Urban Poor: Policy and Practice in Developing Countries*. New Delhi: Vistaar.

Alexander, Amanda. 2012. "'A Disciplining Method for Holding Standards Down': How the World Bank Planned Africa's Slums." *Review of African Political Economy* 39, no. 134: 590–613. https://doi.org/10.1080/03056244.2012.738603

Ali, Daniel Ayalew, Klaus Deininger, and Markus Goldstein. 2014. "Environmental and Gender Impacts of Land Tenure Regularization in Africa: Pilot Evidence from Rwanda." *Journal of Development Economics* 110: 262–75. https://doi.org/10.1016/j.jdeveco.2013.12.009

Alston, Lee J., Gary D. Libecap, and Robert Schneider. 1996. "The Determinants and Impact of Property Rights: Land Titles on the Brazilian Frontier." *Journal of Law, Economics, and Organization* 12, no. 1: 25–61. https://doi.org/10.1093/oxfordjournals.jleo.a023360

Amnesty International. 2003. *Angola: Mass Forced Evictions in Luanda: A Call for a Human Rights Based Housing Policy*. London: Amnesty International.

Anderson, Terry L., and Laura E. Huggins. 2009. *Property Rights: A Practical Guide to Freedom and Prosperity*. Stanford, CA: Hoover Institution Press.

Angel, Shlomo, Egypt Brown, Dessislava Dimitrova, David Ehrenberg, Jim Heyes, Peter Kusek, Giancarlo Marchesi, Viany Orozco, Lauren Smith, and Ernesto Vilchis. 2006. *Secure Tenure in Latin America and the Caribbean: Regularization of Informal Urban Settlements in Peru, Mexico and Brazil*. Princeton: Princeton University.

Ashforth, Adam. 1998. "Witchcraft, Violence, and Democracy in the New South Africa [Sorcellerie, Violence et Démocratie Dans La Nouvelle Afrique Du Sud]." *Cahiers d'Études Africaines* 38, no. 150/152: 505–32.

Ashforth, Adam. 2005. *Witchcraft, Violence, and Democracy in South Africa*. Chicago: University of Chicago Press.

Austin, Peter C., Paul Grootendorst, and Geoffrey M. Anderson. 2007. "A Comparison of the Ability of Different Propensity Score Models to Balance Measured Variables between Treated and Untreated Subjects: A Monte Carlo Study." *Statistics in Medicine* 26, no. 4: 734–53. https://doi.org/10.1002/sim.2580

Ayittey, George B. N. 2006. *Africa Unchained: The Blueprint for Africa's Future*. New York: Palgrave Macmillan.

Bah, El-hadj M., Issa Faye, and Zekebweliwai F. Geh. 2018. "The Housing Sector in Africa: Setting the Scene." In *Housing Market Dynamics in Africa*, 1–21. London: Palgrave Macmillan. https://doi.org/10.1057/978-1-137-59792-2_1

Barzel, Yoram. 1997. *Economic Analysis of Property Rights*. 2nd ed. Cambridge: Cambridge University Press.

Berg, Julie, and Wilfried Scharf. 2004. "Crime Statistics in South Africa 1994–2003." *South African Journal of Criminal Justice* 17, no. 1: 57–78.

Berry, Mike. 2014. "Neoliberalism and the City: Or the Failure of Market Fundamentalism." *Housing, Theory and Society* 31, no. 1: 1–18. https://doi.org/10.1080/14036096.2013.839365

Besley, Timothy. 1995. "Property Rights and Investment Incentives: Theory and Evidence from Ghana." *Journal of Political Economy* 103, no. 5: 903–37. https://doi.org/10.1086/262008

Block, Fred, and Margaret R Somers. 2014. *The Power of Market Fundamentalism: Karl*

Polanyi's Critique. Cambridge, MA: Harvard University Press. https://doi.org/10.4159/harvard.9780674416345

Bloom, David E., and Tarun Khanna. 2007. "The Urban Revolution." *Finance and Development* 44, no. 3: 9–14. https://www.imf.org/external/pubs/ft/fandd/2007/09/pdf/bloom.pdf

Blum, Terry C., and Paul William Kingston. 1984. "Homeownership and Social Attachment." *Sociological Perspectives* 27, no. 2: 159–80. https://doi.org/10.2307/1389016

Boudreaux, Karol. 2006. "The Effects of Property Rights in Langa Township, South Africa." *Maercatus Policy Series Policy Comment*, no. 4. https://papers.ssrn.com/sol3/papers.cfm?abstract_id=1027012

Bray, Rachel, I. Gooskens, L. Kahn, S. Moses, and J. Seekings, eds. 2010. *Growing Up in the New South Africa: Childhood and Adolescence in Post-Apartheid Cape Town*. Cape Town: HSRC Press.

Breetzke, Gregory Dennis. 2010. "Modeling Violent Crime Rates: A Test of Social Disorganization in the City of Tshwane, South Africa." *Journal of Criminal Justice* 38, no. 4: 446–52. https://doi.org/10.1016/j.jcrimjus.2010.04.013

Bromley, Daniel W. 1991. *Environment and Economy: Property Rights and Public Policy*. Hoboken, NJ: Blackwell.

Bromley, Daniel W. 2006. *Sufficient Reason: Volitional Pragmatism and the Meaning of Economic Institutions*. Princeton: Princeton University Press.

Bromley, Daniel W. 2008. "Resource Degradation in the African Commons: Accounting for Institutional Decay." *Environment and Development Economics* 13, no. 5: 539–63. https://doi.org/10.1017/S1355770X08004427

Buckley, Robert M., and Jerry Kalarickal, eds. 2006. *Thirty Years of World Bank Shelter Lending: What Have We Learned?* Directions in Development Infrastructure. Washington, DC: World Bank.

Burgin, Angus. 2012. *The Great Persuasion: Reinventing Free Markets since the Depression*. Cambridge, MA: Harvard University Press.

Burn, E. H., and John Cartwright. 2011. *Cheshire and Burn's Modern Law of Real Property*. 18th ed. New York: Oxford University Press.

Butcher, Sian, and Sophie Oldfield. 2009. "De Facto v/s de Jure Home Ownership: Women's Everyday Negotiations in Lusaka and Cape Town." *Feminist Africa* 13 (2009): 45–63.

Cain, Allan. 2004. *Livelihoods and the Informal Economy in Post-War Angola: ISS Monographs*. Pretoria: Institute for Security Studies.

Cain, Allan. 2013. "Luanda's Post-War Land Markets: Reducing Poverty by Promoting Inclusion." *Urban Forum* 24, no. 1: 11–31. https://doi.org/10.1007/s12132-012-9173-x

Calderón, Julio. 2004. "The Formalisation of Property in Peru 2001–2002: The Case of Lima." *Habitat International* 28, no. 2: 289–300. https://doi.org/10.1016/S0197-3975(03)00072-9

Cantuarias, Fernando, and Miguel Delgado. 2004. "Peru's Urban Land Titling Program."

In *Reducing Poverty, Sustaining Growth: What Works, What Doesn't, and Why a Global Exchange for Scaling Up Success*. Washington, DC: World Bank. https://documents1.worldbank.org/curated/en/851001468775839619/pdf/308120PE0Land0Titling01see0also0307591.pdf

Cassidy, John. 2009. *How Markets Fail: The Logic of Economic Calamities*. New York: Picador.

Central Statistics Office Zambia. 2015. "2015 Living Conditions Monitoring Survey Report." Lusaka: Central Statistics Office, Government of the Republic of Zambia. https://prais.unccd.int/sites/default/files/2018-08/LCMS%202015%20Summary%20Report.pdf

Centre for Affordable Housing Finance in Africa. 2022. *2022 Yearbook: Housing Finance in Africa*. Johannesburg: Centre for Affordable Housing Finance in Africa. https://housingfinanceafrica.org/app/uploads/2022/11/2022_English-Yearbook-compressed-FINAL-12-Dec.pdf

Chabal, Patrick, and Jean-Pascal Daloz. 1999. *Africa Works: Disorder as Political Instrument*. Bloomington: Indiana University Press.

Chancel, Lucas, Thomas Piketty, Emmanuel Saez, and Gabriel Zucman. 2022. "World Inequality Report 2022." World Inequality Lab. wir2022.wid.world

Chang, Ha-Joon. 2002. *Kicking Away the Ladder: Development Strategy in Historical Perspective*. London: Anthem.

Choplin, Armelle, and Elizabeth Dessie. 2017. "Titling the Desert: Land Formalization and Tenure (in)Security in Nouakchott (Mauritania)." *Habitat International* 64 (June): 49–58. https://doi.org/10.1016/j.habitatint.2017.04.003

Cleminshaw, Dot. 1985. "From Crossroads to Khayelitsha to . . . ?" *Reality: A Journal of Liberal and Radical Opinion* 18, no. 2: 331–51.

Cook, Gillian P. 1986. "Khayelitsha: Policy Change or Crisis Response?" *Transactions of the Institute of British Geographers* 11, no. 1: 57. https://doi.org/10.2307/622070

Cook, Gillian P. 1992. "Khayelitsha: New Settlement Forms in the Cape Peninsula." In *The Apartheid City and Beyond: Urbanization and Social Change in South Africa*, edited by David M. Smith, 125–35. Johannesburg: Witwatersrand University Press.

Croese, Silvia. 2010. "Angola: Rebuilding by Demolishing." *Pambazuka News*, March 25, 2010. https://www.pambazuka.org/governance/angola-rebuilding-demolishing

Croese, Silvia. 2013. "Post-War State-Led Development at Work in Angola: The Zango Housing Project in Luanda as a Case Study." PhD diss., University of Stellenbosch. https://citeseerx.ist.psu.edu/document?repid=rep1&type=pdf&doi=d71aa5c4762ee9ba49636869c48829030ee927cd

Czaja, Ronald, Johnny Blair, and Edward Blair. 2014. *Designing Surveys: A Guide to Decisions and Procedures*. 3rd ed. Los Angeles: Sage.

Davies, Glynn, Monty Narsoo, and Mary Tomlinson R. 2007. "Are Hernando de Soto's Views Appropriate to South Africa?" In *Are Hernando de Soto's Views Appropriate to South Africa? Papers Delivered at a Colloquium Hosted in June 2006 by the*

Graduate School of Public and Development Management of the University of the Witwatersrand, and the Development Bank of Southern Africa, 7–12. Johannesburg: University of the Witwatersrand.

Davis, Mike. 2006. *Planet of Slums*. London: Verso.

Deininger, Klaus W. 2003. *Land Policies for Growth and Poverty Reduction*. A World Bank Policy Research Report. Oxford: Oxford University Press.

Deininger, Klaus W., and Daniel Ayalew Ali. 2022. "How Urban Land Titling and Registry Reform Affect Land and Credit Markets: Evidence from Lesotho." Policy Research Working Paper 10043. Washington, DC: World Bank. http://hdl.handle.net/10986/37458

Demsetz, Harold. 1966. "Some Aspects of Property Rights." *Journal of Law and Economics* 9 (October): 61–70. https://doi.org/10.1086/466619

de Soto, Hernando. 2003. *The Mystery of Capital: Why Capitalism Triumphs in the West and Fails Everywhere Else*. New York: Basic Books.

Di Tella, R., S. Galiant, and E. Schargrodsky. 2007. "The Formation of Beliefs: Evidence from the Allocation of Land Titles to Squatters." *Quarterly Journal of Economics* 122, no. 1: 209–41. https://doi.org/10.1162/qjec.122.1.209

Di Tella, Rafael, Sebastian Galiani, and Ernesto Schargrodsky. 2012. "Reality Versus Propaganda in the Formation of Beliefs about Privatization." *Journal of Public Economics* 96, no. 5–6: 553–67. https://doi.org/10.1016/j.jpubeco.2011.11.006

Doebele, W. 1978. "Concepts of Urban Land Tenure." In *Urban Land Policy: Issues and Opportunities*. Washington, DC: World Bank and Oxford University Press.

Domeher, Daniel, and Raymond Abdulai. 2012. "Access to Credit in the Developing World: Does Land Registration Matter?" *Third World Quarterly* 33 (1): 161–75. https://doi.org/10.1080/01436597.2012.627254

Dowall, David. 1998. "Making Urban Land Markets Work: Issues and Policy Option." Washington, DC: World Bank. http://documents.worldbank.org/curated/en/162861468765004717/Urban-land-policy-issues-and-opportunities

Dowall, David, and Michael Leaf. 1991. "The Price of Land for Housing in Jakarta." *Urban Studies* 28, no. 5: 707–22. https://doi.org/10.1080/00420989120080881

Dower, Paul, and Elizabeth Potamites. 2005. "Signalling Creditworthiness: Land Titles, Banking Practices and Access to Formal Credit in Indonesia." *Bulletin of Indonesian Economic Studies* 50, no. 3: 24–27. https://doi.org/10.1080/00074918.2014.980376

Durand-Lasserve, Alain, Edesio Fernandes, Geoffrey Payne, and Carole Rakodi. 2007. *Social and Economic Impacts of Land Titling Programmes in Urban and Peri-Urban Areas: A Review of the Literature*. Washington, DC: World Bank.

Durand-Lasserve, Alain, and Lauren Royston, eds. 2002. *Holding Their Ground: Secure Land Tenure for the Urban Poor in Developing Countries*. London: Earthscan Publications.

Durand-Lasserve, Alain, and Harris Selod. 2009. "The Formalization of Urban Land Tenure in Developing Countries." In *Urban Land Markets*, edited by Somik V. Lall,

Mila Freire, Belinda Yuen, Robin Rajack, and Jean-Jacques Helluin, 101–32. Dordrecht: Springer Netherlands. https://doi.org/10.1007/978-1-4020-8862-9_5

Dyzenhaus, Alex. 2021. "Patronage or Policy? The Politics of Property Rights Formalization in Kenya." *World Development* 146 (October): 105580. https://doi.org/10.1016/j.worlddev.2021.105580

The Economist. 2020. "Parcels Plots and Power: The Quest for Secure Property Rights in Africa." September 12. https://www.economist.com/middle-east-and-africa/2020/09/12/the-quest-for-secure-property-rights-in-africa

Emmet, Tony. 2003. "Social Disorganisation, Social Capital and Violence Prevention in South Africa: Original Contribution." *African Safety Promotion* 1, no. 2: 4–18.

Engels, Frederich. 2004. *The Origin of the Family, Private Property and the State*. Chippendale, New South Wales, Australia: Resistance Books.

Fanon, Frantz, and Richard Philcox. 2004. *The Wretched of the Earth: Frantz Fanon*, translated by Richard Philcox. New York: Grove Press.

Fauveaud, Gabriel. 2020. "The New Frontiers of Housing Financialization in Phnom Penh, Cambodia: The Condominium Boom and the Foreignization of Housing Markets in the Global South." *Housing Policy Debate* 30, no. 4: 661–79. https://doi.org/10.1080/10511482.2020.1714692

Feder, Gershon, and Raymond Noronha. 1987. "Land Rights Systems and Agricultural Development in Sub-Saharan Africa." *World Bank Research Observer* 2, no. 2: 143–69.

Field, E. 2007. "Entitled to Work: Urban Property Rights and Labor Supply in Peru." *Quarterly Journal of Economics* 122, no. 4: 1561–1602. https://doi.org/10.1162/qjec.2007.122.4.1561

Field, Erica. 2003a. "Fertility Responses to Urban Land Titling Programs: Roles of Ownership Security and the Distribution of Household Assets." Harvard University. https://scholar.harvard.edu/field/publications/fertility-responses-land-titling-roles-ownership-security-and-distribution-househ

Field, Erica. 2003b. "Property Rights, Community Public Goods, and Household Time Allocation in Urban Squatter Communities: Evidence from Peru." *William and Mary Law Review* 45, no. 3: 837–87.

Field, Erica. 2005. "Property Rights and Investment in Urban Slums." *Journal of the European Economic Association* 3, no. 2/3: 279–90.

Field, Erica, and Maximo Torero. 2006. "Do Property Titles Increase Credit Access Among the Urban Poor? Evidence from a Nationwide Titling Program." https://scholar.harvard.edu/files/field/files/fieldtorerocs.pdf

Flores-Fernandez, Rosa Amelia, and Bernard Calas. 2011. "The Kibera Soweto East Project in Nairobi." *Les Cahiers d'Afrique de LEst* 44 (September): 129–45. https://doi.org/10.4000/eastafrica.536

Food and Agriculture Organization. 2002. "FAO Land Tenure Studies: Land Tenure and Rural Development." Rome: FAO Rural Development Division.

Free Library. 1997. "Housing Policy in Zambia: Chiluba Doles Out Houses." *Free Library*. https://www.thefreelibrary.com/Chiluba+doles+out+houses.-a020326613

Friedman, Jeremy Scott. 2021. *Ripe for Revolution: Building Socialism in the Third World*. Cambridge, MA: Harvard University Press.

Friedman, Joseph, Emmanuel Jimenez, and Stephen K. Mayo. 1988. "The Demand for Tenure Security in Developing Countries." *Journal of Development Economics* 29, no. 2: 185–98. https://doi.org/10.1016/0304-3878(88)90034-X

Galiani, Sebastian, and Ernesto Schargrodsky. 2004. "Effects of Land Titling on Child Health." *Economics and Human Biology* 2, no. 3: 353–72. https://doi.org/10.1016/j.ehb.2004.10.003

Galiani, Sebastian, and Ernesto Schargrodsky. 2010. "Property Rights for the Poor: Effects of Land Titling." *Journal of Public Economics* 94, no. 9–10: 700–29. https://doi.org/10.1016/j.jpubeco.2010.06.002

Gandelman, Néstor. 2010. "Property Rights and Chronic Diseases: Evidence from a Natural Experiment in Montevideo, Uruguay 1990–2006." *Economics and Human Biology* 8, no. 2: 159–67. https://doi.org/10.1016/j.ehb.2010.05.005

Gastrow, Claudia. 2017a. "Cement Citizens: Housing, Demolition and Political Belonging in Luanda, Angola." *Citizenship Studies* 21, no. 2: 224–39. https://doi.org/10.1080/13621025.2017.1279795

Gastrow, Claudia. 2017b. "Aesthetic Dissent: Urban Redevelopment and Political Belonging in Luanda, Angola." *Antipode* 49, no. 2: 377–96. https://doi.org/10.1111/anti.12276

Gastrow, Peter, and Mark Shaw. 2001. "In Search of Safety: Police Transformation and Public Responses in South Africa." *Daedalus* 130, no. 1: 259–75.

Gilbert, Alan. 2000. "Financing Self-Help Housing: Evidence from Bogotá, Colombia." *International Planning Studies* 5, no. 2: 165–90. https://doi.org/10.1080/13563470050020176

Gilbert, Alan. 2004. "Helping the Poor through Housing Subsidies: Lessons from Chile, Colombia and South Africa." *Habitat International* 28, no. 1: 13–40. https://doi.org/10.1016/S0197-3975(02)00070-X

Gilbert, Alan. 2012. "De Soto's *The Mystery of Capital*: Reflections on the Book's Public Impact." *International Development Planning Review* 34, no. 3: v–xviii. https://doi.org/10.3828/idpr.2012.15

Glynn, Sarah, ed. 2009. *Where the Other Half Lives: Lower Income Housing in a Neoliberal World*. London: Pluto Press.

Gontsana, Mary-Anne. 2020. "Housing Backlog Exceeds Half a Million in Western Cape." *Daily Maverick*, March 26, 2020. https://www.dailymaverick.co.za/article/2020-03-26-housing-backlog-exceeds-half-a-million-in-western-cape/

Government of the Republic of Zambia. 1996a. *Circular Number 2 of the Ministry of Local Government and Housing: Revised Procedures for Sale of Council Houses*. Lusaka: Ministry of Local Government and Housing.

Government of the Republic of Zambia. 1996b. *Zambia National Housing Policy*. Lusaka: Ministry of Local Government and Housing.

Government of the Republic of Zambia. 2011. "Lands Newsletter." Lusaka: Ministry of Lands, Natural Resources and Environmental Protection.

Government of the Republic of Zambia. 2020. *National Housing Policy 2020–2024: Affordable and Decent Housing for All by 2030*. Lusaka: Ministry of Housing and Infrastructure Development.

Guo, Shenyang, and Mark W Fraser. 2015. *Propensity Score Analysis: Statistical Methods and Applications*. Los Angeles: Sage.

Gurney, Craig M. 1999a. "Pride and Prejudice: Discourses of Normalisation in Public and Private Accounts of Home Ownership." *Housing Studies* 14, no. 2: 163–83. https://doi.org/10.1080/02673039982902

Gurney, Craig M. 1999b. "Lowering the Drawbridge: A Case Study of Analogy and Metaphor in the Social Construction of Home-Ownership." *Urban Studies* 36, no. 10: 1705–22. https://doi.org/10.1080/0042098992782

Hailu, Ziade, Isaac N. Nkote, and John C. Munene. 2017. "Property Rights and Investment: The Mediating Effect of Contract Enforcement." *International Journal of Law and Management* 59, no. 1: 21–34. https://doi.org/10.1108/IJLMA-06-2015-0031

Hailu, Ziade, and Gerrit Rooks. 2016. "Property Rights and Owner-Occupied Housing Investment in Urban Ethiopia." *Property Management* 34, no. 4: 345–57. https://doi .org/10.1108/PM-08-2015-0038

Hansen, Karen Tranberg. 1982. "Lusaka's Squatters: Past and Present." *African Studies Review* 25, no. 2/3: 117–36. https://doi.org/10.2307/524213

Huchzermeyer, Marie. 2008. "Slum Upgrading in Nairobi within the Housing and Basic Services Market: A Housing Rights Concern." *Journal of Asian and African Studies* 43, no. 1: 19–39. https://doi.org/10.1177/0021909607085586

Hydén, Göran. 2013. *African Politics in Comparative Perspective*. 2nd ed. Cambridge: Cambridge University Press.

International Labor Organization, ed. 2018. *Women and Men in the Informal Economy: A Statistical Picture*. 3rd ed. Geneva: International Labour Office.

Jacobs, Jane. 1992. *The Death and Life of Great American Cities*. New York: Vintage Books.

Jenkins, Paul, Paul Robson, and Allan Cain. 2002. "City Profile: Luanda." *Cities* 19, no. 2: 139–50. https://doi.org/10.1016/S0264-2751(02)00010-0

Jewkes, Rachel, and Naeema Abrahams. 2002. "The Epidemiology of Rape and Sexual Coercion in South Africa: An Overview." *Social Science & Medicine* 55, no. 7: 1231–44. https://doi.org/10.1016/S0277-9536(01)00242-8

Jo, Tae-Hee, Lynne Chester, and Mary C. King. 2012. "Beyond Market-fundamentalist Economics: An Agenda for Heterodox Economics to Change the Dominant Narrative." *On the Horizon* 20, no. 3: 155–63. https://doi.org/10.1108/10748121211256856

Jones, Branwen Gruffydd. 2012. "'Bankable Slums': The Global Politics of Slum Upgrading." *Third World Quarterly* 33, no. 5: 769–89. https://doi.org/10.1080/01436597.2012.679027

Kalabamu, Faustin Tirwirukwa. 2019. "Land Tenure Reforms and Persistence of Land Conflicts in Sub-Saharan Africa: The Case of Botswana." *Land Use Policy* 81 (February): 337–45. https://doi.org/10.1016/j.landusepol.2018.11.002

Kemeny, Jim. 1981. *The Myth of Home-Ownership: Private versus Public Choices in Housing Tenure.* London: Routledge.

Kemeny, Jim. 2015. *Housing and Social Theory.* New York: Routledge.

Kenya National Commission on Human Rights. 2015. *Allocation of Housing Units in Kibera Soweto Zone "A" Redevelopment Project under the Kenya Slum Upgrading Programme: A Report Submitted to the High Court of Kenya (Nairobi) by the Kenya National Commission on Human Rights.* Nairobi: KNCHR.

Kingwill, Rosalie, Ben Cousins, Tessa Cousins, Donna Hornby, Lauren Royston, and Warren Smit. 2006. *Mysteries and Myths: De Soto, Property and Poverty in South Africa.* Johannesburg: International Institute for Environment and Development.

Klein, Naomi. 2008. *The Shock Doctrine: The Rise of Disaster Capitalism.* New York: Picador

Kohli, Divyani, Rohan Bennett, Christian Lemmen, Asiama Kwabena, Andres Morales, Andre Pinheiro, Robert Wayumba, and Jaap Zevenbergen. 2017. "A Quantitative Comparison of Completely Visible Cadastral Parcels Using Satellite Images: A Step towards Automation." Conference paper under GIG Working Week 2017, From Digitalisation to Augmented Reality. Helsinki.

Konadu-Agyemang, Kwadwo. 1990. "Home Ownership in Urban West Africa: A Mirage of Increasing Proportions." *Ekistics* 57, no. 342/343: 205–15.

Konadu-Agyemang, Kwadwo. 2001. *The Political Economy of Housing and Urban Development in Africa: Ghana's Experience from Colonial Times to 1998.* Westport: Praeger.

Kongela, Sophia Marcian, and Florencia Bahati Didas. 2021. "Assessing Co-Titling Desirability in Matrimonial Properties in Urban Land Ownership in Tanzania." *Journal of African Real Estate Research* 6, no. 1: 19–42. https://doi.org/10.15641/jarer.v6i1.949

Kuyasa Fund. 2022. "The Kuyasa Fund." http://www.thekuyasafund.co.za

Lanjouw, Jean O., and Philip I. Levy. 2002. "Untitled: A Study of Formal and Informal Property Rights in Urban Ecuador." *Economic Journal* 112, no. 482: 986–1019. https://doi.org/10.1111/1468-0297.00067

Last, John M., ed. 2001. *A Dictionary of Epidemiology.* 4th ed. New York: Oxford University Press.

Lee, Rebekah. 2005. "Reconstructing 'Home' in Apartheid Cape Town: African Women and the Process of Settlement." *Journal of Southern African Studies* 31, no. 3: 611–30. https://doi.org/10.1080/03057070500202998

Lemanski, Charlotte. 2011. "Moving Up the Ladder or Stuck on the Bottom Rung? Homeownership as a Solution to Poverty in South Africa?" *International Journal of Urban and Regional Research* 35, no. 1: 57–77. https://doi.org/10.1111/j.1468-2427.2010.00945.x

Libecap, Gary D. 1989. *Contracting for Property Rights.* Political Economy of Institutions and Decisions. Cambridge: Cambridge University Press.

Lusaka City Council. 2010. "LCC Embarks on Registration of Houses in Kanyama Compound." www.lcc.gov.zm/index.php?option=com_content&view=article&id=23:platform

Mamdani, Mahmood. 2018. *Citizen and Subject: Contemporary Africa and the Legacy of Late Colonialism*. Princeton: Princeton University Press.

McGregor, Ross W. 2014. *Kenya from Within: A Short Political History*. New York: Routledge.

Mdewu, M. 2004. "Housing in Khayelitsha." *Cape Argus Newspaper*, March 9, 2004.

Meagher, Kate. 2019. "Reflections of an Engaged Economist: An Interview with Thandika Mkandawire." *Development and Change* 50, no. 2: 511–41. https://doi.org/10.1111/dech.12481

Meintjes, H. 2000. "Poverty, Possessions and Proper Living." MA diss., University of Cape Town, South Africa.

Meinzen-Dick, Ruth, and Esther Mwangi. 2009. "Cutting the Web of Interests: Pitfalls of Formalizing Property Rights." *Land Use Policy* 26, no. 1: 36–43. https://doi.org/10.1016/j.landusepol.2007.06.003

Méndez, Fabio. 2006. "The Value of Legal Housing Titles: An Empirical Study." *Journal of Housing Economics* 15, no. 2: 143–55. https://doi.org/10.1016/j.jhe.2006.08.002

Meredith, Martin. 2011. *The Fate of Africa: A History of the Continent since Independence*. New York: Public Affairs.

Meredith, Thomas, and Melanie MacDonald. 2017. "Community-Supported Slum-Upgrading: Innovations from Kibera, Nairobi, Kenya." *Habitat International* 60 (February): 1–9. https://doi.org/10.1016/j.habitatint.2016.12.003

Messer, Lynne C. 2008. "Natural Experiment." In *Encyclopedia of Epidemiology*, edited by Sarah Boslaugh. Los Angeles: Sage.

Mills, Sophie. 2007. "The Kuyasa Fund: Housing Microcredit in South Africa." *Environment and Urbanization* 19, no. 2: 457–69. https://doi.org/10.1177/0956247807082825

Mitra, Shreya, Joe Mulligan, Janpeter Schilling, Jamilla Harper, Janani Vivekananda, and Lisa Krause. 2017. "Developing Risk or Resilience? Effects of Slum Upgrading on the Social Contract and Social Cohesion in Kibera, Nairobi." *Environment and Urbanization* 29, no. 1: 103–22. https://doi.org/10.1177/0956247816689218

Mitullah, Winnie. 2003. "The Case of Nairobi, Kenya." In *Urban Slums Reports*, 1–22. Nairobi: UN-Habitat.

Moser, Caroline, and Andrew Felton. 2007. "Intergenerational Asset Accumulation and Poverty Reduction in Guayaquil Ecuador (1978–2004)." In *Reducing Global Poverty: The Case for Asset Accumulation*, edited by Caroline Moser. Washington, DC: Brookings Institution.

Moss, Todd, and Danielle Resnick. 2018. *African Development: Making Sense of the Issues and Actors*. 3rd ed. Boulder: Lynne Rienner.

Moura, Mauricio José Serpa Barros, and Rodrigo D. Losso da Silveira Bueno. 2009. "How

Land Title Affects Income." Anais do XXXVII Encontro Nacional de Economia (Proceedings of the 37th Brazilian Economics Meeting) from ANPEC—Associação Nacional dos Centros de pós-graduação em Economia (Brazilian Association of Graduate Programs in Economics).

Mulenga, C. L. 2003. "The Case of Lusaka Zambia." In *Understanding Slums: Case Studies for the Global Report on Human Settlements*. Nairobi: UN-Habitat.

Mususa, Patience. 2010. "'Getting By': Life on the Copperbelt After the Privatisation of the Zambia Consolidated Copper Mines." *Social Dynamics* 36, no. 2: 380–94. https://doi.org/10.1080/02533951003790546

Mususa, Patience. 2012. "Topping Up: Life Amidst Hardship and Death on the Copperbelt." *African Studies* 71, no. 2: 304–22. https://doi.org/10.1080/00020184.2012.702971

Muyeba, Singumbe. 2016. "The Effects of State-Subsidised Housing on Poverty in Cape Town." *Development Southern Africa* 33, no. 5: 628–43. https://doi.org/10.1080/0376835X.2016.1203757

Muyeba, Singumbe. 2018. "Does Strength of Tenure Rights among the Urban Poor Improve Household Economies? Contrasting Matero and George in Lusaka City." *International Journal of Urban Sustainable Development* 10, no. 1: 16–31. https://doi.org/10.1080/19463138.2017.1383257

Muyeba, Singumbe, and Jeremy Seekings. 2011. "Race, Attitudes and Behaviour in Racially-Mixed, Low-Income Neighbourhoods in Cape Town, South Africa." *Current Sociology* 59, no. 5: 655–71. https://doi.org/10.1177/0011392111408679

Muyeba, Singumbe, and Jeremy Seekings. 2012. "Homeownership, Privacy and Neighbourly Relations in Poor Urban Neighbourhoods in Cape Town, South Africa." *South African Review of Sociology* 43, no. 3: 41–63. https://doi.org/10.1080/21528586.2012.727546

Mwingyine, Darius Tuoninuo, Millicent Awialie Akaateba, and Wolfram Laube. 2020. "Elite Capture of Land Commodification and Land Use Planning in Peri-Urban Northern Ghana." In *"Civilizing" Resource Investments and Extractivism: Societal Negotiations and the Role of Law*, edited by Wolfram Laube and Aline Rose Barbosa Pereira, 185–208. Zürich Wien: LIT.

Neimark, Benjamin, Camilla Toulmin, and Simon Batterbury. 2018. "Peri-Urban Land Grabbing? Dilemmas of Formalising Tenure and Land Acquisitions around the Cities of Bamako and Ségou, Mali." *Journal of Land Use Science* 13, no. 3: 319–24. https://doi.org/10.1080/1747423X.2018.1499831

Neuwirth, Robert. 2006. *Shadow Cities: A Billion Squatters, a New Urban World*. London: Routledge.

Nina, Daniel. 2000. "Dirty Harry Is Back: Vigilantism in South Africa: The (Re)Emergence of the 'Good' and 'Bad' Community." *African Security Review* 9, no. 1: 18–28. https://doi.org/10.1080/10246029.2000.9628033

North, Douglass C. 1990. *Institutions, Institutional Change, and Economic Performance.*

The Political Economy of Institutions and Decisions. Cambridge: Cambridge University Press.

Obeng-Odoom, Franklin. 2020. *Property, Institutions, and Social Stratification in Africa*. Cambridge Studies in Stratification Economics. Cambridge: Cambridge University Press.

Obeng-Odoom, Franklin. 2021. *The Commons in an Age of Uncertainty: Decolonizing Nature, Economy, and Society*. Toronto: University of Toronto Press.

Oldfield, Sophie. 2000. "The Centrality of Community Capacity in State Low-income Housing Provision in Cape Town, South Africa." *International Journal of Urban and Regional Research* 24, no. 4: 858–72. https://doi.org/10.1111/1468-2427.00283

Oldfield, Sophie. 2004. "Urban Networks, Community Organising and Race: An Analysis of Racial Integration in a Desegregated South African Neighbourhood." *Geoforum* 35, no. 2: 189–201. https://doi.org/10.1016/j.geoforum.2003.08.006

O'Sullivan, Michael. 2017. *Gender and Property Rights in Sub-Saharan Africa: A Review of Constraints and Effective Interventions*. Policy Research Working Paper 8250. Washington, DC: World Bank.

Palmer, Robin. 2000. "Land Tenure Insecurity on the Zambian Copperbelt, 1998: Anyone Going Back to the Land?" *Social Dynamics* 26, no. 2: 154–70. https://doi.org/10.1080/02533950008458698

Parnell, Susan, and Edgar Pieterse, eds. 2014. *Africa's Urban Revolution*. London: Zed Books.

Payne, Geoffrey. 2001. "Urban Land Tenure Policy Options: Titles or Rights?" *Habitat International* 25, no. 3: 415–29. https://doi.org/10.1016/S0197-3975(01)00014-5

Payne, Geoffrey. 2004. "Land Tenure and Property Rights: An Introduction." *Habitat International* 28, no. 2: 167–79. https://doi.org/10.1016/S0197-3975(03)00066-3

Payne, Geoffrey, Alain Durand-Lasserve, and Carole Rakodi. 2009. "The Limits of Land Titling and Home Ownership." *Environment and Urbanization* 21, no. 2: 443–62. https://doi.org/10.1177/0956247809344364

Pecha, Camilo J., and Inder J. Ruprah. 2010. "Are Homeowners Better but More Conservative Citizens? A Meta Impact Evaluation for Latin American Countries." Washington, DC: World Bank. https://web.worldbank.org/archive/website01542/WEB/IMAGES/PAPER_BE.PDF

Pieterse, Edgar. 2011. "Rethinking African Urbanism from the Slum." *Power* 26, no. 14: 40–48.

Piza, Caio, and Mauricio José Serpa Barros de Moura. 2016. "The Effect of a Land Titling Programme on Households' Access to Credit." *Journal of Development Effectiveness* 8, no. 1: 129–55. https://doi.org/10.1080/19439342.2015.1057859

Poggio, T. 2006. "Different Patterns of Home Ownership in Europe." In *ENHR, Home Ownership and Globalisation Working Group*. Delft, the Netherlands: Delft University of Technology.

Polanyi, Karl. 2001. *The Great Transformation: The Political and Economic Origins of Our Time*. Boston: Beacon Press.

Porio, Emma, and Christine Crisol. 2004. "Property Rights, Security of Tenure and the Urban Poor in Metro Manila." *Habitat International* 28, no. 2: 203–19. https://doi.org/10.1016/S0197-3975(03)00068-7

Porteous, David. 2005. "Setting the Context: South Africa." *Housing Finance International* 20, no. 1: 34–39.

Potts, Deborah Helen. 2020. *Broken Cities inside the Global Housing Crisis.* London: Zed Books.

Prassana, Mora Mudalige Anura. 2007. "Impact of Secure Land Tenure on Income Generating Activities in Urban Informal Settlements: A Case of Dar Es Salaam, Tanzania." MS diss., International Institute for Geo-Information Science and Earth Observation, Enschede. https://webapps.itc.utwente.nl/librarywww/papers_2007/msc/upla/mudalige.pdf

Prindex. 2019. "Global Perceptions of Urban Land Tenure Security: Evidence from 33 Countries." London: Prindex. https://www.prindex.net/reports/global-perceptions-urban-land-tenure-security-report-evidence-33-countries/

Rakodi, Carole, and Ann Schlyter. 1981. *Upgrading in Lusaka: Participation and Physical Changes.* Stockholm: National Swedish Institute for Building Research.

Ramphele, Mamphela. 2002. *Steering by the Stars: Being Young in South Africa.* Cape Town: Tafelberg.

Ray, Debraj. 1998. *Development Economics.* Princeton: Princeton University Press.

Reerink, Gustaaf, and Jean-Louis van Gelder. 2010. "Land Titling, Perceived Tenure Security, and Housing Consolidation in the Kampongs of Bandung, Indonesia." *Habitat International* 34, no. 1: 78–85. https://doi.org/10.1016/j.habitatint.2009.07.002

Republic of South Africa. 1994. "White Paper on Housing 1994." Pretoria: Department of Human Settlements.

Republic of South Africa. 1996. "Growth, Employment and Redistribution: A Macroeconomic Strategy." Pretoria: Department of Finance, Republic of South Africa.

Republic of South Africa. 2013. "Delivery of Serviced Sites and Houses/Units from the Provincial Human Settlements Development Grant (HSDG)." Pretoria: Department of Human Settlements.

Riano, Yvonne. 2001. *Informal Land Use in Peripheral Barrios of Quito: Planning Problem, Development Obstacle or Poverty Alleviation?* https://www.researchgate.net/publication/239607856_Informal_Land_Use_in_Peripheral_Barrios_of_Quito_Planning_Problem_Development_Obstacle_or_Poverty_Alleviation

Robinson, James A. 2010. "Property Rights and African Poverty." *Defining Ideas: A Hoover Institution Journal.* March 15, 2010. https://www.hoover.org/research/property-rights-and-african-poverty

Rodney, Walter, Angela Y. Davis, Vincent Harding, Robert A. Hill, William Strickland, and Abdul Rahman Mohamed Babu. 2018. *How Europe Underdeveloped Africa.* Brooklyn: Verso.

Rohe, William M., and Michael A. Stegman. 1994. "The Effects of Homeownership: On the Self-Esteem, Perceived Control and Life Satisfaction of Low-Income People." *Journal of the American Planning Association* 60, no. 2: 173–84. https://doi.org/10.1080/01944369408975571

Rohe, William M., and Leslie S. Stewart. 1996. "Homeownership and Neighborhood Stability." *Housing Policy Debate* 7, no. 1: 37–81. https://doi.org/10.1080/10511482.1996.9521213

Rohe, William M., Shannon van Zandt, and George McCarthy. 2013. "The Social Benefits and Costs of Homeownership." In *The Affordable Housing Reader*, edited by J. Rosie Tighe and Elizabeth J. Mueller, 145–92. London: Routledge.

Ronald, Richard. 2004. "Home Ownership, Ideology and Diversity: Re-evaluating Concepts of Housing Ideology in the Case of Japan." *Housing, Theory and Society* 21, no. 2: 49–64. https://doi.org/10.1080/14036090410033295

Ronald, Richard. 2007. "The Social Production of Homeownership: Towards a Typology." In *ENHR International Conference on Sustainable Urban Areas*. Rotterdam: European Network of Housing Research.

Ronald, Richard. 2008. *The Ideology of Home Ownership*. London: Palgrave Macmillan. https://doi.org/10.1057/9780230582286

Rose, S. 2006. "Tenure Security and Household Labour Decisions: The Effect of Property Titling on Labour Force Participation in Urban Ecuador." MA thesis, Georgetown University, Washington, DC.

Rosenbaum, Paul R., and Donald B. Rubin. 1984. "Reducing Bias in Observational Studies Using Subclassification on the Propensity Score." *Journal of the American Statistical Association* 79, no. 87: 516–24. https://doi.org/10.1080/01621459.1984.10478078

Ross, Fiona C. 2005a. "Urban Development and Social Contingency: A Case Study of Urban Relocation in the Western Cape, South Africa." *Africa Today* 51, no. 4: 19–31.

Ross, Fiona C. 2005b. "Model Communities and Respectable Residents? Home and Housing in a Low-Income Residential Estate in the Western Cape, South Africa." *Journal of Southern African Studies* 31, no. 3: 631–48. https://doi.org/10.1080/03057070500203038

Ross, Fiona C. 2021. *Raw Life, New Hope: Decency, Housing and Everyday Life in a Post-Apartheid Community*. Claremont, South Africa: UCT Press.

Rubin, Donald B. 2006. *Matched Sampling for Causal Effects*. Cambridge: Cambridge University Press.

Rust, Kecia. 2007. "Supporting the Housing Asset Triangle: South Africa's Real Housing Challenge." In *Are Hernando de Soto's Views Appropriate to South Africa? Papers Delivered at a Colloquium Hosted in June 2006 by the Graduate School of Public and Development of the University of the Witwatersrand, and the Development Bank of Southern Africa*. Johannesburg: University of the Witwatersrand, Graduate School of Public and Development Management.

Saunders, Peter. 2022. *A Nation of Home Owners: Housing Policy and Home Ownership*. Oxfordshire: Routledge.

Schlyter, Ann. 1998. "Housing Policy in Zambia." *Habitat International* 22, no. 3: 259–71. https://doi.org/10.1016/S0197-3975(98)00010-1

Schlyter, Ann. 2002. *Empowered with Ownership: Privatisation of Housing in Lusaka, Zambia*. Maseru: National University of Lesotho, Institute for Southern African Studies.

Schlyter, Ann. 2004. *Privatization of Council Housing in Lusaka, Zambia: Our Common Estate*. London: RICS Foundation.

Schramm, Sophie. 2017. "People's Room for Manoeuvre in a Fragmented City: State Housing in Kibera, Nairobi." *Transformation: Critical Perspectives on Southern Africa* 93, no. 1: 116–41. https://doi.org/10.1353/trn.2017.0005

Seekings, Jeremy. 2008a. *Beyond "Fluidity". Kinship and Households as Social Projects*. CSSR Working Paper no. 237. Cape Town: Center for Social Science Research.

Seekings, Jeremy. 2008b. "The Continuing Salience of Race: Discrimination and Diversity in South Africa." *Journal of Contemporary African Studies* 26, no. 1: 1–25. https://doi.org/10.1080/02589000701782612

Seekings, Jeremy. 2017. "State Capacity and the Construction of Pro-Poor Welfare States in the 'Developing' World." In *States in the Developing World*, edited by Miguel Angel Centeno, Atul Kohli, Deborah J. Yashar, and Dinsha Mistree, 363–79. Cambridge: Cambridge University Press.

Seekings, Jeremy, Johan Graaff, and P. Joubert. 1990. *Survey of Residential and Migration Histories of Residents of the Shack Areas of Khayelitsha*. Stellenbosch: Research Unit for Sociology of Development, University of Stellenbosch.

Seekings, Jeremy, Tracy Jooste, Singumbe Muyeba, Marius Coqui, and Margo Russell. 2010. *The Social Consequences of Established "Mixed" Neighbourhoods: Does the Mechanism for Selecting Beneficiaries for Low-Income Housing Projects Affect the Quality of the Ensuing "Community" and the Likelihood of Violence Conflict?* Cape Town: Centre for Social Science Research, University of Cape Town.

Shaanan, Joseph. 2017. *America's Free Market Myths*. Cham: Palgrave Macmillan.

Shioda, Kayoko, Leonard Cosmas, Allan Audi, Nicole Gregoricus, Jan Vinjé, Umesh D. Parashar, Joel M. Montgomery, Daniel R. Feikin, Robert F. Breiman, and Aron J. Hall. 2016. "Population-Based Incidence Rates of Diarrheal Disease Associated with Norovirus, Sapovirus, and Astrovirus in Kenya." Edited by Rodney D. Adam. *PLOS ONE* 11, no. 4: e0145943. https://doi.org/10.1371/journal.pone.0145943

Soares de Oliveira, Ricardo. 2015. *Magnificent and Beggar Land: Angola since the Civil War*. Oxford: Oxford University Press. https://public.ebookcentral.proquest.com/choice/publicfullrecord.aspx?p=5825837

Spiegel, Andrew, Vanessa Watson, and Peter Wilkinson. 1996. "Domestic Diversity and Fluidity among Some African Households in Greater Cape Town." *Social Dynamics* 22, no. 1: 7–30. https://doi.org/10.1080/02533959608458599

Stiglitz, D. Joseph. 2009. "Moving beyond Market Fundamentalism to a More Balanced Economy." *Annals of Public and Cooperative Economics* 80, no. 3: 345–60. https://doi.org/10.1111/j.1467-8292.2009.00389.x

Strønen, Iselin Åsedotter, and Margareth Nangacovie. 2016. "Violence against Women in the Context of Urban Poverty in Angola." *CMI Brief* 15, no. 16: 1–4. https://www.cmi.no/publications/5976-violence-against-women-urban-poverty-angola

Syrjanen, Raakel. 2008. *UN-Habitat and the Kenya Slum Upgrading Programme: Strategy Document*. Nairobi: United Nations Human Settlements Programme.

Tissington, K., N. Munshi, G. Mirugi-Mukundi, and E. Durojaye, eds. 2013. *"Jumping the Queue," Waiting Lists and Other Myths: Perceptions and Practice around Housing Demand and Allocation in South Africa*. Cape Town: Community Law Centre at the University of the Western Cape and Socio-Economic Rights Institute of South Africa.

Todaro, Michael P., and Stephen C. Smith. 2020. *Economic Development*. 13th ed. London: Pearson.

Tomlinson, Mary, R. 2007. "Are Title Deeds a Silver Bullet for Accessing Credit?" In *Are Hernando de Soto's Views Appropriate to South Africa? Papers Delivered at a Colloquium Hosted in June 2006 by the Graduate School of Public and Development Management of the University of the Witwatersrand, and the Development Bank of Southern Africa*, edited by Glynn Davies, Monty Narsoo, and Mary R. Tomlinson, 7–12. Johannesburg: University of the Witwatersrand Graduate School of Public and Development Management.

Turner, John F. C. 1976. *Housing by People: Towards Autonomy in Building Environments*. London: Marion Boyars.

Turner, John F. C., and Robert Fichter. 1972. *Freedom to Build: Dweller Control of the Housing Process*. New York: Macmillan.

Tvedten, Inge, Gibson Lazaro, Eyolf Jul-Larsen, and Agostinho Mateus. 2018. "Urban Poverty in Luanda, Angola." Luanda and Bergen: CMI. https://www.cmi.no/publications/file/6497-urban-poverty-in-luanda-angola.pdf

UNDESA Population Division. 2017. "Household Size and Composition around the World." *Population Facts*. https://www.un.org/en/development/desa/population/publications/pdf/popfacts/PopFacts_2017-2.pdf

UN-Habitat. 2003. *Handbook on Best Practices, Security of Tenure and Access to Land: Implementation on Habitat Agenda*. Nairobi: United Nations Human Settlements Programme. https://unhabitat.org/sites/default/files/download-manager-files/Handbook%20on%20Best%20Practices%2C%20Security%20of%20Tenure%20and%20Access%20to%20Land%20-%20Implementation%20of%20the%20Habitat%20Agenda.pdf

United Nations. 2009. "Legal Empowerment of the Poor and Eradication of Poverty. Report of the Secretary General A/64/133." United Nations General Assembly. https://www.un.org/esa/socdev/documents/reports/Legal%20empowerment%20of%20the%20poor.pdf

United Nations. 2022a. "Household Size & Composition, 2022." https://population.un.org/Household/index.html#/countries/

United Nations. 2022b. *Sustainable Development Goals Report 2022*. United Nations Department for Economic and Social Affairs. https://unstats.un.org/sdgs/report/2022/The-Sustainable-Development-Goals-Report-2022.pdf

Van de Walle, Nicolas. 2001. *African Economies and the Politics of Permanent Crisis, 1979–1999*. Cambridge: Cambridge University Press.

van Gelder, Jean-Louis. 2007. "Feeling and Thinking: Quantifying the Relationship between Perceived Tenure Security and Housing Improvement in an Informal Neighbourhood in Buenos Aires." *Habitat International* 31, no. 2: 219–31. https://doi.org/10.1016/j.habitatint.2007.02.002

van Gelder, Jean-Louis. 2009. "Legal Tenure Security, Perceived Tenure Security and Housing Improvement in Buenos Aires: An Attempt towards Integration." *International Journal of Urban and Regional Research* 33, no. 1: 126–46. https://doi.org/10.1111/j.1468-2427.2009.00833.x

Varley, Ann. 1987. "The Relationship between Tenure Legalization and Housing Improvements: Evidence from Mexico City." *Development and Change* 18, no. 1987: 463–81.

Vogl, Tom S. 2007. "Urban Land Rights and Child Nutritional Status in Peru, 2004." *Economics and Human Biology* 5, no. 2: 302–21. https://doi.org/10.1016/j.ehb.2007.01.001

Vorster, J., and J. Tolken. 2008. "Western Cape Occupancy Study, 2008. Report Commissioned by the Provincial Government of the Western Cape." Stellenbosch: University of Stellenbosch. https://www.westerncape.gov.za/Text/2012/8/hs_wc_occupancy_study_2008.pdf

Waldorf, Pétur. 2014. "The Informal City: Candonga, Governmentality and Corruption in Post-Conflict Luanda." PhD diss., McGill University.

Wallerstein, Immanuel. 2020. *World-Systems Analysis: An Introduction*. Durham: Duke University Press. https://doi.org/10.1515/9780822399018

Watson, Vanessa. 2014. "African Urban Fantasies: Dreams or Nightmares?" *Environment and Urbanization* 26, no. 1: 215–31. https://doi.org/10.1177/0956247813513705

Weil, David N. 2013. *Economic Growth*. 3rd ed. Boston: Pearson Addison-Wesley.

Weimer, David Leo, ed. 1997. *The Political Economy of Property Rights: Institutional Change and Credibility in the Reform of Centrally Planned Economies*. Cambridge: Cambridge University Press.

Western, J. 2002. "A Divided City: Cape Town." *Political Geography* 21, no. 5: 711–16. https://doi.org/10.1016/S0962-6298(02)00016-1

Wilkinson, Peter. 2000. "City Profile." *Cities* 17, no. 3: 195–205. https://doi.org/10.1016/S0264-2751(99)00059-1

World Bank. 1980. "Shelter." Washington, DC: World Bank.

World Bank. 1993. "Enabling Markets to Work." Washington, DC: International Bank for Reconstruction and Development.

World Bank, ed. 2002. *Building Institutions for Markets.* New York: Oxford University Press.

World Bank. 2015. "Stocktaking of the Housing Sector in Sub-Saharan Africa: Challenges and Opportunities." Washington, DC: International Bank for Reconciliation and Development. https://documents.worldbank.org/en/publication/documents-reports/documentdetail/551311468194953133/main-report

World Bank. 2018. *Overcoming Poverty and Inequality in South Africa: An Assessment of Drivers, Constraints and Opportunities.* Washington, DC: World Bank. https://documents1.worldbank.org/curated/en/530481521735906534/pdf/Overcoming-Poverty-and-Inequality-in-South-Africa-An-Assessment-of-Drivers-Constraints-and-Opportunities.pdf

World Bank. 2022a. "World Development Indicators Database." https://data.worldbank.org/indicator/NY.GDP.PCAP.CD?locations=ZG

World Bank. 2022b. "The International Bank for Reconstruction and Development." September 22. https://www.worldbank.org/en/who-we-are/ibrd

World Bank. 2022c. *Poverty and Shared Prosperity 2022: Correcting Course.* https://doi.org/10.1596/978-1-4648-1893-6

World Bank Group. 2016. *Poverty and Shared Prosperity 2016: Taking on Inequality.* Washington, DC: World Bank. https://doi.org/10.1596/978-1-4648-0958-3

World Food Programme. 2016. "Supporting National School Meals Programme in Kenya." https://www.wfp.org/publications/supporting-national-school-meals-programme-kenya

INDEX